THE
FIELD & STREAM

TREASURY OF

TROUT FISHING

THE
FIELD & STREAM

TREASURY OF

TROUT FISHING

Edited by
LEONARD M. WRIGHT, JR.

Illustrated by Gordon Allen

THE LYONS PRESS

Printed in the United States of America

10   9   8   7   6   5   4   3   2   1

Library of Congress Cataloging-in-Publication Data

The field & stream treasury of fly-fishing / edited by Leonard M. Wright, Jr. ; illustrated by Gordon Allen.
    p. cm.
  Originally published: New York : N. Lyons Books, c1986.
  ISBN 1-58574-229-5 (hardcover)
  1. Trout fishing. I. Title: Field and stream treasury of fly-fishing. II. Wright, Leonard M. III. Field & Stream.

SH687 .F54 2001
799.1'757—dc21
                                                                    2001018932

Contents

Introduction

Since its historic first issue back in 1895, FIELD & STREAM has published several thousand articles on trout fishing—far more than on any other fish. These range from hard-core, "how-to" instructions to poetic musings on the essence of the sport, yet nearly all are punctuated with memorable or revealing fishing incidents.

The earliest pieces may seem quaint in some ways, but remember: they depicted a world vastly different from ours. Around the turn of the century, cars and paved roads were rarities once you left the cities and so were even simple amenities like telephones, electric lights, and flush toilets. A fishing trip into southern Canada from, say, Philadelphia, could be a near-heroic expedition.

The tackle and tactics used in those days may surprise the modern angler, too. Bait or spinner fishermen had to lob or slip-cast their offerings with a long bamboo fly rod and thick enamel line, severely limiting both their range and their presentation. Fly fishers were restricted to chuck-and-chance-it methods with a team of large, gaudy wet flies.

The numbers and the naiveté of the quarry more than made up for these limitations, though. East of the Mississippi, including the upper Midwest, wild brook trout were numerous, innocent, and eager. On the east slope of the Rockies you'd encounter mostly cutthroats and, to the west, rainbows—both in Utopian sizes and quantities.

A few things have remained pretty much the same. The uncanny ability of boots and waders to leak or ship water, the anticipation at the start of a day's angling, and the sudden, stubborn strength of a newly hooked trout against the bend of the rod haven't changed one iota.

Unfortunately, our ancestors—even the "sports"—kept every decent trout they caught and this was killing the goose that laid those 24K eggs. Already, some streams near major population centers were being reported as fished out and many rivers, even then, had become too warm or polluted to support native trout.

The solution to these problems seemed to lie in stocking the hardier and smarter brown trout from Europe. Though this fish had been imported three decades earlier, it was neither numerous, widely distributed, nor much admired until after World War I. This more demanding trout, plus dwindling populations, challenged anglers to adopt more sophisticated tactics from Europe and to experiment on their own.

During this transition period in American trouting, the dry fly and the nymph—for years popular artificials on Britain's choicest rivers—were adopted on our waters. Leaders became longer and lighter. Flies grew smaller, drabber, and more imitative.

Perhaps the biggest revolution of all, though, occurred right after World War II. Detailed entomologies and biologies were published, guiding the trout fisher toward more accurate imitations and presentations of aquatic foods. New monofilament lines and fixed-spool reels allowed the bait man and spinner to toss their wares half way into the next county and to fish them with greater control. Synthetic materials for rods, lines, and leaders caused the price of efficient fly tackle to plummet. Add in suddenly higher incomes, shorter working hours, plus more cars and it's no wonder the number of anglers multiplied almost overnight.

Over the past ninety years, FIELD & STREAM has printed literally millions of words on trout and trouting. Obviously, this volume can contain only a tiny fraction of that staggering total so the reader deserves some explanation of how a final selection was made.

Although FIELD & STREAM, as the leading outdoor publication, attracted contributions from famous authors, statesmen, and world-travelers as well as noted sportsmen, this book makes no attempt to be the Who's Who of trout fishing. Neither does it try to be a "where-to" guide or a "how-to" manual. And yet, on the following pages, you'll outwit picky trout with Ray Bergman, take a trip to New Zealand's trout waters with Russell Chatham, tangle with the trout of a lifetime with John Taintor Foote, chase rainbows with Corey Ford, catch steelhead with Zane Grey, learn the killing curve cast from George M. L. LaBranche, visit a legendary fly tyer and rooster-raiser with A. J. McClane, tie and fish deadly ant imitations with Ernest G. Schwiebert, and land huge fish on the lightest fly rod in history with Lee Wulff—all without having read much more than a quarter of the contents.

The FIELD & STREAM *Treasury of Trout Fishing* was, simply, edited to be the book you would turn to first when faced with a long, troutless winter night— the one you would read and reread, whatever your mood, for enjoyment, for adventure, for humor, for the sheer joy of it. In short, it was designed to make the sort of reading that only the most blasé and tepid trout fisherman could pick up without wanting to devour the whole thing.

LEONARD M. WRIGHT, JR.
March 1986

THE
FIELD & STREAM
TREASURY OF
TROUT FISHING

PART ONE

THE EARLY YEARS

The Trout and the Indian

GENERAL JOHN McNULTA

Back in the 1840s, when leaders were made of horsehair instead of gut, fly fishers were a rarity. A Civil War hero describes the angling of his youth. (May 1900)

From my infancy I had heard tales of the Big Woods, but do not remember ever having then seen anyone who had been in them. A party was being made up to go there, and my father, when the time for starting came, on account of feeble health was prohibited from making the trip, as he had intended. I was in despair, as I was to be left behind, and all of the fond hopes that I had nourished were to be shattered—the big trout, the deer, the bears, the panthers, the wildcats and other varmints that I expected to kill, I would not see. And then, most of all the Indians, real wild Indians, but friendly, in whose wigwams I was going to rest, I would not see them. I was almost heartbroken. One of the party, however, with whom my father and I had been on a stream, volunteered out of pure sympathy to look after me.

Consent was then given that I might go, but the apprehensions under which I labored lest it be withdrawn, of which there was strong indication, are among the most painful reminiscences of my life.

We finally set off, three strong men and one small, freckled, scrawny boy. As one of the party facetiously remarked: "He is about the size of a pound of soap after a hard day's washing." And another said: "About two good mouthfuls for an ordinary bear," and my particular champion replied: "A small but very lively bait."

We got off on a steamer with a deck passage to Albany; fare one dollar for man, fifty cents for boy; canal boat from Albany to Utica. This was in 1847 or '48, and the New York Central Railroad was, I think, being operated between Albany and Syracuse. We took the canal boat because it was cheaper than the railroad, and we also took a freight boat because it was cheaper than the packet boat—being one cent a mile, instead of two. It was slower, but time was of no value to us.

At Utica we hired a man with a team and wagon for the trip, but I do not remember the cost; it was approximately about what a sleeping-car porter would now expect as a tip for like time.

We went through Trenton over to Alder Creek and the big Black River Dam, where digging for a canal to Rome had just been started. Here we struck the primeval forest—no habitations beyond in that direction. A Mr. Williams had a sawmill at the dam, and there were a few small houses. We had traveled more than half the time in the woods after we left Trenton, often many miles at a time without seeing any sign of human life beyond the rough road over which we passed. A few miles before we reached Alder Creek, there was considerable clearing and a settlement of Welsh people, who were starting dairy farms.

From Alder Creek we diverged to the left and to the west, then northwest through the Steuben Hills, and again southwest on to Booneville, and there our team left us and went back to Utica. Here we met our guide, a Canadian-Frenchman voyageur named Marienne, who expressed in emphatic mixed English and Canadian-French his disapprobation of taking that puny, sickly petit garçon in the woods, who might get wet and die there.

After several days' delay we got started. There had been provided for me as a special guide and caretaker an Ojibway Indian of Herculean proportions, fully 6 feet 2½ inches in his moccasins, and weighing, I judge, about two hundred pounds.

My long-desired wish to meet the Indians had been gratified, but the effect was not what I expected. I was afraid of the Indian, and it soon became evident that the Indian entertained grave apprehensions of some kind about me. I was constantly uppermost in his mind, whether for good or evil I could not determine, but feared the latter, and always felt great relief when he put away a big butcher knife that he carried in a leather sheath on a belt around his waist. I avoided being left alone with him, and as he did not know a dozen words of English and I did not know one word of Indian, our conversation was limited. My desire to know Indians had become fully satisfied, yet I thought if I could meet this particular Indian when he had no knife—in the city in the presence of a good-sized squad of policemen—it would be more satisfactory. I avoided being left alone with him and shied away from him on our journey. When we came to a stream I would slip out a few yards from camp and try my flies, and soon he left me to my ways.

At one of our camps I found an exceptionally good place for casting near the top of a rapid; the only place, however, to get room for a back cast was from a point of vantage on a tree fallen across the stream, upon which I crawled out. When in the act of making the first cast my feet slipped and down I went in the cold, swift water over head and ears, the current holding me up against the submerged limbs and body of the tree under which I was partly drawn with my head still under, but perfectly composed and with no apprehension, being a good swimmer and diver. With a good hold I was about to make a supreme effort to raise myself against the current, when I was pulled, almost jerked, straight up out of the water and found myself being held up in the air at arms' length by the Indian, about as he would hold up for inspection a muskrat that he had caught by the nape of the neck. He looked me in the face, made a grunt, and carried me to the bank. When he saw that I stood up and was all right, he gave two or three more grunts with a different inflection, while the expression of his countenance indicated satisfaction. Then it dawned upon me that the Indian thought I was in danger of being drowned, which I was disposed to resent as a reflection upon my resourcefulness as an angler, my skill as a diver and my all-around qualities as an amphibian.

An impulse came over me to make a run for camp and get away from him, but I could not run, as my boots were full of water. All men and boys wore boots then—calfskin boots, coming near to the knee. Boots indicated the line of demarcation between babyhood and boyhood. Then it occurred to me if I did start to run, the Indian could catch me before I reached camp. I pulled off my boots and rolled up my trousers ready for a run. Then I observed the Indian was without his butcher knife, and he beckoned me to come out on the fallen tree and hold the rod while he released the line from its entanglement. I did so because I was afraid to refuse, and reeled up while he released the hard-braided, heavily waxed linen line. When he came to the horsehair leader and single-hair snells and artificial flies on tiny hooks he was amazed and charmed. He had not only never seen but never heard of such an appliance. It was to him incredible that a fish could be caught without bait, on that imitation of an insect, and impossible to hold the fish on a single hair after he was hooked, or that that little hook would hold anything larger than a minnow. He made manifest his feelings in pantomime, and also indicated a desire to see the thing tried. This gave me some confidence in him, and I immediately began to gratify his desire.

A few casts brought up a good trout, fairly hooked and nicely held in the stiff current until successfully landed, the light rod showing all the curves from the straightness of an arrow to and beyond the perfect arch, the standard of a rod's capacity, to almost a perfect loop—the point of desperation, where nothing further in the way of line can be yielded, and where the only alternative is to hold or break. The little twig and single horsehair held in that swift current a vigorous two-pound trout—a true *Salvelinus fontinalis*.

The stoicism of the Indian melted away and was all gone; he was bubbling over with enthusiasm and continued to bubble until, without moving from that fallen tree, I had landed a full dozen, one a double of about a pound and a half each.

Radically opposite in race, in aspiration and traditions and physical endowments, two kindred spirits now communed together and understood every thrill and emotion that moved each. The man regarded the boy as he would a little weak bird fluttering between life and death, prematurely separated from the nest and brood. And the boy, terrorized by being alone in the wilderness with this gigantic savage, whose queer actions and dress filled him with distrust.

And then the desire of the Indian to witness a practical test of the angler's skill touched the boy's vanity. The interest and enjoyment of the Indian made a soul communion and coalescence, and all fears and distrusts were dissipated by confidence.

The two were children of one father, the one true and ever-living God, with like thoughts and aspirations. They became friends and remained so for life.

The Sportsman Tourist

JOHN A. LANT

How good were the "good old days"? Would you believe two-and-a-half-pound wild brook trout just twenty-six miles from Manhattan?
(July 1900)

A few years ago I found my domicile in famed Sleepy Hollow, near Tarrytown. The little brook that passed my door leaped into the Pocantico nearby the rock whereon the oldest inhabitant averred that Irving sat and fished. It was an ideal spot to lure a dreamer. The living waters of three brooks met and mingled. Well, indeed, might this spot be hallowed in the memory by the legend, which recalls the brook "with just murmur enough to lure one to repose," hard by the then old schoolhouse.

In an idle moment, I, too, sat upon that rock, with, by chance, rod and line. A quiet, cool, refreshing spot, indeed. A limpid pool below formed near an old wall, over which a wooden bridge was thrown. Swirling bubbles gathered, lingered, and then strung off as the ripples danced along. Overhanging branches nearly touched the water, and vines trailed along the banks. By no special direction my line floated down to this spot. In a lazy, listless way I drew the line back too quickly. I had unconsciously perpetrated a skilful play. A sturdy fish rose to seize the bait. I saw the white belly and sudden splash. My former experience gave me to understand that I had lost a beautiful trout. I was not long in solving the secret. By cautious lingerings I lured many trout. Knowledge came with experience, and day by day I took practice lessons at my door. With confidence and courage I ventured to adjacent streams and favorite pools, always with success, when the strictest caution was observed. I studied the habits of the trout and lured him with every variety of seasonable bait and color. I was loth to deceive the noble trout with artificial fly, preferring the natural variety, but occasionally added a bit of color, which may have appealed to a passion other than that of gluttony.

My earliest and best rods were improvised from that stately purple-crowned, jointless weed known as "Pride of the Meadow." In the spring they may be seen in great clusters, brown and bare, of ample length for fishing. I found them admirably light, but at times insufficient. It occurred to me they might be strenghened by inserting a slender one inside another, and then bind on a handle upon which to fasten the reel. A better rod could not be devised for trout. The "admirable apparatus" of the artist angler has many a scar in its polished surfaces, not dreamed of by my more natural substitute.

The result of my first season's catch, and it was a short one, footed up four hundred and seven good trout, within twenty-six miles of the great metropolis, and my second, in a single month's opportunities, and a dry season at that, footed eighty-seven.

No trout was counted or taken which was less than seven inches. Numerous evidences of these catches can be seen in my fishing books of fins, skin and tails. The skin of a two-and-a-half-pounder in part, forms a cover decoration for this volume.

I record these investigations along brooks in the immediate vicinity of Tarrytown, twenty-six miles from New York, the Pocantico, the Saw Mill river, and the Bronx. The Sprain, near Yonkers, is a good trout stream, also the lower Saw Mill river. These are accessible by rail, boat or wheel. Several experts have satisfactory stories to tell that would astonish the yearning angler, whose dreams encompass the Adirondacks.

The past year I visited that region, the Catskills, and wandered far into the Green Mountains of Vermont, but at last yield the palm of success to my native brooks as above.

Fly Fishing for Trout on a Canadian Lake

WALTER GROAVES

At the turn of the century, a one-day trip could include train, steamer, and a stiff hike, but the size and numbers of fish, even when they weren't hitting well, were impressive. (August 1903)

Early on May 24 Throop Hayes, Deslaurier and I left Hull for Buckingham, where we arrived at 9.20 and found our man waiting for us with a good team. After a very pleasant drive of three miles we reached the Hedmore then ready to start up the river with a bright and merry party of ladies and gentlemen on board, bound for the High Falls to spend the holiday there, namely, the late Queen Victoria's birthday. We made good time and arrived at our destination at noon, where we found Isaac and his boy waiting for us with a horse and jumper. It did not take long to get things snugly packed on the jumper, and by one-thirty we were at the Lake. It would have surprised many people to have seen the places over which Isaac's horse took the load. It seems to understand every word he said to it, and actually walked along single logs while drawing quite a load too. I have seen a good deal of this kind of work done before, but I never saw a horse to equal this one.

We found the boats in good shape and by two o'clock were at the point where we pitched our tent, a nice level spot close to a beautiful stream of clear running water about three feet wide. After partaking of a light lunch we got our rods and tackle together and started for the evening's fishing, Throop and I going in one boat and Hayes and Deslaurier in the other. We did not anchor, but kept constantly moving about, one paddling and the other casting. By this means we covered a large expanse of water, picking up fish here and there, chiefly from under the bushes and fallen trees close to the shore. The day was, however, very bright, not a cloud in the sky, and for that reason, doubtless, the trout did not rise very well.

When we returned to camp we found we had eighteen nice trout between us. Hayes and Deslaurier had some good ones too and related having lost some much larger (not an unusual circumstance with fishermen I fancy). They did not move about much, but fished not far from camp, using both bait and fly. Throop and I used only the fly. We found the most killing patterns to be the Grizzly King, Alexandra and Zulu, and they seemed to show a marked preference for the former. The largest trout, however, was caught by me on a fly I made without any particular pattern. It was dressed thus: body, dark brown seal's fur, brown hackle, tied palmer; wings and tail well marked pin tail. The largest trout weighed two and one-half pounds, and we had several others nearly as large.

Next day was just about as bright as the previous one and the result about the same. We returned to camp about half past eight somewhat tired after having been up since about four in the morning, and at work all day with the exception of about an hour for lunch. The black flies were very troublesome on the Lake, but we fortunately did not have many near the camp. We had different kinds of fly oils with us, but found the tar preparation recommended by "Nessmuk" to be the best, but even that required renewing frequently.

We were out early again on the third morning, and fished until ten o'clock, when we returned to camp and packed up, after partaking of a good meal. At the end of the portage we found Isaac waiting and it did not take us long to get down to the river, where we divided the fish and repacked them with ice. The steamer arrived about four, and we reached Buckingham at five-thirty. We had our tea at a small, clean hotel near the station, and a good tea we had, too, after which we smoked and chatted until the train left, reaching home at ten-thirty, after what we all agreed had been one of the pleasantest short fishing trips we had ever enjoyed. Not a single thing occurred to mar our enjoyment, and nothing whatever went wrong with any of our arrangements or calculations.

During the whole fishing I used my Chubb split bamboo Murray trout rod and found it simply perfect in its action. The rest used greenheart rods and I regret to say they broke three or four joints in a manner that would have been quite impossible, I believe, with the one I was using. They were all good fishermen and no blame can be attached to them. Greenheart appears to me to be very unreliable unless one can get hold of a very good piece of wood, and this is a very difficult thing to do. It appears to get powdery and snaps off with the slightest sudden jerk, at times, and in a most unexpected manner. Split-bamboo and lancewood are decidedly preferable to my thinking.

About the Brown Trout

SAMUEL G. CAMP

Once the brown trout was almost universally despised in America. This early fly fisherman, while relegating the brown to second-class citizenship, pleads for its consideration as a true game fish. (March 1907)

Possibly you have heard some old trout fisherman—a man who has passed a good portion of his life in the woods and on the rivers and lakes of New England, fly-fishing for the red-spotted brook trout and hunting the white-tailed deer and the ruffed grouse—discourse concerning the game qualities and characteristics in general of the German or brown trout, *Salmo fario*, "made in Germany" and imported in 1882. If so, you have heard no good of the brown trout. You have been more or less forcibly informed that the brown trout is a coarse fish; that he grows at the rate of one pound a year and fattens on the smaller red-spotted trout; that he lacks sporting blood and rises reluctantly to the artificial fly; that when hooked he furnishes a poor sort of fight compared with that of a speckled trout of equal size; that he is not as handsome a fish as the speckled trout; that, in fact, as a sporting proposition the brown trout is not to be considered.

 Now the old trout fisherman is more or less correct in his conclusions; correct in so far, and only so far, as he assumes that the brown trout is not to be compared with the red-spotted brook trout, *Salvelinus fontinalis*; for no game fish, with the exception, possibly, of the salmon, which is very far beyond the dreams of most of us, will ever be so favorably esteemed as *fontinalis* has been, is now, and, thanks to the fish culturists, always will be.

In England, trout fishing means fishing for this same brown trout, and there they certainly consider it a true game fish. The reason why the brown trout has never come to his own in this country is because American anglers insist on comparing it with the "little salmon of the springs," to the inevitable detriment of *fario*.

Considered by itself, on its own merits, and leaving aside all odious comparison, the brown trout is a mighty good game fish. Its place, however, is not in the same stream with the speckled brook trout, for the very good reason that the growth of the brown trout, being almost a pound each year, as above stated, is much more rapid than that of *fontinalis*, and where the two co-exist, the brown trout preys upon his smaller speckled relative rapaciously, and to the latter's ultimate extinction.

Many of our former good trout waters have been rendered unfit for the red-spotted trout by logging operations, the introduction of foreign matter, and through various other causes. When the axemen have blazed their trail to the head waters of a trout stream, and cleared away the cool, green forest growth from its natal springs and tributary brooks, where the trout spawn and the fry grow to fingerlings, and the sun has had its way with the dismal "clearing," that stream is ruined for the native red-spotted trout; its temperature is raised beyond the point where the native trout will prosper and, in addition, with the removal of the overhanging foliage there is a consequent reduction of the insect food upon which *fontinalis* most thrives. It is in just such a stream that the brown trout, which does not demand water of a low temperature, and is naturally a tougher, hardier fish, will do well. A stream such as the above will yield good sport when planted with the brown trout. Do not conclude from this, however, that the brown trout is a coarse fish. It is not. The red-spotted brook trout, you must remember, is a charr, and the brown trout a salmon trout; and as salmon trout, *Salmo fario*, is no more a coarse fish than is any other similar member of the *Salmonidæ*.

A certain trout stream that I have fished many times is inhabited by brown trout, running in weight up to five pounds, of course rarely, for although the books credit the brown trout with a capacity of attaining truly colossal proportions, we do not find them at all frequently; at least I have yet to raise one—I do not say catch.

It happened that one day I fished this stream in company with a friend who is much the sort of a trout fisherman that I have alluded to above—an expert, experienced, dyed-in-the-wool fly-fisherman, with an overweening admiration for the speckled brook trout and a small opinion of the brown trout.

We had fished down the stream until late in the afternoon with ordinary success, catching a fair number of native trout, but none of large size. There were now only two good pools left to fish, and the Old Angler was fishing ahead. The Old Angler started in on the Bridge Pool and I took the one upstream around a sharp bend. Leading down to the Bridge Pool is a pretty stiff riffle running on the left under overhanging cedars. The still water begins directly beneath the bridge, and a very little lower down there are two large submerged rocks. Between these two rocks there is generally a big brown trout; but the Old Angler did not know this. When I arrived it was all over. The Old Angler stood in mid-stream looking thoughtfully at a smashed fly-rod that dangled down into the water from his shaking hand. Also he was swearing softly, but with admirable taste and fluency. The Old Angler has since been heard to admit that possibly the brown trout has been maligned.

The fight of the brown trout is not as brilliant and erratic as that of the native, but it is, in its way, fully as effective. You will lose, in a day's fishing, just as many brown trout as native. As a general thing as much time must be taken to safely land a brown trout of, say, half a pound, as is needed for a red-spotted trout of equal weight. The red-spotted trout fights faster, but the brown trout puts a bulldog strain on the line and keeps it there; and he is never your fish until he is in the basket. Also, the brown trout, when hooked, will occasionally leap from the water and shake himself like a bass; a feat in which the native trout seldom or never indulges unless the fisherman is holding him too hard.

The brown trout rises to the artificial fly very freely, and any of the standard trout flies, hackles especially, when properly presented and seasonably used, will be successful. In habits the brown and red-spotted trout are very similar and consequently you should follow the same methods in fishing for either. There is a difference, however, in the manner in which they take the fly. A large red-spotted trout, when he has concluded that he wants a certain gaudy but palatable looking insect—perhaps a Royal Coachman—comes up leisurely, rolls over and sucks it in. But a brown trout will more often go at the fly like lightning, leaping clear of the water in his efforts, and if he misses he will do it again. He takes the fly viciously.

If there is a long rapids in the river, plentifully studded with rocks, you will find the brown trout lying in the fastest water, using the rocks as a shield from the current. Cast your flies for him directly into the foaming swirl below one of these rocks and very close to the rock itself. When hooked he immediately hurries down stream for a nice long distance, and you find yourself separated from your victim by many yards of roaring, white water. Then you may pursue two courses of action. You may, if you can, scramble down to your fish; or you may stand on a rock, with your rod bent double and yell. If you follow the latter course your fish whips himself off the hook in a little time; if you decide on the former you may make a killing or you may break a leg. In either event it is safe to say that, if you are without prejudice, you will acknowledge the brown trout a game fish.

Why Do Trout Sometimes Not Rise to the Artificial Fly?

M. P. KEEFE

The author gives thirteen possible answers to fly fishing's oldest co-nundrum and cannily avoids committing himself. What's your theory?
(April 1907)

This is a question that interests all anglers, without regard to nationality, and one that will perhaps never be answered satisfactorily.

It is essential to an interesting discussion that the subject should be discussable and that it should be worthy of being discussed. Are we all agreed as to the reasons why trout do not rise to the fly on particular occasions?

Let us begin the inquiry by asking the question, Why do trout at any time rise to the artificial fly? The answer being restricted to trout, it may confidently be given that it is because they think it a real fly, or, at least, something eatable. Then why do they not always take it when presented? The most obvious answer

16

is that they are then not hungry. But this does not seem satisfactory, when one thinks of days when fish rise and take the fly during its whole course, morning, noon and night, and other days, often in succession, when hardly a rise can be seen. This would assume a wholly unnatural caprice of appetite. A more reasonable assumption is that on these occasions the trout can get no natural flies, or have something more tempting to feed upon under the surface. While it is true that during or after a spate, when there has been an abundance of worms and insects washed into the water, the trout are specially on the lookout for them, even this assumption will not quite meet the case, because it is notable that trout frequently rise suddenly and stop as suddenly without any apparent difference in the number of natural flies on the water and—but here comes the rub—without any change of any sort, that we as yet know of definitely.

We are now led to consider the causes which have been advanced in explanation of the non-rising of trout. For the sake of clearness we may number these causes and say:

(1) Because they are not hungry.

(2) Because there are no natural flies, and trout not expecting them do not come to the surface.

(3) Because they have a plentiful supply of bottom food.

(4) Because of over-fishing.

(5) Because the angler has not the correct fly.

(6) Because they see the angler's tackle or himself.

(7) Because of the presence of otters or predatory birds.

(8) Because the air is too cold.

(9) Because the wind is in the wrong direction.

(10) Because there is mist on the water.

(11) Because of varying barometric pressure.

(12) Because the electric tension of the atmosphere is too great, which in common parlance is because there is thunder in the air.

(13) Because the light is bad.

We may now consider the conditions in which trout rise to the fly, and yet do not take it, "short-rising" as it is familiarly called. There is something particularly mysterious in trout rising to the fly and so affecting it as to cause a distinct twitch of the line, and yet not hooking themselves. This happens often, not for an hour only, but for hours in succession. All forms of striking and want of striking on such occasions end only by one or two being hooked by the mouth or by the back fin. Whether they nibble at the flies or strike them with their tails it is difficult to say, and as difficult to say why they do not more frequently get hooked.

We may now ask the question, Is there ever a time when trout can be depended on to rise? As regards the season, most authors are agreed that in spring and in autumn trout rise best to the fly. That in the early spring and late autumn they rise best in the middle of the day, and at other times in the morning and evening, and all this in relation to the sun conditions.

What is the conclusion of the whole matter? Shortly, this—that there is a great deal about the question of rising and not rising of trout that we know little or nothing about. Instead of giving up the problem in despair, we should watch narrowly the facts as observed in Nature, note them down carefully at the time, compare them with those of brother anglers on occasions such as this, and out of all evolve theories which when reduced to practice, will be found to have carried us nearer to the truth. And, further, the doing of this will not do away with the romance and delightful uncertainty of angling, but rather add to the zest with which we carry it on.

This is very good advice, freely given—and by the way, advice is more easily given than reliable information in a case like this. Nevertheless fly-fishers should consider, says Dr. Henshall, the noted authority, that a "condition, not a theory confronts anglers in the rising or non-rising of a trout to an artificial fly, and that we should endeavor to ascertain if such be possible, just what conditions are present to account for the peculiar actions, at different times, of those elusive creatures of the adipose fin, that according to popular opinion seem to have as many moods as specks or spots." He goes on to say:

"There is one feature of this subject, however, that I have never known to be alluded to, which is this: That the rising or not rising of trout may depend on the scarcity or abundance of the fish. In regions where trout are usually abundant I have never, in my experience, known them to fail to rise to the artificial fly, at any time of day, or under almost any condition of wind or weather. It is only in sections that are much fished, and fish consequently scarce, or 'educated,' as some term it for want of a better reason, that trout fail to respond to the solicitations of the fly-fisher.

"In the wilds of Canada I have had trout rise to my fly by the dozen, day after day, so that all semblance of sport disappeared, and only enough were taken for the frying-pan. In Yellowstone Lake the merest tyro can take the red-throat trout until his arms ache, at any time of day, beneath clouds or sunshine. And in the river below the lake one can stand on the bank in plain sight of the trout, which with one eye on the angler and the other on the fly, rushes to his doom by snapping up the tinselled lure, contrary to all conventional lore. This is an extreme case, of course, for the trout are extremely abundant.

"One can imagine that in the clear and shallow streams of England, which have been thrashed by the flies of anglers, good, bad and indifferent, for centuries, and where trout are consequently and necessarily scarce, or 'educated,' that they fail to rise—in other words they are not always there. This, I think, is the reason that dry fly-fishing is becoming the vogue in that country, where the angler waits patiently by the stream until a trout rising to a natural fly proclaims its presence. The rest is easy."

We will be glad to hear from the readers of FIELD & STREAM on this subject.

June Fly Fishing for Trout

DR. JAMES A. HENSHALL

Although mainly remembered as "Mr. Bass," the good doctor was also
one of the most enthusiastic and expert trouters of his day. (June 1907)

June is one of the best months for the fly-fisher for brook trout. Some streams, however, are likely to be occasionally swollen or roiled by spring rains or the June rise. At such times, when not too much discolored for fly-fishing, the angler will do well to avoid the channels of the stream and cast his flies along the edges, where the water is clearer. This tip may add many a fish to an otherwise scanty creel.

When the stream is at its ordinary stage, and clear, the riffles and eddies are the most likely places at this season, and will be pretty sure to reward the careful angler. In fishing such places, the flies should be floated over them, allowing them to sink below the surface occasionally. The stone fly, gray drake and brown drake, will be found useful, especially in localities where the May-fly or sand-fly puts in an appearance.

Churning the flies up and down, or wiggling and dancing them, should be avoided; the only motion, if any, should be a very slight fluttering, such as a drowning insect might make as it floats down stream. Strike lightly. Should the trout leap after being hooked, as it sometimes does in the shallow water of riffles, lower the tip slightly for half a second, but recover it immediately—in other words, it is simply a down-and-up movement about as quickly as it can be done.

While talking of lowering the tip, it may not seem out of place to make a few observations concerning that proceeding, which some anglers do not seem to understand, or at least do not fully appreciate. The rule of lowering the tip to a leaping fish is a very old one, centuries old, in fact, and is founded on the experience of anglers for many generations past. Its usefulness and reasonableness are as manifest in the twentieth century as at any former time.

But because some thoughtless anglers at the present day have succeeded in landing a leaping and well-hooked fish without observing the rule, they decry it as entirely unnecessary, and declare that it ought to be relegated to the limbo of obsolete and fanciful notions and useless practices. The iconoclast usually attacks his images without thought or reason, and often in sheer ignorance. A little reflection might enlighten him and cause him to stay his hand.

The rule originated in Great Britain and pertained, particularly, to fly-fishing. The very small hooks on which trout flies were tied offered but a slight hold on the mouth of the fish, and in case a leaping fish threw its weight on a taut line and raised rod, it was almost sure to break away—hence the rule to lower the tip and release the tension for a brief moment. As the fish regained the water the tip was raised and the former tension resumed. It must be understood, however, that "lowering the tip" does not mean to touch the water with the tip, but as the rod is usually held at an angle of forty-five degrees, a downward deflection of the tip for a foot will usually suffice.

So far as my observation goes the objections to the rule have been raised by black bass bait-fishers, who use heavy rods, strong tackle and large hooks. Under these circumstances, a fish is usually so securely hooked by a vigorous yank that the lowering of the tip, when it leaps from the water, is not so essential, inasmuch as the angler has a cinch on his quarry, whether the line be slack or taut.

But even in bait-fishing, with a light rod and corresponding tackle and a small hook, it is a wise plan to follow a leaping fish back to the water by slightly lowering the tip, especially on a short line—with a long line it does not matter so much, as the "give" of a pliant rod and long line is usually sufficient to relieve the increased tension when a fish is in the air.

The question as to the best fly to use at certain seasons, or at any season, is a vexed one. Whether it is the colored dressing of the fly, or its form, that is most enticing to the fish, will perhaps never be known, except approximately. Of the long list of named artificial flies the choice of most anglers has been narrowed to a score or two, and for the only reason that they have been more or less successful with them. We are apt to look at the matter from our own view-point, and often without reference to that of the fish.

Reasoning from the appearance of artificial flies in general, it would seem that on a fretted surface almost any one of the many hundreds should get a rise from a fish, if in a biting mood, and indeed this is, in a measure, true. But one swallow does not make a summer. There are times and places where any old thing, even a bit of colored rag, will coax a rise. I have had good success with a bit of the skin of a chicken neck with the feathers attached. Then there are times when nothing but natural bait proves alluring.

We may assume as almost a self-evident proposition that a fish takes an artificial fly under the delusion that it is a natural one, or something good to eat—otherwise, it would not take it at all. If this assumption is correct, then it would follow that the best imitations of natural flies or insects should be the most successful. This is, in the main, a reasonable conclusion, though on the other hand certain flies that are universally considered and used as good ones, do not, to our eyes at least, bear any resemblance to any known insect—for instance, the coachman, professor, and other so-called fancy flies.

An artificial fly on the ruffled surface of the water presents a very different appearance to the same fly when held in one's hand, even to our own eyes; what then does it look like to the fish? That's the question. I have often attempted to solve it by diving beneath and viewing the fly on the surface. If the water was perfectly clear and calm, without a ripple, it simply looked like a dark fly, no matter what its color, though I could sometimes discern the lighter color of the wings when formed of undyed mallard or wood-duck feathers. When the surface was ruffled, it was so indistinct that a bit of leaf would have seemed the same. A somewhat similar experiment may be performed, in a minor degree, by placing a mirror at the bottom of a barrel of water and viewing the reflection of the fly on the surface.

We can surmise that fish are not color-blind, otherwise there would be no object in the beautiful colors that many male fish assume during the breeding season. Fishes are possessed of keen vision, and possibly have the faculty of distinguishing colors in a fly, even when on a fretted surface, where, to our eyes, they are very indistinct, and where even the form can not be well defined.

We may assume, then, that as trout are in the habit of feeding on such flies and insects as resort to, or are hatched in, the water, that the best imitations of such natural flies, from the trout's viewpoint, would be the most alluring. I think it goes without saying, that all past experience has proven that the imitations of some of the commonest aquatic insects have been the most successful under all conditions. This would include not only the image, but the larva, as represented by the various hackle flies.

Practical Dry-Fly Fishing for Beginners

EMLYN M. GILL

A year before the first American book on dry-fly fishing was published, its author describes a revolutionary, new technique recently smuggled in from England. (September 1911)

"What is a dry fly?"

This question rather startled me for a moment, as I well knew that the man who asked it had been a thorough outdoor man all his life; had visited nearly all the haunts of big game in this country and in Canada; had shot at different times mountain sheep, mountain goat, moose, bear, antelope, elk, caribou, various kinds of deer, and other varieties of wild animals, and had as a rule carried at least one fishing rod with him on most of his trips, if not on all. Also I well knew that he had been successful in luring the finny fighters, as I had seen some of his records; and had also examined, mounted in his office, very fine, large specimens of bass, silver trout, ouananiche, muscalonge, and other game fishes.

A day or two before he asked me this question the July issue of FIELD & STREAM had appeared containing an article that I had written on the dry-fly; this article did not attempt to go into the methods and technicalities of dry-fly fishing, but was simply intended to be a question put to American anglers, as to why this very fascinating branch of the sport was not practiced more generally in this country.

"The only mistake in your article," said this friend, "was that you did not even tell us what a dry-fly was. If you did not desire to go into technicalities, you should at least have described to us the fly mentioned."

And I apologize.

I had fully realized for several years that the vast majority of American fly fishermen had used only what are known as "wet flies," and that the knowledge of dry-fly fishing, as it has been practised in England for many years, had been very limited in this country. But I must confess that I did not appreciate the fact that there was a very large body of anglers still in total ignorance of the meaning of the word "dry fly." English angling literature has been full of it for years; many books have been written upon the subject in England; in fact, books and sporting magazines have not only contained much about dry-fly fishing, but countless pages have been taken up with disputes about dry-fly methods between what are known as the "purists" and those who fish in other ways.

The dry-fly "purist," as he is known, casts his fly only when he sees a trout rising; he "stalks" the stream; if he sees a rise, he goes within casting distance of the spot, carefully places his fly so that it falls exactly where the trout had risen, or just above it, so that the fly will float down over the fish. If he does not get a rise, it is not incompatible with his code of ethics to try a fly of a different pattern; if he finally gives up in his attempt to catch this particular fish, he again "stalks" the stream, but does not make another cast until he again sees a rise. If no rises occur within his vision during the day, he does not fish.

This method of angling, sportsmanlike and commendable though it may be, and undoubtedly fascinating to its English devotees, is not, I believe, the kind of dry-fly fishing that would appeal to the majority of American anglers. Some of the strict "purists" call those who use other methods of dry-fly fishing "poachers," and it may be imagined that the disputes between the two schools are not always conducted in the most amiable manner. Whether or not we watch with amusement the more or less heated arguments among the various schools, over technical and what may appear to us minor details, yet we must give British anglers enormous credit for the deep, careful, scientific study that they have given for many years to the art of angling.

First, the expert English angler is an entomologist and knows upon what insects the trout feed, and as a rule finds out upon which insect they are feeding on that particular day and hour that he is on the stream; and from his fly box he selects a fly tied in exact imitation in size and color of the insect. Can that be said of the average American fly-fisherman?

He also endeavors to present the fly to the fish in the most natural manner possible. He knows that weak flying insects cannot swim against a current with the speed of a torpedo boat, and that they do not move about under the surface by fits, starts and jerks. He reasons that if a winged insect is on the surface of a running stream it can have but one motion; that is the motion imparted by the current. In other words, the fly simply *floats* on the surface of the water; and so his artificial lures are known as dry-flies or *floating flies*.

From this comes the whole theory of dry-fly fishing: To use a fly tied in exact imitation of a natural insect and so made that it will not easily sink; to allow it to float down over the trout, with no other motion than that imparted by the current. If any other movement is given to the fly the theory is that the trout will look upon it as entirely unnatural—something that it has learned to know that live flies will not do—and that therefore the lure will have no attraction whatever for the fish.

It is not probable that the average American angler would care to go on a stream and not cast a fly until he had seen a rise, even at the risk of the long-distance ignominy of being called a poacher by some of the English "purists." In the first place, he enjoys the practice of casting, whether the fish rise or not. Then again abundant experience has taught our American dry-fly fishermen that on some of our nearby streams they can often pass an entire day without seeing a trout rise at a natural insect. So the dry-fly fisherman of this country begins casting when he reaches the stream more or less "for general results," as the Englishman might think; but it may be said that the work of an American expert is not at all a bungling performance, and there is very little "hit-or-miss" about it. His methods may differ from those of the English "purist" in that instead of casting at the rise, he casts at what seems to him to be "likely spots"—that is, at those places where his experience has taught him that the trout hide, live and seek their food. There is nothing prettier to watch on a stream than the casting of a dry-fly expert. It is seldom except when watching them that I have seen flies light "like thistledown"; or that I have been deceived into thinking for a moment that an artificial fly was a natural insect as I saw it flutter down through the air to the surface of the water.

For the benefit of my friend of the Camp Fire Club who asked me the question which appears at the beginning of this article, and for those anglers to whom the arts of dry-fly fishing still remain as a hidden book—in other words, for the very *beginner* in dry-fly fishing—I will try to explain as simply as possible the methods of dry-fly fishing as they are commonly practiced by some of our American anglers.

First, as to the equipment—rod, line, leader, flies and one or two other specialties used in dry-fly angling. I shall assume that the reader is thoroughly familiar with the rest of the equipment, such as clothing, waders, reel, creel, etc.

The rod for this form of angling should have plenty of what is commonly known as "back bone"; that is, it should not be weak or "whippy." It may be 9, 9½ or 10 feet long, though perhaps the 10 foot rod is the favorite. It is impossible to describe a rod by giving weight for length, for the very simple reason that one 9-foot rod of 6 ounces may have much less power, back bone and resiliency, than another rod of the same length weighing only 4½ ounces. What are known as 4 oz. or 5 oz. tournament rods, weighing 4¾ oz. and 5½ or 5¾ oz., respectively, are in my opinion ideal rods for the purpose. Not, however, that tournament rods are at all necessary; I have several rods that are ideal for dry-fly fishing— one in particular, 9½ feet long, and weighing 5½ oz., full of back bone, snap and ginger, and easily capable of handling an English waterproofed "D" tapered line; and still it was not built or intended for tournament casting. There are several reasons for selecting a strong, powerful rod for dry-fly work. A heavier line is used than is commonly used in ordinary fly fishing for reasons that will be explained later; the rod also is called upon to do much more work, for in using the dry-fly, after each cast there must be several casts in the air or "false casts," for the purpose of drying the fly, before the insect again touches the water. Therefore your rod should be powerful, though not necessarily heavy; in fact, unless one likes to have a tired wrist at the end of the day, an unnecessarily heavy rod is anything but desirable.

As to the line, expert anglers will advise without qualification a waterproofed silk-line. While nothing can equal the best American-made split bamboo rods, the best English fly lines, while very expensive, are well worth the price and the trouble of getting them. They are waterproofed in a vacuum, so that the "dressing" may permeate every part of the line. Then they are rubbed down, and afterward dressed again. Just how many times this operation is repeated I do not know. But the completed product is a line of great beauty, smoothness and flexibility, and the angler who has not used one has a fresh pleasure before him in fly-casting. As to the size of the line, the same thing that was said of "weight for length" in rods may be said of lines, changing the expression to "weight for size." In a line it is the weight that counts; and lines of different makes designated by the letters "D," "E," or "F," vary both in size and in weight. It is probable, however, that the beginner in dry-fly fishing will be perfectly safe if he buys a good size "E," though I often use with much pleasure a "D" line. And by all means, whatever anyone else may tell you to the contrary, buy a tapered line, and have it tapered at both ends.

Next comes the leader. There are various opinions as to whether this necessary article should be tapered or not, and also as to the exact length that should be used. The beginner may study all these things out later, and be guided both by his own experience and that of others whom he will meet on the stream. It is safe to say that a large majority of dry-fly anglers both in England and America use a tapered leader, 9 feet long, and dry-fly leaders are commonly listed in this

way in nearly all catalogues. It is true that a long, light leader is difficult to
manage against a strong head wind, and in these weather conditions a leader of
6 feet might be better. The conventional dry-fly leader is tapered, and is rather
coarse at the line end, tapering down to from fine drawn gut to the finest undrawn
at the end where the fly is tied. Personally I prefer the fine undrawn gut for
general fishing.

It has already been made plain that the flies are "tied dry"; that is, so that
they will float. It is therefore necessary that the bodies of dry-flies shall be made
of some material that will float readily, and that it will not become water-soaked
easily. There are certain objections to the use of silk, as it changes color when
wet, and "dubbing," commonly used for the bodies of flies, becomes easily water-
soaked and the fly consequently "soggy." So that now Mr. Halford, the English
expert, recommends quill, horsehair and Rafia grass for dressing the bodies of
floating flies. This, however, properly belongs to the fly-dressers' art, and not to
beginners.

Most of our dry-flies come from England, though handled by the best American dealers, and all are tied as nearly as possible in exact imitation of live insects.
It is customary to "paraffine" the flies from time to time to make them float better.
For this purpose carry along with you on the stream a small bottle of parafine
oil, or one of the several preparations made especially for this purpose. It will
also pay to buy a small "dry-fly oiler" made to carry this oil when you are on
the streams. After tying the fly to the leader, put a small quantity of oil on the
hackles and body of the fly. Carry a rag or old handkerchief with you, and with
it "squeeze out" the superfluous oil.

The majority of dry-fly men also own a small tin of deer fat, though some
consider its use unnecessary. With it they grease their line occasionally, or at
least from 10 to 30 feet of it. The deer fat is best put on the line with the thumb
and forefinger of one hand, and the line is then carefully rubbed down with a
soft rag to remove the superfluous fat. The idea of the use of deer fat is to make
the line float more readily. It is also claimed that it preserves the line.

While it has been made very plain that these words are written for the beginner
only, yet I hope that the exact type of beginner that I have in mind will be
equally well understood; he is not the tyro who has never as yet had the pleasure
of using a fly-rod, or the man who has no knowledge of trout streams or the
habits of trout. I assume that those who have asked me recently to write some
dry-fly instructions of the simplest kind for the beginner are already good anglers.
It is my hope that this article will be of some slight assistance to those who are
fly fishermen, but who have not as yet tasted the pleasures of luring the trout
with the dry-fly. It is not difficult to believe that the step from the expert wet-
fly fisherman to the dry-fly expert is a comparatively short one, and easily accomplished by one willing to devote some thought to the subject, and some time

to practising on the streams. In this way it is probable that all our best American dry-fly anglers have become experts. They have first been expert wet-fly anglers; then their attention has been drawn to the dry-fly; they have received a few "points" from friends—enough to start with; they have practised on the streams, perhaps somewhat crudely at first; they have read much of the very fine literature written in England upon the subject; they have been quick to understand the methods used by our English cousins; they have adapted and changed the English ideas to meet the conditions upon our streams, and in a comparatively short time they have become successively our pioneers and our experts in dry-fly angling.

It has already been noticed, possibly, what a part *naturalness* plays in dry-fly fishing; we have learned that the fly is an exact imitation of the natural insect; it must be presented to the trout in an absolutely natural way, and when the fly is on the water, it must have a natural motion. It is not a case of hoping that by some lucky chance the trout may possibly take the feathered lure for "something good to eat," without knowing exactly the nature of the food presented. The trout must see that the fly is an insect upon which he has fed many times before; it must light on the water as he has seen thousands of other insects light; it must float down the stream in precisely the same manner that he has been accustomed all his life to see other insects float with the current. In other words, the very naturalness of the entire game must deceive the trout absolutely.

You must fish upstream, or up and across stream, and the beginner will make no mistake in following this advice blindly without being influenced by the arguments made pro and con by the wet-fly fishermen as to whether it is better to fish upstream or down. True it is not desirable that you cast directly ahead of you on the stream, so that you will "line the fish" as it lies with its head upstream. By "lining the fish" is meant casting the fly above the trout so that the leader comes down directly over its head and body, thus placing the fly, the head and tail of the fish and the angler all in a direct line. It is obvious that the fish may get a good view of the leader before it sees the fly, or that he may see the fly and leader simultaneously.

Before taking the beginner to the stream, even at the risk of repetition, it may be well to recapitulate and bring together the principal points of dry-fly fishing that we have already covered in a general way: 1. Use but one fly and that an imitation of a natural insect, and a fly that floats; 2. Cast this fly upstream, at or slightly above a spot where you know there is a trout, through having seen it rise, or a spot where your "fish sense" tells you that a trout may be; 3. Let the fly float down with no motion whatever except that naturally imparted by the current; 4. After the fly has floated down well below the place where you think the trout may lie, lift it very gently from the water and prepare for the next cast; 5. Make at least three or four casts in the air both to dry your fly, and to lengthen your line, and do not let the fly touch the water again until you see that the fly will strike the exact spot that you have picked out for it to land; 6. If you "bungle" your cast—this is, if the fly does not light at the spot that you intended—or if it does not light properly, with wing nicely "cocked" in the air, do not allow yourself to become excited and immediately jerk the fly from the water; let it float down as if you had made the finest cast possible, and then lift it out gently as before. By following this course you will lessen much the chances of frightening the trout, which may take the fly at the next cast as if nothing unusual had happened.

About making the casts in the air a word of explanation may be necessary, as this is something that is seldom practised in wet-fly fishing. Strip the line from the reel with the left hand. Work the rod backward and forward as in regular casting, but hold the tip well up and allow the fly to move back and forth in the air without touching the water. But for several reasons do not swing your rod as if you were practising with Indian clubs or beating a carpet, or as if you were taking any kind of daily exercise to strengthen your muscles. Let the wrist and spring of the rod do all the work. Let the tip of the rod describe only a small arc; that is, let it go only slightly beyond the perpendicular on the forward or on the back cast. Let the movement of the rod be gentle, and avoid all quick, sharp motions. In addition to being much better casting, the motion of the rod is not nearly so liable to alarm the trout. Before beginning to make these "false casts," your eye has picked out the exact spot on the water where you wish the fly to drop. When you see that you have enough line out, allow the fly to light very gently. Keep practising until the fly falls as lightly as a small live insect would fall. Then let the fly float down with the current. As it comes down strip in the slack with the left hand, but do not strip so fast that you impart any unnatural motion whatever to the fly. When ready, lift the fly from the water as gently as possible, and then begin another series of "false casts."

Dry-flies are tied in two ways: First, with wings, which are generally upright; Second, they are tied "buzz," or with hackles and without wings. The winged fly should float on the water with its wings upright or "cocked." If the beginner cannot always make a fly light in this way, he need not be discouraged—the expert cannot do it either; often, very often, the fly will light on its side. Incidentally it may be interesting to know that the fly lights on the water with its wings "cocked" more often with the horizontal cast than with the overhead cast.

Where to Use the Dry Fly

E. B. RICE

Despite British "purist" pleas for dry-fly exclusivity, here's common-sense advice on when and where to (and not *to) use the floater on our faster waters.* (October 1911)

The "Dry Fly" on American trout streams is, and has been for some time, the subject of animated discussion amongst anglers far and wide, though its use is limited to a comparatively few individuals of more courage and initiative than their brothers.

There is no reason in the world, except for lack of exact knowledge on the subject, why we should not all use, in its proper place and at the proper time, the dry fly, and here lies, I think, the real cause of uncertainty amongst the majority of fly fishermen regarding the employment of this method.

The floating fly, commonly called the dry fly, is a development of the artificial fly brought about by the condition of water obtaining on the "chalk streams" of England. Streams of the most marvelous clarity, quiet streams generally, as compared with the average American trout stream, where the greatest care in casting and the finest quality of tackle are necessary, not only to be successful, but to kill any fish at all. It was found that fish were more easily deceived with a fly which floated in a natural manner upon the surface, than with the submerged fly, and flies were specially tied to produce this result. There are no American streams that present exactly the same difficulties to the fly fisherman. Difficulties we have to overcome, but they are not the difficulties of the English chalk stream.

As the streams of this country are different from those upon which the dry fly art was born and reared to its present state of perfection, so also must the method of its employment in this country be different.

In the first place, let me state that *all* English streams are not well adapted to the exclusive use of the dry fly, nor is the dry fly used to the exclusion of the wet method on *all* English streams.

One of the foremost principles of dry fly fishing on the English chalk streams is that of "fishing the rise," which means never to cast except to a rising fish. As to the merits of this, there seems to be some difference of opinion, but of one thing we may be certain, it would be time wasted to do the same on American streams. English streams may be well suited for "fishing the rise," but on American streams one should "fish the water," which means to cast in every likely spot.

"Val Couson" reminds us in an interesting article in the *Fishing Gazette* of May 6th, 1911, in "The Excommunication of the Wet Fly," that we must keep in mind the fact that the dry fly was invented and is now employed, because it will kill more fish in certain waters than the wet fly. This notwithstanding that some American, and many English anglers, claim that it is used because it is more scientific and sportsmanlike. Let me impress that upon you—while the dry fly method is the more spectacular means of taking trout, it is not more scientific nor more sportsmanlike than the wet method.

If you doubt this ask your expert dry fly friend if it is not easier to take fish from a quiet, glassy still, stretch of water (though difficult at best) with a dry fly than a wet. Individual anglers may develop greater skill in the use of one than in the use of the other, and the dry fly method being new to many of us, we are apt to look upon it, on account of its spectacular features, as requiring a greater degree of skill than that which we have been used to, the wet.

Now we come to the best method of using the dry fly on our own streams, and the purpose of this article being to discuss the merits and uses of the dry fly rather than to give instruction in casting, I will leave that part to others, in the hope that you may find a better teacher.

To begin with, I think you will agree that the typical American trout stream is one in which the water alternates between hurrying rifts and deep and quiet pools, and it is perfectly reasonable to assume that trout are more easily deceived in quick water than in the quiet, glassy stretches where they so often lay in plain sight, to the distraction of the fisherman. I refer particularly to our hard fished Eastern streams, where in many cases brown trout predominate and furnish the major part of the sport—streams upon which it is a greater feat of skill to take one single twelve-inch trout, than to fill a boat with bigger ones in wilderness waters.

It is a pretty generally accepted theory that the larger a trout grows the lazier he becomes, and his surface feeding diminishes as time goes on until finally he reaches an age where he apparently ceases to take food on the surface altogether. Witness the comparative sizes of large trout taken on the fly and those taken with bait. This is especially striking in streams where brown trout are abundant.

I have never heard of brown trout being taken on a fly in our Eastern streams of over 3¾ lbs., and even a 2½ pounder is a monster.*On the other hand, I know personally of many large fish from 4 lbs. up being taken on bait, two of these weighing 6½ lbs. apiece, and in the same streams, where the largest trout, to my knowledge, taken on the fly was 3¾ lbs. It is therefore reasonable to assume that trout grow lazy as they advance in years and, as I have said, feed less and less upon the surface.

Keep these things in mind when you fish, and do not *overdo* the dry fly. The angler who uses either method to the exclusion of the other (regardless of the water) diminishes his chances of success.

In every stream of my acquaintance there are stretches of quiet water from which the casual fly fisherman seldom or never takes a trout, and yet the fish may be seen lazily watchful of the angler's every move. These glassy spots are just the places for the employment of the dry fly method. If the fly is submerged the fish perceive the deception instantly, but often, to the carefully cast and floating fly, will come these wily fellows whose position is an impregnable one to the wet fly angler.

I remember well an instance of this sort. Some years ago I was fishing with a friend, a dry fly enthusiast. I came to a beautiful pool where deep and rapid water at the head slowly shallowed and flattened out toward the tail of the pool, presenting for two-thirds of its lower length quiet, clear, transparency, the Waterloo of the wet fly man. At the head, however, was a most alluring stretch of wet fly water and in my haste to reach this upper stretch, the kind of water, I must admit, which has always appealed to me as ideal trout water, I did not take the trouble to remove my dropper fly and fish the lower part of the pool with floating fly, as I knew I should do, but simply used the wet fly method right over the whole water, being well content to take two nice fish from the upper part; not a rise did I have in the quiet glassy lower part of the pool. As I reached the head my friend appeared and asked what luck I'd had. I showed him my fish and told him of the lack of rises in the lower part. "I think I will float a fly over that water," he remarked, and going below he dropped a whirling dun, cocked

*Except in the Field & Stream Prize Fishing Contest, 5¼ lbs.—Editor.

and floating over near the opposite bank. Nothing resulted from this first cast and I was beginning to think my judgment correct for not having bothered much with the lower water, when he dropped it once more on the farther side and a yard above the first cast. Splash! swirl! a slight raising of the rod tip and my friend was fast in a fine fish.

One instance of this kind might prove nothing, but I have seen it many times since, the dry fly angler succeeding with that method, where the wet fly man had failed, and failed, and failed to score.

Indeed it does not pay to overlook the dry fly. On the other hand, it would be, in my opinion, as unwise, on our home streams, to discard the wet fly method, as it would be to leave unlearned the adaptation of the dry.

We are often prone to overdo the new inventions, with which we are continually being blessed in these enlightened years of progress, too apt to forget the virtue in our old friends while contemplating the wondrous attractions of the new.

While it is true that the dry fly method will take fish that would not even notice the submerged fly, it is likewise true that certain fish can be reached by a well sunk fly which seldom or never could be had by floating fly. I refer now to those fish, to catch which is the ambition of every angler—those record-breakers of which we dream and dream, the catching of one of which will live with us in after years, like the killing of our first deer—the fish which grow lazy with age and cease their surface feeding.

I am aware that some dry fly enthusiasts will not agree with me here, but these differences of opinion only serve to make the subject more interesting, and on this point I personally find no room for doubt. I have seen the thing so many times,—the dry fly angler and his wet fly friend, each most confident in his own particular branch of the art. They take their fish in different places, the wet fly man making little progress in the still and mirrored water and the dry fly man seldom killing in the best water for his friend. And what is the result? As to numbers there is but little difference, but in size the wet fly man has often had one or two much larger fish to show. Of course, the question of individual skill plays an important part in the game, but I most assuredly believe that any of our skillful American anglers, using both methods in their proper places, will find that they get bigger fish while fishing wet. Why should they not? Certainly the well sunk fly offers an easier tid-bit to the big and lazy fish than does the floating fly, and if we are correct in our thinking that fish grow lazy with advancing years, certainly the wet fly is an easier prey.

I was fishing with a friend two years ago, a dry fly man of the very best, down on the Brodhead Creek, Pa., and after a little lunch and a smoke beside a splendid pool, he took his rod while I sat by and watched. Deftly and surely the floating insect found its mark in three good fish, each about eleven inches long, and then there came a fish which rose short and never touched the fly. This was at the head of the pool where the water was swift though clear. Presently he rose again, and again did not touch the fly but we saw him clearly this time, and he was a beauty. For some minutes longer my friend floated his fly over this fish and then asked me to take his rod and try. I did so and after extending the line I sunk the fly above the fish and he took it, at least ten inches under the water on the very first cast. A sixteen-inch brown trout was added to my creel.

Now here was a fish which was just large enough to move too slowly in this rapid water to get the floating fly. He came for it, to be sure, but it was whisked away by the rapid current before he reached it. Who can say that this same fish, after missing untold numbers of floating flies, would not have ceased ere long to be a surface feeder? It seems very probable.

And after we have all had our say and given to the expectant world our weighty opinions, there still remains that vast expanse of water which is neither "wet" nor "dry," where all of us, brothers of the angle, may beg to differ as to flies and methods, and where the embryo expert may develop or may not, as the red gods dictate.

It would be a poor and sorry game if we could lay out rules for every inch of every stream, and we should be thankful that, beyond a certain point, each of us has to work out his own salvation.

Up to this point I have referred, in speaking of the use of the dry fly, to the method and not to the fly itself. Let us briefly consider the fly itself and compare it with the ordinary wet fly.

In the first place, the whole fly is constructed more carefully and with greater effort to imitate some insect, but the chief difference is noted in the position and character of the wings and hackle. The best winged floating flies (with the exception of the May flies) are tied with double wings in such a manner that the wings stand up from the body and apart, in a most lifelike and natural position, and add greatly to the floating quality of the fly. When laid side by side with a wet fly, the rankest novice would choose the dry fly for his fishing.

It has been my habit, and that of many of my friends, for some years past to use in both *wet* and *dry* fly fishing, nothing but dry flies, that is, flies tied specially to use as floating flies. The dry fly when *sunk* makes a much more attractive lure than the wet fly *sunk*. It may be fished after the wet method in all the water along the stream which your intuition and experience tells you is best suited for a submerged or sunken fly, and then when you come to some stretch of dry fly water you can, with little trouble, remove your dropper and, by making a dozen or two dry casts, float the fly perfectly.

Stock up your fly boxes hereafter with none but dry flies and use them in fishing either method.

Do not paraffine your flies at all unless you have a great deal of dry fly water ahead of you, and then do not resort to oil until you are actually on the stream, treating each fly as you need it. Do not dose up a number of flies with paraffine in expectation of future use, for you will surely want to use one of these flies *wet* if you do, and they cannot be used *wet*, after being treated with paraffine, with any degree of comfort.

The Shank of the Trout Season

O. W. SMITH

Tips on early-season tackle and tactics (including worm fishing) that are every bit as helpful today as they were before World War I. (April 1913)

All my life I have been a trout-fisher. I can say, without a smack of conceit, that I know something of troutology, and am not exactly an ignoramus in the matter of tackle, though I am ready to admit that upon neither matter is my word final. What student of fish has not been surprised again and again by some strange antic or, shall we say, acquired habit of this beauty of the brooklets; and as to tackle, well, may not the most experienced old hand secure valuable hints even from the veriest tyro? All of which goes to prove that no man knows it all, and that that wise guy of ancient days was right when he said, "In a multitude of counselors there is safety."

The habits or, perhaps we had better say, ways of trout change with the varying seasons. He who hopes to fill his creel in the quixotic month of April must seek the creek beauties in the deep holes and larger streams, for it is not until the temperature of the water begins to rise and the insect life to multiply that this speckled aristocrat seeks out the spring-fed brooklets and densely shaded pools. A party of my friends a few seasons ago visited a famous Wisconsin stream shortly after opening day, and though they fished assiduously for two days secured only a few small trout; then on their way home one member of the party cast an experimental fly upon the surface of the larger river into which the famous stream disembogues. In less than two hours he had creeled thirteen trout, the combined weight of which was something over twenty pounds. Early in the season the deeper, more sluggish streams are preferred by trout; even in the smaller streams, when you find them it will be in the quiet, snag-infested pools.

I have a theory, based on my own experience, that trout will not rise to flies while ice is found along the marge of the stream; as a rule, will not strike at the feathers with any degree of savageness until the natural insect is found upon the surface of the water. Whether or not flies are out in April will depend altogether upon the season; I have seen certain early forms out in force even upon opening day, though, as a rule, they do not hatch much more before the first week in May. Oh, I have caught trout on a fly, if you can so dignify it, by trolling a silver doctor, bass size, deep in the water as you would a spoon hook; even when the fish would not look at an ordinary fuzzy-wuzzy lure skipped lightly over the surface, though such fishing never appealed to me; almost as soon use a spoon and be done with it. Some years ago I secured three large trout by trolling a scarlet ibis, large bass size, in a deep hole below a dam, when every other bait or lure proved unattractive. Just why the fish struck at the thing is more than I can imagine, unless out of mere curiosity, for surely they could not have supposed it a thing good to eat, even though all members of the *fontinalis* tribe are notorious gourmands.

Early in the season, unless the season be in advance of the calendar, in order to secure even a respectable mess of trout there are times and streams where one must resort to the much-maligned earthworms. Freely and gladly, even enthusiastically, I will agree that worms are not the ideal bait, but if between worms and an empty basket, what will you? I prefer six trout on feathers to twelve on worms, but I also prefer the twelve trout caught on worms to the gaping mockery of an empty creel. I have always held that a man can be a true sportsman even though he use such a bait as "garden hackle." To me there is a right and a wrong way of using bait. I never vary my tackle one iota, whether using worms when the feathers prove unattractive, or when using the feathers exclusively. Why should I? It is playing the fish, fighting him to the point of exhaustion, the bending of the rod and the singing of the line that makes angling, spring or summer, the fascinating sport it is. I had rather three trout would escape than that I should be guilty of hauling even one sparkler incontinently out upon the bank.

I well remember one square-tailed monster that had taken up his home at the foot of a little rapid below an old dam, in a favorite early spring stream of mine,

mine because fished by me. (You own a stream in the same unreal, real way, do you not?) Well, a full half-dozen times I visited that rapid. Always I caught a glint of the fish's irradiant sides or saw the shape of his disappearing tail. Once for a brief, glorious moment I was connected with him by a thrumming line, and therefore knew him for as goodly a bunch of ichthyic trouble as ever wore gills, but, alas, an outreaching timber of the old dam caught the ripping line and—well, the world became dark suddenly. Once again, after imagination had juggled with memory until he had become a leviathan, I hooked him, played him for fifteen minutes or so in the deep pool below the rapids; then, because to reach him with the landing net there was an impossibility, contrary to all law and precedent, successfully led him *up* through the rushing water; but just as I reached down with the net a last, spasmodic flop tore out the hook, and the monster— never had he seemed so large as at that instant—floated away with the current. He must have left the pool forthwith, for I neither hooked nor even caught a glimpse of his square tail again. At the time I was desperately angry, but now I am as well satisfied, for perhaps, probably, he was not so large as he seemed.

I was fishing with worms and using a very light fly rod, because of which some say I lost him; if so, well and good. I hope he still is at liberty. I repeat what I said a moment ago, "I never vary my tackle one iota, whether using worms when the feathers prove unattractive, or when using the feathers exclusively." Employ as light a rod as your experience and skill will permit, and as good a one as you can afford. A good split bamboo will cost from, say, eighteen dollars up to the limit. I know of one light rod, in split bamboo, that weighs in the neighborhood of four ounces, for which the manufacturers charge an even five dollars, the only dependable cheap rod of which I know. Understand me, I do not mean that that little rod in any way compares with the more expensive tools, but it is good enough for a host of us; even though we possess more expensive fly wielders, we will be glad to take the cheaper rod on those hard trips where an accident is apt to occur.

With a light fly rod it is possible to cast a worm—don't laugh—in a manner impossible with the ordinary, stiff bait rod, not to mention the convenience of having the reel below the hand. Trout will *rise to* worms in the spring with as much vim and life as, later in the season, they strike at flies. Do not for a moment think that you must weight down the line with a chunk of lead and sink the bait to the bottom. A worm cast close up to an overhanging bank, or just at the outer edge of a snag or rock, will bring out a bit of living rainbow with a rush that will do your heart good. Fish downstream, by all means, casting over obstructions which form little pools in the bend of the stream. A small boulder will sometimes cause quite a deep pool to form on the lower side, a pool the advantages of which a trout is quick to discover. Cast just where the current sets around and let the worm go dancing along down upon the surface and see what will happen. Cast the worm; be as nice and exact about it as you would were you using the feathers. Right and left, hitting every possible lurking place of a fish, working down stream slowly. Fish *all* the water.

Of course there are times when one must reel, the alders lay close upon the surface of the water, and casting is an absolute impossibility, but beneath the brush is water, plenty of it, sometimes a deep pool. I know rods of stream where casting, casting anything, is out of the question from one end of the season to the other; surely in such places bait reeling is legitimate. Again, never use a sinker. Let the worm go adventuring down among the brush at the mercy of the current; it will carry along the "line of least resistance." You can reel back if you do not hurry, and should you hook a fish your patience will be tried to the utmost. However, I have more than once taken several trout from such places, one after the other. To hook a branch away below is serious and spells trouble unless some obliging trout comes along and unhooks it for you.

Last summer I was fishing and taking pictures on the Pine River, in Waushara County, Wisconsin. I came to just such a place as I have been describing, let out about a hundred feet of line, then laid my rod over the tops of the brush and went back to set up my camera. Now there was a very strong current at that particular place, and every moment or two I would hear the reel give tongue. Of course I slipped on the click before I left it, but, being engaged with the focusing of my picture, I did not pay much attention. Just as I was laying out the rubber tube, preparatory to making the exposure, there came a *fortissimo* shriek from the reel, which sent me sprinting down the bank. But I was too late; I arrived just in time to see the end of my best line whip through the guides. Then I remembered all about *not* tying the line to the spool, for I had planned to rewind it onto another reel. Of course I had an extra line and reel in my pocket, but the line that had disappeared cost me three dollars, and was the new idea of a certain maker, which had strongly commended itself to me. I poked around the brush with a crooked stick, said things which afterward I was sorry for, but failed to find a trace of it. (Water is a mighty poor medium in which to look for tracks.) Well, I gave it up, put on another reel, then went back and took my picture. I caught two fish by reeling, and now comes the strangest part of the yarn. I got a strong bite, and in due time reeled up a fine fish, and snarled about his head was the other line. Evidently he had crossed it somewhere on the way up. Then I found the end, put on the empty reel and began to wind. Imagine my surprise when I found that the first fish was still on, and I landed that, too. Beat this yarn if you can, and it is the unvarnished truth, too.

In the matter of reels, there is not much to be said, or, rather, was not until recently. As I use worms exactly as I do flies, the balance handle of the multiplier makes that reel a vexation, if not an impossibility; of course, when one reels, the multiplier is much more convenient, though, owing to the out-reaching handle,

I have always confined myself to the lighter, single-action click. I am glad to state that recently I secured a multiplying reel in aluminum, built with an ingeniously arranged handle, which cannot possibly entangle the line; however, it is somewhat expensive, costing in the neighborhood of twelve dollars, if I mistake not, but it is worth it, every cent. Of course, always, the reel for a fly rod should be light, cannot well be too light, though it should be large enough to spool fifty yards of line. Here, you see, we use more line than we do in regular fly fishing, where thirty yards is plenty. Ordinarily I do not use over thirty yards of line in my bait fishing with a fly rod, but for the seldom spot, where one must let the line down under brush, the extra twenty yards is a great convenience.

The line is a matter of supreme importance, for it must be strong and of sufficient weight to cast with ease. I use a regular enameled fly line, the same line that I use when employing feathers; indeed, it would be hard to handle my bait, as I handle it, with the oiled line usually recommended for bait fishing. There is a "general purpose" line upon the market, with which I have experimented to some extent, said to be equally good for bait casting or fly fishing, which I have found satisfactory, so far as I have used it. Remember, if you expect to reel much, that the line should be strong enough to break the hook every time, otherwise it may break at the reel. A good line is too valuable to sacrifice, and a poor one is of no value anywhere. I am willing to pay a good price for a line. Then I care for it as the apple of my eye, drying it in the shade after each trip and coating it with "deer fat" now and then.

When I first began fishing with fly-rod worms I used a long leader, nine feet, but to-day I use only three, for all fishing. I find that length more convenient in the small streams to which I resort when the red gods call. Such a leader is not so apt to break, will not snag in the brush, and is a whole lot more convenient when it comes to landing fish. We all expect to land fish; that, I take it, is what we fish for. With the light fly rod, the long leader I have found to be a delusion and a snare always. I pay just about as much for my leader as I used to when I purchased the nine-foot length; you see, what I have subtracted from price I have added to quality. Never get a poor leader; buy the best.

So I have reached the end of the line, have arrived at the hook. I get a good, hand-made hook in small size, one that line and leader will break, for reasons set forth above. As to the particular bend and make, I honestly think that purely a matter of individual choice; personally, I am converted to the "square bend," for which some of my angling friends laugh me to scorn. Certainly a square-bend hook from the shop of a man who produces a good article is a better implement than a trade article, a matter which holds true of all shapes. All along you will note that I have urged the best quality of tackle, not alone because there is a certain satisfaction in possessing the best—for the mere possession's sake. No one dare say a well-made article, into which the maker has put the best of his mind and heart, is not more durable than a cheap, machine-made one. Now, if the tackle maker be a devotee of the gentle art, as nine times out of ten he is, you are going to get class and quality as well as durability.

I am ready to admit that I am fastidious about my tackle, a fastidiousness that extends even to the worm which I use on my hook. He, or it, must be just so so, in the pink of condition, or I will not use him. For three days I "scour" him in moss, then when he glows red I loop him on my hook. The point is to hook the worm in a natural manner so that when he strikes the water he will appear as though a gift from the sun; don't know where else he could drop from. Experience has proven that a single worm fastened to the hook in a proper manner is 90 per cent more alluring than a wad of them bunched on promiscuously.

Colorado Trouting

T. NASH BUCKINGHAM

A western angling adventure by Nash Buckingham, who was to become one of America's favorite gunning authors. Trout in the accompanying photos, by the way, appear to be well into the three- to five-pound category. (June 1913)

CASTING CHARACTERS

A Southern Colonel.
An Eminent Jurist.
"Me and Bunk."

FIRST JOINT

My cabin door banged open and in cluttered the Eminent Jurist, bringing with him an aroma of cigar smoke and leaving behind a path of brilliant sunshine.

"Get up if you're going fishing," he bawled, suiting action to the command by seizing a corner of my blankets and bracing himself for a lusty pull. I squinted at him through rebellious lids and craftily twisted what cover I could beneath me in order to resist an impending attack. Or perhaps I might out-talk him and gain a few precious moments.

"Bin'ner brek'fus?"

42

"Nope! But I'm on the road there and you're going with me—pretty pronto—too. Come on! Resistance is useless, my fine fellow, right *now*—or I uncover you to the world."

"Gim'me five minutes mo'."

"Not a frazzling second."

"Spare me, Mister Man."

I felt the blankets tighten.

"Peccavi—have mercy—Judge!"

"At *three*—I yank," gritted the Jurist—"one—*two*——"

"Oh! all right," I grumbled, "I'll get up." And so I did, crawling out from the hay tick and blankets like an old "stove-up" hunting dog, stretching until my ribs seemed ready to burst through the skin. But, by the time I'd manipulated the tooth brush and been soused off with a bucket of snow water that the Jurist gleefully fetched from the crick, my eyes were not only wide open but dancing. Then we hit off up the breakfast route.

What a bully morning it was, with beaming day not long come into its own; the pasture agleam beneath its melting nightcap of near frost; lemon-splotched side hills shading aspen belts into the darker folds of spruce, and, towering above all, the gnarly, gray, uncompromising barriers of the Divide. Full two moons ride from the screech of a locomotive, amid a network of lakes and close beside a white-capped, throaty little river—in short—at the E Bar X—old Sam Himes' ranch in the White River country of Colorado.

Above the cook cabin a drool of smoke filtered into the brisk air, and when we drew nigh a most fetching odor of frying bacon and fragrant coffee assailed the senses. Opening the door of the sawdust-floored dining-room discovered the Colonel and Bunk (she's my one and only best bet) seated vis-a-vis at the long linoleum-covered table. Above them arched the magnificent outlines of a noble elk's head and a bright, cheery log fire snapped and steamed in the cavernous rock fireplace. Entered Mrs. Himes with a pleasant "Good morning, folks," and a tin platter piled high with smoking, pink-fleshed trout. In addition to a surplice of corn meal each fish was delicately browned in boiling bacon grease, covered to withhold the juices, and stuffed, by way of good measure with a sliver of crisped pork.

"These heah fish," began the Colonel (having first applied a most chivalrous response to the greeting of Mrs. Himes), slipping his knife under a trout and accomplishing the transfer without the loss of a single stir to his coffee, "have literally got my goat. Befo' I started fishin' in this heah country there war'n't nothin' better to me, nor is there for that matter, than a slice of ole' blue channel catfish steak cooked like ole Wes' used to turn the trick. But, fo' goodness, I declare the way Mrs. Himes cooks these fellows is paramount, simply paramount." This trout eulogy was interrupted here by the deft paramounting of the

Colonel's fork. The Eminent Jurist, having by this time gone into action, looked up from his silent destruction of a trout whose prodigious size forbade the presence of other edibles upon his plate, and nodded vigorous approbation, being unable to voice support of the Colonel's sentiment owing to a large section of fish in his mouth. Having ultimately finessed this, he spoke.

"I am deeply impressed, my dear Colonel, with your discriminating appetite and broad sense of justice which holds you loyal to the lowly but much beloved catfish. Now to my mind a bit of broiled pompano with, say, a drawn butter sauce and lemon, or a crab omelette or——"

"My dear suh," testily interrupted the Colonel, "back in Mississippi my ole fren' Sykes Lauderdale, who has prob'ly caught an' et mo' fish than any man livin' in Monroe county to-day, assures me on his own puf'ctly good authority that in no way can the pomp'no stack up aginst the channel cat. I am with him, suh, to the death. His feelins' are so strong on the subjec' that on one occasion to which I was a silent but admirin' witness, he fully demonstrated his unswervin' loyalty on the question of supremacy." The Colonel paused and stoked a stack of fish in order to strengthen himself for the defense.

At this juncture a relay of low-flying hot-cakes dipped into the Colonel's killing zone and his trusty blade flipped two of them from the flock. The Eminent Jurist brought down the survivors and for a while, following a tremendous buttering and douches from the molasses jug, their attention was focused upon the flapjacks. At length, however, they finished. Our ponies, tethered at the hitch rack were embellished with slickers and rod cases. The Jurist with the agility of scantier years was soon aboard, while the Colonel, first lighting a long black Bayou Regalia, scrambled up and we were off. Bunk and I swung ahead into the wagon road that led down the valley and before long only a heavy cloud of Bayou Regalia smoke marked our path at a point where the trail branched off toward the canyon.

SECOND JOINT

Six miles below we corraled our ponies at Missouri Park, Sam's winter home, given over now to sunshine and packrats and an open-house policy of hospitality to any who desired to drop off and camp for the night. What a wealth of reminiscence lingered about the squat log cabin, its unfloored dog-trot and gloomy potato cellar. How many winters had engulfed it, roof deep in ponderous drifts, until the warm sunshine of late spring burst into the valley and sent the river a-roaring with a sluicing from the melt of the heights. It was here that "Grandpa" Himes "took-up" years agone, when he, among the first hardy adventurers, lowered their packs from the range cliffs and scanned the horizon for the dribbling signal fires of the Utes.

"It's ten-thirty now," said the Colonel, consulting his Ingersoll, "we'll meet here at—say—twelve-thirty for lunch—and you may make the coffee and biskits, Bunk."

"I'll be right on the job, Daddy," voiced that worthy, busily engaged in jointing up her little Divine and bending on a Royal Coachman first and a Heather Moth second.

"Up stream for mine then," said the Colonel, striding off across the timothy. "We'll stick around down here," called the Jurist, "and catch some fish!"

The Colonel whirled in his tracks.

"Two drinks of ole Patterson to one that I'll git mo' fish than the two of you!"

"Done and double the bet," cinched the Jurist, "it's a good one if I lose—at that rate."

What are more delightful than one's emotions when approaching a trout stream for the initial cast? Two miles above us the canyon spat the river down in tumultuous prospect and allurement. Log jams stemmed it here into green depthed holes and released it—there—into wide banked oily rapids.

Down a grassy bank I plunged, through the alder fringe and out onto the purl of a wide pebble strewn shoal. Behind me came Bunk, headlong, squeaking a bit when the icy torrent climbed above her spiked boots and clutched through her overalls. Up stream we toiled, around a bend to where, plunging over a half buried gigantic boulder, the surge eddied into a foamy greenish rapid.

"Get your Coachman into the white water above and let it carry down into the spume," I advised, and Bunk, with a neat little flick, behind which went many a day of experience, sent her lure right where the rule book said. Down it swept.

Zip! Bingo! A snap of the wrist! Snitched!

"Oh! you Bunk!" And away she went, stumbling, hooked hard and fast to a fighting Turk, meeting him at every jump and right in her element.

"Where there's so much smoke there's bound to be fire," I yelled, "gim'me fair play, men"—and in I whipped. Nothing doing!

Once more. *Wham!!* A leaden thud and the Leonard did a loop-the-loop.

"Clear the track!" I bellowed above the roar of the stream, "The whole river for this gent, please, he's enough for lunch by himself."

Out of the spray he came, a regular Tartar, knowing he was up against it and bulldogging to a fare-thee-well. Matters were flying like a moving picture film and from the corner of my eye I saw Bunk, with her trout clutched through its gills, beating a retreat to the shallows. The Big Fellow had me in the wide white riffles now and I gave him the run of the place for a second. Away he shot, full steam ahead upstream, and I barely held him off the slog of the murderous, hook-twisting rollers. At this moment the Jurist rallied on the flag, appearing knee deep in the riffles below, waving his landing net and shouting his battlecry.

"Avast down there," I screeched, "here he comes, get under him——"

So saying I turned Mr. Trout's head downstream. Gee!! but he hit the high places. But we put the deal across, for the Jurist, with a deft sinking swish, sacked him to a flopping finish. The battle was over and Mr. Skillet had claimed one more victim. "The bigger they come the harder they fall," said the Jurist!

Then he, too, decided to take a fall out of the big rapid and after tossing his hat into the ring a few times "tied-in" with a fairly shifty gent who waltzed off down stream almost as fast as my late customer had done. Bunk, meanwhile, was serenely testing out a lower eddy and had creeled four fair-sized floppers when I cut in ahead of her and attempted to ford the hurly-burly of the river to reach a fallen tree across the way. Right in the middle of the boiling waste my footing, or nerve, or something slipped and I did a surpassing Kellerman, but managed to cling to my rod and ship only a trifle of ice over the waders. But along the side of that tree trunk I garnered four "beauts" and then laboriously recrossed to sound "retreat" for lunch. But Bunk, bless her fat little heart, had already jingled a fire and had rustled coffee and biscuits. You all know what it takes to ease trout into the frying pan. A few rips of the old Barlow, wallow-wallow, over-and-over-in-the-meal-splutter-sputter-bread-and-butter!!! Then the Colonel puffed in—beaten in the count-up by one lonesome trout—but a gallant loser.

I must tell the truth about that lunch. We ate everything in sight; trout, hashed spuds, biscuits, doughnuts, hot coffee and all. Then we loafed for an hour while Bunk explored the cabin. What tales the old broken snowshoes and discarded skis could tell; what yarns the ponderous single-shot Buffalo gun might spin; what visions the cozy chimney corner conjured up—of steely stars glinting down upon the frozen wastes and the wilderness echoing to the howls of gaunt wolves giving hot-breathed racing voice to the pangs of hunger. But the Colonel couldn't see that picture at all, expressing, as he put it a "v'ey decided longin' for Dixie an' a cotton bale 'bout that time!"

"Just the right time to begin serious fishing," decided the Jurist finally, "we'll hike uptrail and do the cañon thoroughly—what say ye, men and women?" Then he turned to the Colonel. "I'll just spot you the fish you have in your creel—for two more drinks."

"Done ag'in, suh," grunted the Colonel, "an' I sincerely hope I lose!"

THIRD JOINT

The cañon is truly heart's delight in the fishing line. For a mile or more a shelving slather of black bed rock, sheer wall of shale on one side and a beetling spruce cliff on the other. Thence t'wixt steep side hills rifted here and there with wild-oat-strewn niches where a pony could be left to feed in safety while his rider whipped a seeming convention place for ravenous trout. Beneath green-coated logs and thunderous spouting falls the big rascals lay and from behind current-splitting boulders we took others—the latter citizens coming, as a rule, about one influential member to a package. The Colonel, whose years forbade the utmost daring fished a masterful race, while the Jurist, intent upon victory, gained steadily. At one pool of generous proportions the contestants met, but with indecisive result, drawing off with two monsters each, the Colonel, however, claiming a shade for his larger trout. Bunk, meanwhile, was fishing her usual careful, steady pace. Occasionally I caught sight of her leading a victim to an advantageous landing beach, or breasting the stream to gain better ground. And so it went. Back and forth we struggled, lending assistance to one another when needed, whipping, encouraging, working hard and enjoying the tug of our ever weightning creels. At one point the Colonel went to his knees battling with a monster and once the Jurist attempting to defeat a huge battler, became involved in a sweating tangle of fish, line, flies, alder bushes and profanity, and emerged minus his hat. I was fortunate enough, however, to spear the latter as it sped round a bend.

The afternoon sun was taking leave of our cañon before a lusty call from the Colonel fetched us from the onslaught. Bunk retreated into a hidden nook and soon emerged clad in warm, dry raiment of her sex. Home we hiked, our gingery bronchos hitting the narrow sidehill trail for all they were worth. Day was making a last stand when we tumbled off at the ranch and I delivered our superb catch to the culinary mercies of Mrs. Himes.

In the homelike warmth of their cabin the Eminent Jurist twirled his watch charm and meditated deeply. He gazed up the valley, to where, on the Chinese Wall above Trapper's Lake, a lingering daybeam was tracing a fantasy of colors. Then he arose, and taking the Colonel by a sturdy flannel-shirted arm led him to their rudely hewn threshold and directed his gaze out upon the vista of magnificent distances. Said he:

> "Then to this Earthen Bowl did I adjourn
> My Lip the secret Well of Life to learn
> And Lip to Lip it murmur'd 'While you live
> Drink!' For once Dead you never shall return."

The Colonel listed in an attitude of polite and admiring attention.

"As ole Wes' used to say, suh, 'You have spoke a Parable,' " he commented. The Eminent Jurist's arm degreed an arc of darkening east.

"It has not changed," he continued, his voice rising in tones of measured, sonorous oratory, "in lo! these many years. When Cæsar led his armies into the fields of the Remii; when Cyrus hurled back the Lydian hosts; when all Gaul was as yet unsubdivided; when Napoleon was beating it out of Moscow—*this*— was all here, just as we see it now. Fantastic shadows came and went, the eagle wheeled in the cloudless skies, seasons spun their wheels and sunshine bathed the land——"

"And," took up the Colonel, "that trout I hooked an' lost this afternoon was prob'ly jus' a minnow an' that made it harder to lose 'im. Why! my dear suh, he was *that* long, I *saw* him." The Colonel expanded his bristling white mustachios and stretched his hands far apart in definite yet elastic demonstration of the dimensions of his lost leviathan. Purely by accident his fingers came in casual touch with the bottle of Old Patterson. His grip closed like a vise about its neck. From the direction of the cook cabin came the faint note of a horn. It was a dramatic moment.

"Bless us," exclaimed the Colonel, "I believe that's the supper bell."

"I am convinced that it is the dinner signal," corrected the Jurist, ignoring the Colonel's sixty odd years of subservience to a "supper bell."

"You owe me two drinks, Colonel, remember?"

"I am here to pay my debts, suh, po' yo' liquah!"

"With pleasure, my dear Colonel."

Nothing broke the stillness save a limpid gurgling and clinking with a touch of stirring, familiar to all true fishermen.

"So help me Shiloh," vowed the Colonel, using his most profound oath of determination, raising a beaded glass and tossing off its contents with that quick whip and fervid smack of deep-rooted approval which comes only with sincere and intimate dealing extending over a long period of years, "I'm goin' to snake that big trout out of that hole befo' I leave the country."

Said the Jurist, sipping his shot with the delicate observation of rare flavor that betrays the connoisseur:

> "Ah! fill the Cup, what boots it to relate
> How wily trout escape both flies and bait
> Uncaught to-day and lost yesterday
> Why fret about him if To-morrow mean his Fate."

"In my country, suh, we don't admit defeat of no kind; an' I pledge you my word that onc't my fightin' fishin' blood is roused, thoro'ly roused, that that there trout don't stan' no mo' chance of stayin' out the fryin' pan than a watermelon stands in a Levee camp. I fully inten' to devote my pussonal attention to him." The Eminent Jurist rinsed his glass in the water pail.

"Shall we go down to supper?"

The Colonel passed an arm about the Jurist's shoulder and together they made off down a winding path.

THE EXTRA TIP

At the mess-hall door they paused and the Colonel's voice assumed a low, confidential note.

"I'm goin' to use a fly on that fellah t'-morrow, suh, that I have never used befo'. One of my own make. Pulled the hackles outer Henry George, my ole game rooster's tail an' underpinnin' an' som-t'hothers outer The'doh Roosevelt, my private mallard decoy, named for a gentleman, who, tho' of unfortunate political tendencies, I admiah ve'y much as a man. I believe it'll prove a killer-sho'!"

The Jurist's instinct asserted itself.

"Granting that it turns out a success, Colonel, I shall attempt to borrow one from you."

"What is mine is yo's, suh."

"Colonel, I thank you!"

The door swung inward.

"After you, suh."

"Age and beauty before youth, Colonel."

"Yo' langwidge is a tribute to yo' ability to pack yo' liquah, suh, like a man."

And then they were engulfed in a medley of clattering tinware, of lamplight and the sounds and odors of good cheer.

PART TWO

BETWEEN THE WARS

Life and Death of Speckles

EUGENE V. CONNETT, 3rd

A fictional, but all-too-true, epic struggle between angler and fish by the man who brought us the incomparable Derrydale Press. (April 1923)

A biography which contained anything but facts would be less than perfect. With this thought in mind, I shall strive to cleave very closely to the truth in this history of Speckles S. Fontinalis. His middle name was Salvelinus, but one can hardly blame him for not wanting this known among his playmates.

To begin at the beginning, I wish to record a very fervid romance which took place seven years ago come November. Lord and Lady Brook Trout were on their honeymoon: they had been traveling upstream by easy stages for more than a month before they reached the gravelly shallow over which they decided to take up household cares together. His lordship was dressed in quite the most resplendent raiment you can imagine; his tastes ran all the way from olive green and brown to burnt orange and vermilion. His shirt front was of the most shimmering white—with just a touch of the laundry bluing still in it. Picture to yourself a suit of clothes with the brightest of blue spots, in the center of which was a dab of the brilliant red! Jacob would have looked as though he were dressed in sackcloth and ashes compared to Lord Brook Trout on his honeymoon. The bride's trousseau was not quite so gay, but she had a sweeter expression, fortunately lacking the ugly hooked underjaw of her husband. He found good use for this "mug" when he started to build the nest, and I do not doubt but what one look at him was enough to warn intruders away from her ladyship.

Well, seven years ago come November next, Lady Brook Trout deposited about 500 nice white eggs in the nest just referred to; they varied somewhat in size, but averaged three-sixteenths of an inch in diameter. No sooner had she accomplished this feat than his lordship ejected milt over them, his slowly fanning tail and the gentle current of the stream combining to mix the fertilizing fluid among the little white globules. In each of these there was a minute hole through which the life-giving germ might penetrate the shell. This matter satisfactorily attended to, the bride and groom proceeded to cover the eggs with pebbles, knowing that hungry carp and countless other marauders might visit the nest after they had left it. Then they started down stream to seek a deep pool in which to spend the winter.

You may recall that at this time the weather was quite mild; in fact the temperature of the water in this brooklet was about fifty degrees, which accounted for the fact that Speckles first saw the light of day some seven weeks after his egg was laid. If it had been very cold, and had the temperature of the water been as low as forty, his birthday would have been another seven weeks later than it actually was.

When Speckles broke through his shell overcoat he was about as queer a looking little duffer as you could imagine. Stuck onto him where his stomach should have been was the yolk sack of his egg, and he found it pretty hard work to move around much with such a big balloon hanging to him. He was about half an inch long, and his scientific name was *alevin*. It was a fortunate thing that he did have this cumbersome yolk sac attached to him, as it contained a little drop of oil on which he was nourished for some time. His one object in life seemed to be to get underneath his brothers and sisters, in order to hide, I suppose; as all his immediate relatives had precisely the same object in life, they were an amusing lot to watch. Every now and then he would make an aimless sort of journey for the great distance of two or three inches, and then sink to the bottom exhausted.

Soon Speckles's yolk sac began to disappear, and when this was an accomplished fact our little friend graduated into the *fry* class. He began to forage around for food, but spent most of his time stemming the gentle current, seizing the tiny particles in the water as they came down to him. From now on his life was simply a question of avoiding the mouths of larger fish, and securing enough food so that he would grow up to be a big one himself. One day a water snake made a pass at him, but he managed to scoot under a rock just in time. When he had reached the stage of *fingerling*, and was about an inch and a half long, a kingfisher struck at him. All that saved him from an untimely end was the fact that the bird did not allow quite enough for the refraction of the water and missed Speckles by a fin's breadth. Another time he was foraging around near the edge of the brook and swam almost under a heron, who was roosting in the shallow water on one foot: if a mink hadn't given the heron something to think about besides Speckles, the latter would have become breakfast food instead of a big trout. Somehow or other he managed to pull through until he was a year old, at which time he had reached a length of six inches. When he was two years old he was eleven inches long, and at three he measured fourteen inches and weighed fourteen ounces. Some of his brothers, who had remained in the small brook of their birth, were only seven or eight inches long at three years, but the lads who sought the larger waters, where they could get plenty to eat, grew at the same rate as Speckles.

When he was two years old springtime came for him in August, and his young trout's fancy lightly turned to thoughts of love. He worked his way slowly upstream, keeping his eye open for a likely looking lady. He was dressed up in the most gorgeously bright colors; small wonder that it was not very long before he found a right nice mate. Together they kept on toward the very headwaters of the stream, and here they spawned. *Some* yearling trout will spawn, but *all* two-year-olds do; if a six-inch trout is found spawning it usually means that it is a two-year-old fish which has not grown very fast. The most ideal wedding day to a trout's mind is one on which a warm rain is falling; next to this in popularity is a warm, sunny day following a frosty night.

Speckles had had several unpleasant experiences with creatures known as anglers by this time, and it did not take him so very long to find out that when they approached him he was in danger of grabbing a fly that had steel in its makeup. After a while he realized that these fellows were throwing the dangerous flies over him, and when he saw one come floating down to him with a thin line attached to it he used to try to put the corner of his tail against the tip of his nose and wiggle it. This often caused him to make a swirl near the imitation flies, and he enjoyed seeing the anglers jerk them off the water. Sometimes he didn't notice the thin gut line on the fly, and he would grab it; usually he found that he could spit it out before the hook was stuck into his jaw. But when he was just under a year old he had a very unpleasant experience; the hook was sunk into his lip before he knew it, and he was hauled out from behind his rock. In a moment he was flopping in the meshes of a net, and then the angler had him in his hand. Imagine his relief when the man exclaimed, "Damn these five-inch sprats," and threw him back into the stream.

It was not until his fourth year that he was hooked again; he weighed over a pound and a half, and was in prime condition; it was his wonderful strength that saved his life. Indirectly it was also the cause of his final downfall. This is what happened: he rose to a fly that he did not suspect was an imitation until the instant before he reached it; then he turned to return to his hole, and the hook stuck in his tail. In his surprise he dashed off at top speed, and when the angler tried to check his rush he snapped the tiny leader as though it were a cobweb. It was several months before he got rid of that hook with its trailing piece of gut, and to his dying day he carried a little scar on his tail to remind him of the experience. The angler never had another peaceful minute after this; he was convinced that he had hooked the biggest trout that ever lived, and he swore by the cork in his dry-fly oil bottle that he would catch Speckles if it took him ten years to do it.

The next year our finny friend had reached a weight of about two pounds, and by strength and daring had appropriated for his own a very choice spot under a fall in the river. He was safely out of reach of imitation flies here, as no man had ever been able to cast across the big pool below the fall. During the daytime he played around in the churning white water, or lay deep down in the green depths of the whirlpool. At night he would drop downstream to a swift run below the pool and feed on minnows and flies here undisturbed. He thought that he had things worked out to a nicety and that his days of worry were over; but he reckoned without the angler who had hooked him foul the year before. This fellow decided to spend his vacation on Speckles's river, and he made up his mind to accomplish just one thing during this time: the taking of this big trout. He had a week in which to do this and he took his time in starting. He spent most of the first day in locating Speckles, and then most of the evening in watching the run below the pool; he had developed a theory that his quarry would probably feed at the surface at night in a less turbulent stretch of water than the bottom of the falls offered. By the time that Speckles dropped down to feed it was pitch dark, but a silent and solitary figure was patiently sitting on the bank, hunched over the glowing bowl of his pipe. It is easy to believe that the angler was almost asleep when the indistinct sound of Speckles sucking in a juicy fly reached his ears. Instantly he was fully awake, seeking by sight and hearing to determine exactly where the big trout was feeding. He spent another half hour before he was satisfied that his fish lay under the overhanging branches of a beech tree which glimmered faintly in the darkness. Speckles, of course, had no inkling of the much-to-be-feared enemy's presence, and fed as freely as if he were already in trout heaven, where no anglers are.

The next morning, while our finny friend reveled in the ærated waters below the dam, the man was carefully casting experimental flies over the spot where Speckles had fed the night before. After an hour of this preparatory work the angler retired, well satisfied that the trout was measureably nearer his basket. He must have fished another part of the river during the day, for by the time that he returned to the farmhouse for supper he had a half dozen trout in his creel. The evening meal finished, our angler slowly approached the run below the whirlpool; Speckles also moved down there for his nightly repast. He fed for some time on little midges, hoping that before long some larger flies would drift down to him. Out of the tail of his eye he thought he saw a slight disturbance on the water and he immediately sank toward the bottom to watch for further signs of danger. For ten minutes he waited, seeing no other indications of an enemy, and, deciding that a muskrat had been responsible for the tiny wave on the surface of the water, he began to feed once more. He was delighted to see that during the interval he had laid low larger flies were floating down, and he started the second course of his meal with much gusto. He noticed a darker looking fly among the others every minute or two, but as he was enjoying the more plentiful variety he did not bother with the others. Gradually the lighter colored flies became fewer and fewer, until only an occasional one floated over him; it might be a good idea to top off his dinner with a few of the darker ones, thought he.

No sooner said than done, but to his horror he felt a tiny, sharp steel hook embedded deeply in his jaw. Speckles' first thought was one of rage: he was mad clean through at having been disturbed at his evening meal. He sank to the bottom, frantically trying to loosen the hook with his tough, sharp tongue; if it had not been for the continual strain pulling the hook into his jaw he would have been able to tear it loose. Then he made a mad rush in the direction from which the pull came, but he found that he was dragging a long length of line behind him, and that the strain was still on the hook. In another second he felt the steady pull which he recognized as coming from the trembling tip of a rod. The leader which tied him to his tormentor seemed to be a very light one, so he determined to try brute strength against it; he swam downstream as fast as his fins would carry him, until he lay in a piece of very fast water. He shook his head from side to side, he ran around a rock, and then around another. He turned his body broadside to the current and pulled for all his might. In a minute he heard the angler coming toward him, his reel clicking faintly along the line, as he recovered most of that which Speckles had run out. The trout waited until the angler, who was feeling for a foothold among the slippery rocks that carpeted the rapid, was very close to him; then he tore up into the run above, weaving in and out among all the rocks that came in his way, until he reached the big whirlpool below the dam. Here, just as he had run out all the angler's line, he was forced to rest; could he have found the strength to continue his rush for another ten feet he might have had his freedom.

Speckles realized that he could not make any more such dashes as the last, and he worked his way into the eddy, so that he might face downstream toward the angler; then he waited for his enemy to make the next move. He would have been encouraged, could he have seen that the angler was as tired as he was, but the fight was in the dark and neither antagonist had seen the other. It seemed an hour to both combatants as they waited for each other to reopen the battle. The angler dared no more than a tentative tug now and then, in the hopes of stirring up the fish to further efforts; the trout did no more than probe at the maddening hook with its tongue, always trying to loosen its deadly hold. Neither succeeded at these tactics. At last the man began to wade up toward his quarry, reeling in line a foot at a time, as he slowly lessened the distance between them. Deeper and deeper he waded into the swirling black waters of the pool, until he felt a cold trickle down inside his waders. He slipped on a treacherous rock, had cursed himself for a fool as his waders filled. He began to wish he had never hooked the trout, as he literally fought for his life in those icy, dark depths. Speckles felt the convulsive jerks on the line as the angler struggled to regain his foothold, and not knowing what to expect from them he rushed downstream until he was in the run once more. How could he know that his steady pull on the line was just enough to give his enemy that touch with his balance which saved him from drowning in the pool?

The exhausted man pulled himself to the bank, his angler's instinct keeping his hand clasped tight to his rod. Even before he tried to free himself of the dragging waders, he unconsciously reeled in until he had a firm hold on his fish once more. By the time he had kicked his waders clear he could see a gray streak in the Eastern sky. He shivered with the cold, but a sporting strain in his blood kept him to his determination to kill the trout. Out in the icy waters he waded once more, his numbed feet hardly feeling the sharp rocks as they cut through his woollen socks. With aching wrist he struggled to conquer his all but spent quarry. Poor Speckles had really given up any hope of dislodging the hook by now; he felt his only chance lay in breaking the thin gut strand that chained him to his enemy. With every ounce of strength and determination that was still in him he made dash after dash up and down the run. Slowly he realized that his strength was failing; he had not the power to struggle against the relentless pull on the line; and slowly he came to the surface, quietly rolling over on his side, only to be drawn into the angler's waiting net. As he saw the meshes about to entangle him he summoned every atom of fight that was left in him, and made one more brave struggle for his life; but his conqueror had seen his gleaming spotted sides, and seemed to gain new strength from the sight. In a minute it was over. Speckles died fighting to the last; he was game. So was the angler.

Casting the Curve

GEORGE M. L. LaBRANCHE

The author of the classic, The Dry Fly and Fast Water, *was widely acclaimed as a master of fly presentation. This particular cast is still deadly.* (January 1925)

There seems to have been, recently, considerable discussion abroad of the method of making this cast—"curved," I have called it, although Mr. Marston, of the *Fishing Gazette,* has dubbed it the "Shepherd's Crook." It is known on our streams and rivers as the "loop" cast. Whatever name it may finally come to be known by, it is certain that the success which follows its use will make it popular enough with fly fishermen to prompt them to practise it.

Casting a fly is largely a subconscious act. It requires little or no effort except when distance is desired, and no such mental concentration as is required in golf. For the beginner, perhaps, this statement hardly holds true, but it is not my purpose to give instruction to the novice other than to say: watch a good man on the stream; practice; learn to know the action of the rod, and—practice.

Many works on angling include, with great clarity, descriptions of methods of taking fish, the flies to be used under certain and nearly all conditions, the striking or hooking of the fish, and even instructions in handling the fish after it is hooked. The photographs and diagrams in some of these books showing the position a rod should assume, both on the back cast and on the forward cast, are extremely helpful, and an intelligent and earnest reader may learn to correct many bad habits by studying them. It is hoped, however, that the angler interested enough to read these pages, and who may wish to learn the principle of throwing the curved cast by following the none-too-lucid instructions given, will have learned all of these things before making the attempt.

The purpose of the curved cast is obvious. It may be thrown to either the left-hand or right-hand bank, but one is made in an entirely different manner from the other. Both are rather simple, once the principle is understood, and the knack is easily acquired. The execution of these casts will be dependent, to a great extent, upon the familiarity of the angler with his rod—its action, its power, and the "feel" of the line on both forward and back casts. The dry-fly fisherman whose practice has been to "shoot the line," as it is called, knows instinctively when to let his forward cast go so as to have the weight of the live line—that line which is free of the top—pull after it the loose line that is held in his hand. It is this perfect timing that distinguishes the really expert; and, unless one has mastered the rhythm of casting, there is little to be gained in attempting to control the fly after it has been cast.

The cast to the left bank is rather simple of execution, because the angler has control of his line and fly at all times, and, if the fly appears to be going wrong, it may be retrieved before it has touched the water. A false cast or two will generally send it in the right direction, and it may be dropped when the angler is satisfied that it will fall properly.

Assuming that the angler has selected the spot to which he is to direct his fly, his position with respect to his objective should not be at a greater angle than forty-five degrees unless he has attained rare proficiency. Under no circumstances should the attempt be made with more line than can be kept alive in the air without effort and without bungling. A fair length of line to start with would be about thirty-five feet for a two-handed rod of twelve feet or more. Many anglers are prone to use too long a line—an error that is particularly noticeable on our trout streams. It is very gratifying, of course, to lay out a long, beautiful fly, but as control of the fly is lost after a certain distance is reached, the use of a short line is much more effective where accuracy and delicacy are required. In any event, one must learn to control a short length of line before hoping to attain proficiency with the curve when using the length one has been accustomed to. With thirty-five feet of line that is part of a well-balanced outfit, one should be able to shoot from six to ten feet, or even more, of the loose line held below the hand guide.

The office of the curved cast is twofold on salmon rivers:
  (1) To avoid drag.

(2) To keep as much of the leader as possible away from the fish.

On trout streams there is an added advantage which will be considered later, with the hope that the digression may be overlooked.

For the purpose of illustration, let us assume that the angler has taken his position and is about to assail a fish that is visible to him, and which is lying rather close to the bank in open water which has no varying currents. To reach him properly with the fly, one must first judge the distance as accurately as possible. A great aid in ascertaining this is to cast the fly straight upstream, allowing it to fall upon the water at a point assumed to be the correct distance, and, as it alights, to draw an imaginary line on the surface of the water between the fish and the fly. If this results in producing in the mind's eye a triangle in which the fish, the fly, and the angler appear equidistant, the length of line will be found to be quite correct. This sounds rather difficult and geometrical, but if the angler will try it in practice, with a stone or some other object as the other point of the triangle, it will be found rather easy of accomplishment, and very helpful.

Being satisfied as to distance, the angler makes the preliminary dry or false casts toward the fish, but not directly at it. Selecting a spot upon the water about three feet, or even more, upstream from the fish, and using, of live line and line which is held in the hand, about three feet more than it is calculated will reach the fish, the caster should direct the fly to this point, and, as the line is about to straighten, pull or hold back the top of the rod a trifle, just enough to stop the fly in its forward flight. The effect will be to throw the fly out of the direct course it is taking, thus imparting to the line, and obviously to the fly, the impulse to return as it would if being retrieved. If the checking is timed properly, the fly will be thrown downstream, the leader and forward part of the line falling where they are. A sharp curve will be the result, and what has seemed impossible will prove to be very simple. The length and diameter of this curve will be dependent entirely upon the skill of the angler in his timing of the check. Each degree that the rod is held from the vertical will add to the diameter of the curve until the horizontal or side position is reached, when the greatest curve can be thrown. It is advisable, in beginning the attempt, to make this cast from the horizontal position as nearly as is possible. The curve will be more pronounced, and the angler will be less likely to become discouraged. As a matter of fact, those men who are able to throw the curve with the rod held at an angle of less than forty-five degrees from the perpendicular are rarely met. In my own fishing little is achieved from a more acute angle than this. If there is any merit in the belief that the fly alone should be seen by the fish, with this cast the desired result is obtained. If the theory has no merit, the cast is nevertheless worth while, if only because a fly may be so placed that it will float for a comparatively long time before drag is exerted upon it. Particularly is this so on water where a straight cast would be practically useless. It was this consideration that really prompted its development.

In throwing, either to a fish that may be seen, or to one that is not visible, but which may be lying in an eddy across a swift current, no change in the principle of the cast is involved. One case, perhaps, calls for a nicer display of accuracy than the other, but that is the only material difference.

There are bits of water on salmon rivers, extremely difficult to fish with a wet fly, that are easily and successfully searched with the dry fly fished in this manner. Those narrow, deep eddies or stickles against a ledge past which the river races madly, are cases in point. Salmon love to lie in such water, because there they may rest without continuously battling with the swift current. Unless one is very expert, a wet fly rarely reaches these fish, because it is whisked away so rapidly by the pull of the fast water on the line. Downstream fishing does not aid the angler unless a position can be assumed upon the same side of the stream as the eddy. This is not always possible, and, even where it is, a fly is seldom made to swing properly. With the dry fly, however, these places are not difficult problems, because the angler fishes upstream and across. With the fly floating in the eddy, the leader, which is in the current and upstream from the fly, does not exert any drag until the fly has had quite a long drift.

To make this point clearer, let us picture a run such as I have endeavored to describe where the main current is traveling at, say, three times the speed of that in which the fish are lying, and to which the fly has been cast. If the curved cast is made so that the leader is in the swift water and three feet above the fly, which is in the slower current, the latter will have no pull exerted upon it until the leader has assumed the same curve below it that it had above it. Let us assume, further, for the purpose of illustration, that, if the curve in the leader is a true one (not at all likely, however), it would travel downstream approximately nine feet before it exerted any influence upon the fly if the latter remained stationary—which it does not. This would mean, then, that, while the leader was being carried these nine feet, the fly would have traversed a distance of three feet, entirely unhampered. This would be quite long enough for it to be taken by a fish that was willing, and considerably longer than a wet fly could be induced to remain, unless cast partly upstream by the same method. If the arc formed by the curved leader should have a greater diameter than the three feet used in the calculation, or if the leader were more loosely cast, the fly would naturally ride a longer time in proportionate ratio.

The possibility of some obstacle preventing the proper handling of one's rod to throw the curve suggests the "loosely cast" leader. Where exigency forces the cast to be made with the rod in a position perpendicular to the river, the loose cast is very effective on water where drag must be overcome. It is particularly effective where the fish cannot be reached from below and where the fly must be drifted down from above. The loose cast is accomplished by casting in the ordinary overhead manner, with more line than is required to reach the objective, drawing the fly back sharply just before it alights upon the water. This action causes the leader to fall in rather ragged shape, and is not over-pretty, but, until its convolutions are straightened out by the current, the fly is not greatly interfered with. The time given the fish with this cast is but a fraction of that afforded him by the curved cast, but certainly this short time is better than none.

Rocky Riffle on the Rogue River

ZANE GREY

A pioneering big-game fisherman finally gets the knack—or the luck —to score on fresh-run steelhead. (June 1926)

These Rogue River steelhead must have had a council before my arrival to decide upon the infinitely various and endless tricks they would play upon me. To be sure, they played a few upon my comrades, but the great majority, and the hopeless ones and the terrible ones, fell to my lot.

During those unforgettable ten days I kept secret and accurate account of what happened to R. C. and the boys. Some of this I saw myself; part of it I learned at the general camp-fire narratives of the day's experience, and the rest I acquired by a casual and apparently innocent curiosity.

To some wag of a writer are credited the lines anent the universal fisherman: "he returneth in the evening smelling of vile drink, and the truth is not in him."

I regard this as an injustice to many anglers. The best and finest anglers I have known did not return in the evening redolent of drink. And outside of a little exaggeration, natural to the exciting hour and the desire to excel, the tales of these fishermen could be accepted as truth.

As to R. C. and the boys, the weakness in my argument may be that they did not tell everything, or that they did not observe keenly or remember correctly. At any rate, the monstrous fact seemed to be that, during these ten days, I had as many strikes from steelhead as all of them put together.

But how vastly different the conditions of my strikes! Here was where the fiendish tricks of the steelhead began. For me the river was empty of fish at first; then suddenly they began to rise. They bewildered me. They flustered me. They baffled me.

If I made a poor cast, with a bag in my line, then a steelhead would rush the fly. Another would suck the fly in when it floated deep, and spit it out before I was aware I had a strike. Another would come after the fly as I drew it out to recast. Whenever I cast from an awkward or precarious position I was sure to feel a nip at my fly.

And once—crowning piece of incredible bad luck of that whole trip—when I was wading far out in the river, I had a strike on my back cast. My fly hit the water behind me and a rascally steelhead took it. I thought I was fast to the familiar willow or rock. When I turned to free myself, a big, broad steelhead leaped and savagely shook out my hook. I was stunned, then insulted, then furious. Could anything worse happen?

Many a rosy, silvery steelhead loomed up and out of the dark depths and put his game snub-nose against my fly, as if he meant to gulp it. But he did not. Many a steelhead, always choosing the inevitable and unaccountable instant when I was not ready, would strike my fly hard and jerk the slack line out of my hand. Faithfully I would cast for a whole hour, on the qui vive every instant; then just as I relaxed, or looked away from my leader, or lifted my foot to step—smash!

Along with all these dreadful happenings, occasionally I would hook a steelhead or he would obligingly do it for me. Then he would proceed to show me how quickly he could get off. The time came, however, when I held one for a long hour. I did not see this one rise. But I felt him hook himself. He was heavy. He swam upstream and stayed in the current. R. C. yelled encouragement. I replied with Takahashi's classic expression: "He stick right there!"

Indeed he did. He never leaped, never made a fast run, never frightened me by a sudden move. He plugged deep. He got behind this stone and that one, and under the ledge across the river, and he stayed by each place a long time, tugging at my line. My rod nodded with his jerks. At last, after a half hour or more, he came toward me, and got behind another stone, in a deep eddy. Here he plugged slower and slower.

Several attempts to lead him forth proved futile. But at last he gave up plugging and allowed himself to be led out of deep water. R. C. had decided it was a salmon. So had I. But when I led him into shoal water, I saw the beautiful opalescent glow of a steelhead. When he came clearly into view and I had actual sight of his great length and depth, my heart swelled in my throat.

Still no angler could have handled him more gently. He rolled and twisted —rolled and twisted, and finally he twisted the slight hold loose. I saw him drift on his side, gleaming rosily, then right himself, and swim off the bar into deep water. When I turned to R. C., mute and exhausted, he gave a most capital imitation of Burnham's vociferous execration.

On October 15th we were due in southeastern Oregon, to take a hunt in a new country. I had still several days to fish before we started, and I could prolong the stay a couple of days longer if desirable. R. C. had now eighteen steelhead to his credit, taken on a fly. The boys had added several to their string. And I still cherished unquenchable hopes. Next day I actually caught a steelhead on a fly, so quickly and surprisingly that I scarcely realized it.

I went down the river later than usual, and found Ken and Ed casting from the dry rocks at the head of Rocky Riffle. R. C. was above in midstream. When I rigged up my tackle, I put on an English salmon fly. It was unlike any fly the steelhead had been rising to, and I meant to try it just for contrariness. Wading in fifty feet above Ken, I made a preliminary cast, and let the fly float down.

Tug! Splash! A steelhead hooked himself and leaped, and ran right into the water Ken was fishing. I waded out, ran below, and fought the fish in an eddy, and soon landed it—a fine plump steelhead weighing about four pounds.

"Bingo! Out goes a fly—in comes a fish!" exclaimed Ed. "Say, you're a fast worker!"

Ken cupped his hand and yelled up to R. C. "Hey, Rome, he's busted his streak of bad luck!"

R. C. waved and called back: "Goodnight! Lock the gate!"

I took R. C.'s good-natured slang—an intimation that they would now have to look out for me—as a happy augury for the remaining days. Next day I caught three: a small one, another around four pounds, and the third over five and a half.

"Too late, old boy," quoth R. C. "I have you trimmed. Nineteen to date, and the biggest seven and three-quarters."

"Heavens!" I replied. "Can't you recognize a grateful and innocent angler? I don't dream of equaling your splendid record. Too late, indeed!"

"Well, I reckon I'd better cinch this fishing trip," he said, dryly. "There's no telling how you'll finish. I'll stick on the job."

The day before our last day found me with a total of twelve steelhead, the largest weighing six pounds. I was seven behind R. C. Yet still no ambition or even dream of catching up with him crossed my mind. I was fishing desperately hard to prove something to myself, as well as for the thrill and joy of it.

That day happened to be Sunday, a still, cloudy day, threatening rain. I reached Rocky Riffle ahead of everybody, even the native fishermen that usually flocked there on this day. It was a fishy day if there ever was one. I had before me the pleasure of fishing that quarter-mile of best water all by myself. I seemed to be a different angler from the one who had first waded in there nearly three weeks before. Trial, struggle, defeat, persistence—how they change and remake a man! Defeats are stepping-stones to victory.

The water was dark, mirroring the shade of the green mountain slope opposite. It had amber shadows and gleams. Autumn leaves floated on the swift current. From upstream came the shallow music of the riffle; from below the melodious roar of the channel sliding over the rocks into the deep pool.

Wading in to my hips, I began the day with a cast far from perfect and short of record distance, but I placed it where I wanted to and softly, at the end of a straight leader. Thus I worked downstream.

Suddenly, as the current swept my line down even with me, I saw a wave, then a dim pale shape, seemingly enormous in length. Lazily this steelhead took my fly. When I struck, I felt the fly rip through his hard mouth. He made an angry swirl as he disappeared. "Oh! why can't I hook one of these big fellows!" I muttered, groaning inwardly. And I went on with a grim certainty that soon I would do so.

After making a few casts, I waded down several yards. From the instant my fly touched the water until I withdrew it to cast again, I was strung keen as a whipcord. I had paid dearly for my lesson.

My line straightened out with fly sunk. Then came a vicious tug. Quick as a flash I struck and hooked what felt like a log. Downriver he raced and my reel snagged. He did not leap. With wagging rod held high—no easy task—I began to wade out and down. But I could not make fast enough time. I wallowed, plunged. Then I forgot to hold the loose click on my reel. It slipped off, releasing the drag, and the spool whizzed. I felt a hard jerk—then a slack line.

"That *was* a ten-pounder," I muttered, and then I gave vent to one of the emotion-releasing cuss words. As I pulled out the loops of the tangled line my fingers trembled. At last I got my line in, to find the leader minus a fly. Wading out, I sat down to put on another of the Golden Grouse flies. A glance up and downstream failed to add any other fisherman to the scene.

Below the place where I had hooked that big one there was a flat, submerged rock in midstream. The water swirled round it, with little eddies below. On the second cast my fly floated beyond and round it. I caught a gleam of light as if from a mirror under the surface. I sharply elevated my rod even as the steelhead struck the fly. Solidly came the weight. I knew he was hooked well.

He ran upstream fifty feet, leaped prodigiously, showing himself to be a long, slim male fish. He had bagged the line against the current, and when he leaped again he got some slack. But the hook held. Downstream he turned, and I was hard put to it to hold the click on my reel. Twice it slipped, but I got it pushed back before the spool overran.

Meanwhile the steelhead was running and I was following as fast as possible. Far down the channel he leaped again, then he went into the rapids. When I got to shore, all my line was out. I ran, splashing, scattering the gravel. But I saved the line, and in the pool below I bested this steelhead. He did not weigh much short of seven pounds.

I tied him on a string. Far upstream I made out Ken whipping his favorite hole, and in the riffle above I saw R. C.'s white hat. Rocky Riffle, wonderful to see, was still untenanted by any fishermen save myself. Too good to be true! Where were the native fishermen, all out on Sundays? It occurred to me that fishing must be too good up the river. The clouds did not break, though in places they were light. Ideal conditions improved. My day seemed to have dawned.

Beyond the flat, submerged stone was a deep channel with a ragged break in the ledge. Here the water swirled smoothly. To reach it meant a long cast for me, fully sixty feet, even to the outer edge of that likely spot. Wading deeper, I performed as strenuously as possible, and missed the spot by a couple of yards. My fly alighted below. But the water exploded, and the straightened rod jerked almost out of my hand.

My whoop antedated the leap of that Rogue River beauty. After I saw him high in the air—long, broad, heavy, pink as a rose, mouth gaping wide—I was too paralyzed to whoop. I had established contact with another big steelhead. Like lightning he left that place. He ran up the river, making four jumps, one of them a greyhound leap—long, high, curved. I had to turn so my back was downstream, something new in even that ever-varying sport.

When he felt the taut line again, he made such a tremendous lunge that I lost control of the click, and could not prevent him from jerking my rod partly under water. I was up to my waist, and that depth and the current augmented my difficulties. The fish changed his course, swerving back between me and the shore, and he leaped abreast of me, so close that the flying drops of water wet my face. As I saw him then I will never forget him.

The slack line did not seem to aid him in any way, for he could not shake the hook. I anticipated his downstream rush, and was wading out, all ready when he made it. Otherwise, *goodnight*, as R. C. was wont to say. He leaped once more, a heavy, limber fish, tiring from the furious speed. I followed him so well that he never got more than half of the line. He took me down the channel, through the rapids, along the gravel bar below, down the narrow green curve into the rough water below, where I could neither follow nor hold him.

That fight gave me more of understanding of these game fish and the marvelous sport they afford. As I wearily plodded back, nearly a half mile, I felt sick, and yet I had to rejoice at that unconquerable fish. My tackle was too light, but I would not have exchanged it for my heavy one, with that magnificent fish again fast to my line.

Lady Fingers

ARTHUR R. MACDOUGALL, JR.

Dud Dean stories were great favorites for over two decades. Here's one of the choicer tales from this Maine-woods series. (January 1930)

I have known hushed and mystic hours when I have wished the red gods were not fiction. It was one of those hours when Dud Dean and I sat in front of our lean-to on the shores of one of the Nelhutus lakes. We were a long, long hike from home, under the black shadows of the last large stand of virgin black-growth in Maine.

We had had a tough day. The big trout had been particularly unconcerned with us. So we sat there in the evening quiet—the quality of quiet that a man from civilization can feel soaking in from all around him. Not a tinge of regret remained because of the troutless day. He who angles for big ones must bide their time. I was hoping Dud might presently drift into a story-telling mood.

He did. "Didjer ever study psychology?" he suddenly asked.

"Not much," I guardedly answered.

"What d'yer think on it?"

"Why, I don't know—"

"It's durn tricky stuff," declared Dud Dean. "I useter guide a bird that talked erbout it in his sleep. His name was Stanley B. Goss, an' he came from down in N' York. I never figured out in all the years I knew him whether I liked him

70

er not. Sometimes he was human, an' it 'peared that the milk of human kindness in his breast weren't all soured. Then again he'd act like a pizened pup.

"I needed money in them days, an' guidin' was my way of gittin' a chunk now an' then. This feller Goss telegraphed me one spring." Dud chuckled softly. "Nancy, she 'bout had a fit when it come. 'Oh, dear,' she says, 'Sunone is dead.' Telegraphs was sure scarce in them days. It seemed by the telegraph that Stanley B. Goss was a-comin' up with a couple of fellers, and wanted me to lead the three of 'em round.

"First off I says, 'I won't do it.' But Nancy says, 'Dudley!' So I see I maybe would. Well, I went down to Bingham. In them days the railroad hadn't gone north of Bingham. When folks got off, I see Stanley B. an' his party. One of 'em was a most peecular lookin' cuss. I can't remember ever seein' anythin' more so.

"He was six foot four high and eighteen inches wide. I've got sizable feet on me, but that beanpole had the biggest underpinnin' I ever see. His hands was big, an' his neck—well, you've seen them pie-eyed cranes. Then he had over-big ears. I found out later that his neck was queer-like. He could turn his head a good deal like a owl settin' on a tree. He could look right square round without twisting his body. I'm tellin' yer, I never see anybody looked like that Alphonsa Turrel.

"Soon 's Stanley B. Got me off kinda alone he says, 'Dud, I've made a serious error. This Alphonsa Turrel is a lemon, an' I've sorter picked it. I'm a great jedge of character an' can read a man first off, but this gink was sorter thrust onter me by a friend. In a generous mood I invited him before I see him. We've got to see it through sunhow.'

" 'That ain't hard,' I says, havin' in mind that I'd like to see anyone harder to see through then Stanley B. hisself. Them was the days when the Dimicks, down to Moxie, was prime fishin', an' they ain't the worse now. Ever been in there?"

I admitted ignorance of the Dimicks.

"Moxie Mountain sorta soaks her feet in lakes, figur'tively speakin', as old Doc Brownin' useter say. Thar's the Healds on her southwest, Pleasant Pond on her north, an' the Dimicks on her east. The black-growth's all gone—old stuff, I mean—an' that lets the sunshine inter a nice wild country.

"I planned to take Stanley Barnarbus—that was his middle name—into the Dimicks. We crossed Pleasant Pond down to the south beach. Thar's a little snake of a path from that point to Little Dimick—'bout three miles er so. Goin' in, Stanley B. Got kinda hot an' touchy, I guess. Anyway, he started ridin' this Alphonsa some. Started referrin' to him as Lady Fingers. Every time he done that, Alphonsa would look round at him with those big, sorrowful eyes of his'n, but he didn't say much.

" 'What kinda fishing rod have yer got, Lady Fingers?' asks Stanley B.

* * *

"Alphonsa's face kinda brightened up, an' he says, 'I've got a little dandy. My wife got it fer me, fer Christmas.'

"Stanley Barnarbus sorter snorted and said, 'How much does she weigh?' meanin' his rod, of course.

"Alphonsa looked queer, but he comes back with, 'Almost one hundred pounds.'

" 'What?' explodes Stanley B. 'I mean yer rod. How much does yer rod weigh? Who cares how much yer wife weighs?'

" 'Oh!' says Alphonsa. Guess I might 's well call him Al. 'Oh, the rod. It weighs jest two an' a half ounces.'

"I kinda pricked up my ears at that. I'd never seen s' light a riggin'.

" 'Two an' a half,' says Stanley B. 'My gosh, a woman would pick out a rod like that! I s'pose she knows all 'bout fishin'—like Mister Jonah did.'

" 'On the contrary,' comes back Al, 'she is an expert. She is a much better fly fisherman then I am, I assure you.'

"That made Stanley B. Goss laugh. 'By the jumpin' horn pouts, that's a good one,' he says, almost doublin' up.

"Alphonsa—Al, I mean—just kept walkin' straight ahead, an' never said a word ner cracked a smile. Bine-by we come out to the outlet of Little Dimick. I went huntin' fer a canoe I'd hid back from the pond. Stanley B. went along with me.

" 'Jest's I told you,' he says. 'He's goin' to be a unmitigated nuisance. Damn the luck, anyway.'

" 'He's all right. He ain't a bad sort,' I replies.

"That set Stanley B. t' fairly spittin' blood. 'All right! Him? Say, d'yer mean to tell me that a man that would come way up here with nothin' but a minner pole is all right? What kinda place is this fer parlor fishin'? My tomcat's whiskers! I knew the minute I laid eyes on him jest what he was. I'm a jedge of character, Mister Dean, I am.'

" 'If yer knew what he was the minute yer laid eyes on him, yer did better'n I could,' says I.

" 'Study psychology,' he says, with a self-satisfied smirk.

" 'It don't fit into my business to know too much,' I says. An' then I see some houn' had stole my canoe. Sunhow I felt mad. So we had to go back where the other two fellers was waitin'. I found a raft an' jedged it would hold two, if the heavenly powers consented, as Doc Brownin' useter say.

"The other chap—Herbert Jackson, his name was—offered to stay ashore with me.

" 'I insist,' says Alphonsa, 'that you'—meanin' Jackson—' go out.'

" 'Why should I?' Jackson argued, bein' a good sort.

" 'Because it wouldn't be good fer my soul,' says Al.

"I kinda figured out what he meant by that later. Well, no sense in keepin' you awake tellin' how they chewed that over. Finally they tossed up, an' Al won—that is, he had to go out with Stanley B.

"Jackson an' me started lookin' up some dry cedar to make another raft outer. The fishin' was poor. We watched them two out on the raft. Al sure seemed to be an awful dub with a fly rod. Three-four times he got his flies hooked into Stanley's hat er sunwheres else. When that would happen, Stanley Barnarbus talked right out in meetin'. He raved sunthin' fierce.

" 'Barnarbus'—that's what his friends always called him—'is rawer'n usual,' Jackson says to me. 'He's a funny cuss, an' takes his dislikes too serious.'

"Right thar I made up my mind fer sure that this Jackson was a decent sort; so I see my chance to find out what this psychology was erbout. Jackson explained, an' then he says, "That's half what ails Stanley B.'

" 'What's the other half?' I asks.

" 'Eh?' An' then he begin to laugh kinda quiet-like.

"Well, we fussed round makin' our raft, an' time we was done it was five. 'You go out,' I says to this Jackson, 'an' I'll get some supper ready.' I looked round fer the coffee biler I'd left last time I was in thar. It was one of them big four-five gallon pots, like they use in a lumber camp. They're 'bout eighteen inches high, yer know. While I was lookin' fer it, Jackson told me that Stanley B. had it out on the raft to put fish in. So I had to call 'em in if we was goin' to have anythin' hot to drink. They was glad 'nough to quit, I guess, seein's how the trout weren't comin'.

"Alphonsa was doin' the polin' an' Stanley Barnarbus the talkin'. We could hear 'em all plain, an' I see it made Jackson feel plumb miserable.

" 'As a fly fisherman,' says Stanley B. in a clammy voice, 'I must say ye're a first-class old woman.'

"Thar was a piece of ledge jest stickin' out of the water, in front of the raft. I was goin' to sing out an' warn 'em, when I see Al lookin' right over Stanley B. an' straight at the rock. All of a sudden he give that raft an almighty push, an' it hit the ledge like a batterin' ram at the Siege of Troy, as Doc Brownin' useter say.

"Well, that ledge never budged. Stanley B. had been standin' back to us, an' he went along like the raft hadn't stopped. On his way he stuck one foot in the coffee pot. They was crossin' the channel an' the deepest place in the hull pond. The last I see of him, he was wearin' the coffee can, an' upside down. When he come up, he'd got rid of the pot.

"Alphonsa reached the raftin' pole out to him an' pulled him in. 'I'm 'fraid,' says Al, 'that you've lost that coffee urn.'

"Stanley B. was fit to be baptized all over agin. 'Are yer blind?' he roars. 'Didn't jer see that mountain stickin' outer the lake?'

" 'No. Did you?'

" 'How could I see it?' yells Barnarbus. 'Think thar's eyes in the back of my head? How could I see it? Tell me that!'

" 'An',' says Alphonsa, 'how could I?'

" 'Oh, hell!' says Stanley B., kinda givin' it up.

"Jackson got up from where he'd been kinda half settin' an' half rollin', with his hand half over his mouth. 'Did yer git any fish?' he asks.

" 'Yer can go to—!' says Stanley B., gittin' off the raft, drippin' like a scarecrow in a April shower.

"Jackson come over to me where I was fussin' over the fire. 'I begin to think,' he says, 'that our long-geared friend can play his own game of cards. An' I've got a sneakin' idea that ain't all he's got in his hand, either."

"I had some good grub I'd brought erlong. Some of Nancy's fancy odds an' ends. While we was eatin', the trout begin to jump. Thar was some good ones boilin' up an' a reg'lar spatter of little ones.

" 'What a lovely sight!' busts out Alphonsa. 'Trout dancin' on a lake of jade an' gold.' Just like that. I found out later that he was a reg'lar poet, an' Nancy got a book full of his poems he writ. I may's well tell yer that I got kinda fond of that Alphonsa Turrel, an' him an' me done quite some fishin' together.

"Well, let's see. Oh, yes.

" 'Huh!' grunts Stanley B. 'I'll bet you a hundred that you don't land a fish that weighs over a pound.'

"Al sorter looked out round Little Dimick, an' he see plenty of signs of fish that'd weigh more'n that. 'I'd rather bet you five hundred,' he says, slow an' sober.

" 'D'yer mean it?' snaps Stanley, middle-named Barnarbus.

" 'I never meant anythin' more in my life.'

" 'Then let these gentlemen witness that it's a go.'

" 'Amen!' says Al, grinnin' from one big red ear to tother. An' he got up an' left us. He went down to the outlet, an' waded out to a big flat rock. The outlet's full of rocks—funny-lookin' place. I set out to say sunthin' because that wasn't a very likely place, an' Stanley B. knew it.

" 'Let the damphool go,' he says, raisin' his hand to shut me up.

"I guess I fergot to tell yer that the brook that runs outer Little Dimick runs down to Baker Pond. The Moxie Lake guys that was waitin' on sports had made quite a lot of Baker Pond, an' they'd stocked it with salmon.

"Well, we got up an' went down t'watch Alphonsa Turrel. When we got thar, Stanley B. says, 'I'll be damned!'

" 'Ah,' says Jackson, 'What did I tell yer, Mister Dean, 'bout that last hand?'

"An' thar was Al a-fishin'—fishin', I mean! Yer never saw prettier fly-fishin', never! They was long casts, an' that little rod actin' like a lady bred to the part.

"Crotch!" said Dud Dean. "I keep thinkin' sun day to see that kind of fishin' ag'in." Then he went on.

" 'Ye're a liar if yer say yer wife, er any other woman, can cast better'n that,' shouts Stanley B.

" 'I'll bet yer five hundred more that she can outcast any man in the state,' comes back Alphonsa.

"But Stanley B. didn't take him up that time, ner no time that I ever heared of after that.

"He kept gittin' strikes. I wondered how he got rid of them small trout, but I found out later that the barbs was all filed off his flies. Pretty soon he got a rise like he was lookin' fer. An' then begin the pretty work. That little rod begin to bend, I can tell yer. We was all down to the edge by that time. An' Stanley B., bein' a real fisherman, if I must say, was a-shoutin' directions 'long with the rest of us. But shucks, that bird didn't need no how-to's from us beginners. The trout weren't really big—'bout three pounds, as I recollect. It did a lot of surface rushin'.

"Then sunthin' else happened like a crack of doom. He had three flies on, an' a beaut of a salmon riz up and hit that head-on fly—a Montreal, it was.'

" 'I'm sorry,' says Alphonsa, 'but the show is jest erbout all spoke.'

"But it weren't, not by a jugful of blackberry jam, as old Doc Brownin' useter say when he was swearin' mad. I never see no such comical an' excitin' scrap as that was.

"Suntimes that salmon seemed t' lift that trout right outer the water. All I could think of was one of them Spanish bulls yoked up with a ten-year-old ox. It didn't seem possible that it could last long. I'd have bet a hundred it wouldn't, and at that I didn't know 'bout them d'horned hooks of his'n.

"Jackson turned to Stanley B. 'D'yer b'lieve in prayers?' he asks.

" 'Shut up,' snaps Stanley Barnarbus.

"Up the lake goes the pair, makin' the old reel sing. Every time that trout tried to dig fer bottom, that salmon wanted to show how high he could jump. An' every time the salmon wanted to sound, the trout hung back. I never see a worse actin' team.

"It didn't last long. Yer see, that poet knew more 'bout fishin' then Stanley B. er all the would-be's I ever see. He was a poem hisself, if he did look like a dime novel that had been out in the rain all summer. The trout was dead, 'parently, long afore that salmon was done wantin' ter sky-hoot, which weren't s' long as I wished it was.

"Al brung 'em in—slow and easy. Thar was a minute when I pretty near pinched the arm off Jackson, an' then thar they was, kinda waggin' feeble-like in that big landin' net. I sorter sagged. It was the dumbedest fly-rod stunt I ever see. An don't yer think for a minute that I've lied.

" 'Mister Turrel,' says Stanley B., 'yer win the five hundred.'

"Alphonsa come wadin' to shore. 'Be kind enough never to mention it,' he says. 'My wife don't approve of gamblin'.'

"An' I've never took no stock in psychology from that day to this. As fer Stanley B., I never heard him mention it ag'in."

Midge and Nymph Fly Fishing

EDWARD R. HEWITT

The great angling innovator and master of the Neversink startles readers by recommending flies as tiny as #18, or even #20, and the improvement of wet flies by pruning their wings. (March 1933)

Of late years such great emphasis has been placed on dry-fly fishing that many men forget there are other ways of taking trout which are quite different and quite as enjoyable and have a skilled technique all their own that is rather difficult and extremely interesting to master. These other methods of fishing are usually better than dry-fly fishing in taking numbers of trout, particularly the large ones, for it has been found by the examination of hundreds of trout stomachs that their contents consist only in very small part of surface flies. In fact, over 80 per cent of the trout's diet consists of underwater forms. If this is what the trout mostly feed on, why do fishermen insist on fishing on the surface so much of the time? Because it is easier, they can see the trout rise and take the fly, and they know just when to strike without the endless practice necessary with the other methods of fishing.

As a means of catching trout the dry fly is much over-rated for most of the season. When trout are rising to surface insects, there is no better way than the dry fly; but when they are feeding on under-water forms, it is a poor way to take trout. I often see men fishing with a dry fly when it is almost hopeless to take trout on it, and yet they persist because it seems to have a fascination for them in the very name. I myself felt this way for a long time, until I discovered that it required even more skill to fish in other ways and that fish were caught in numbers which would never have been taken with a dry fly.

Often in the early season we have the experience of seeing trout rising all around and not being able to make them take a dry fly. Such conditions used to get me quite exasperated, and I wondered what could be the matter. Observation finally solved the riddle and made the method of fishing to be employed on these occasions perfectly plain. When trout are feeding on the surface and will not take any kind of dry fly, they are always feeding on midge larvae and midges. The larvae are rising from the bottom, and the midges are on the surface. Midge larvae are much larger than the midges we see in the air and are in the form of little worms, often red in color, but other forms are brown or black.

The rises we see are generally made while the trout are taking these larvae just below the surface, and the fish's back or tail breaks the water. Only a small part of the apparent rises are due actually to taking the midges on the surface. Midge larvae are produced in enormous quantities from the right kind of bottom, and they form a very important part of the trout diet. Consequently an imitation of this form is a most excellent lure for trout.

I have never been able to understand why trout, when taking one particular size of insect, will not readily take something a little larger which we would think would furnish more food; but our ways of thinking and acting are not those of the trout, for they have a single-track mind which, when set on one kind of food, can not easily be diverted to something larger. Anyway, when trout are taking midges and midge larvae, they will not look at any ordinary fly, and it is almost useless to fish for them in this way. If, however, we put on a fly of the same size as the midges they are feeding on, it is surprising how easily they can be caught in any quantity, provided the leader used is fine enough.

It is of little use trying to use a midge fly with any leader more than five-thousandths of an inch in diameter. The trout will come up and look at the midge fly on a coarser leader and turn away. Now how small should a midge fly be? Generally it must be tied on a No. 18 hook, but I have some on No. 20 hooks. You will think at once that trout cannot be held on such tackle. This is the greatest possible mistake, because such hooks in the skin of the mouth will hold far more than the fine leaders it is necessary to use. But you will say you can't strike with such tackle. You don't strike at all, but just tighten up the line and give a very small twitch and keep a steady strain on the fish with no jerk. It is surprising how few trout are lost if they are properly handled.

The fly is fished in two ways. If a surface midge is used, it is oiled and left floating on the surface perfectly still for an appreciable time after casting, then given a minute pull to make it move slightly. Generally the trout strikes when this motion takes place, because it makes little light flashes which attract attention. The floating midge can be of many patterns and colors, but it must be of the right size, which is far more important than the pattern.

I have never been able to buy any good midge flies either here or in England and have been obliged to tie them myself. Those bought are always much too large and heavily tied to take our trout. When, however, you get the fly of the right size, nearly every rising trout can be hooked easily.

The second method of midge fly-fishing is operating the fly to make it behave like the midge larvae coming up from the bottom. Such flies must be even more sparingly tied and, in fact, resemble more a little worm. They are just a body on the hook and no wings. Such flies are either fished by letting them sink a little and then drawing them slowly so as to make them come to the surface like the natural larvae, or are cast and drawn slowly under the surface, allowing them to stop from time to time. These larva flies will catch more fish than the surface midges by far, but you do not see the trout take them so well.

Midge fishing nearly always takes place in fairly still water, because the midge larvae grow only in bottoms such as are deposited by still or very slow-flowing water. You can, therefore, see plainly just what the trout are doing.

On many occasions I have had a lot of fun with my friends in taking them to a place where I knew trout would be sure to be rising freely on midges and watching them cast for the rising fish with all the flies they had in the box. It is only on the rarest occasion that they ever take any trout under these conditions. After a while I put on a midge and begin pulling them out, and they think it is due to superior skill. When I show them the trick, they can get them just as easily as I can.

This type of fishing generally occurs early in the season, usually before the end of May. After that time there are enough larger insects out so that the trout get used to them and will, therefore, take larger flies more readily. Later in the season larger flies are far better, and only on rare occasions are midges preferable.

Every well-equipped trout fisherman should have a few midge flies, both the dry pattern and the sunken pattern, and a few lengths of gut four to six feet long about five-thousandths of an inch in diameter which can be tied to the end of the regular leader if it is necessary to do midge fishing. When trout are rising to them actively, there is no other way I have yet seen to get any fish. No one would want to fish midges all the time, because of the great attention which must be paid to seeing these small flies.

There is one absolutely sure sign when midge fly-fishing must be done, and that is when you see a trout strike at the knot in the leader instead of the fly. Knots are about the same size as the smaller midges. If ever you see this happen, just put on a midge and have some real fun for a while.

In England there is considerable literature about nymph fly-fishing. Mr. Skues seems to be the high priest of this art and to have brought it to a great degree of perfection for chalk streams, where it is a most successful method of taking trout. Unfortunately we have no chalk streams in this country and few streams having any great amount of water plants. We do not, therefore, have the same varieties of nymphs they have in England, and the flies they have developed so successfully are of little use in this country, where most of our streams are gravelly or rocky and the insect life of quite a different character. This is the reason why nymph fly-fishing has made little progress in this country. Men who have tried the English patterns of flies have not had much luck in taking trout and have abandoned the method without giving it the study necessary to adapt it to our conditions.

I had the great pleasure of three fishing trips on the Test at the famous Houghton Club and of seeing how this method of fishing was practiced, and I also spent two days on Mr. Skues' water on the Itchen at his invitation. These streams are full of water weeds. If these are examined, it will be seen that they are full of small insect larvae, much smaller in size than those we have here and with much greater variety of color. Most of the food of the trout consists of these nymphs, and only at certain times of the day do the trout take many surface insects.

Anyone fishing all the time with nymph flies is sure to hook many more trout than when fishing with any form of dry fly. But he must know just which kind of nymph the trout are feeding on, as there is a great variety, and each trout seems to have a preference for one or two kinds. In fact, one trout will take only one kind, and the very next fish be found full of quite another variety. Because of the abundance of the insect food, they can pick and choose as they like and get all they want.

On my last trip to the Test I fished altogether with nymph flies and not at all with a dry fly, and caught many more trout than on the other visits. One experience remains in my memory as of great interest.

Standing on a foot bridge, I saw four trout rising along the bank, below the bridge, about seventy-five feet apart. I was using a nine-foot leader and a small nymph tied with partridge hackle. Going below the lowest trout, I cast the fly about two feet above him and let it float down over him, with the fly about four inches below the surface when it passed him. After three casts the fish sank out of sight and ceased feeding. I had put him down.

I resolved to be more careful with the next, and cast as well as I knew how, the fly lighting just right on the water in just the right position. In fact, I considered the cast perfect, and yet the result was the same: he disappeared after a few casts. The same thing happened with the other two; so I walked to the foot bridge and sat down to think it over.

I seemed to have fished as well as it could be done, and yet all four fish had been put down in succession. This seemed to require an explanation, because I had taken many trout in this same way and yet could not even attract the notice of these fish. On thinking it over I decided to try an experiment if the trout began to feed again, which they soon did.

I cut the leader at the second knot up from the fly and put in five feet of gut of the same size, replacing the same fly and end as before. This gave me a leader of fourteen feet in place of nine, with the same fly and gut next to the fly. The idea I had was that the line had been striking the water too close to the trout, and the impact of the line had taken his attention till the fly had gone past his head. The longer leader would keep the line farther away, and the trout might give heed to the fly in time.

Going below the lowest fish, I cast as before, with the fly falling about two feet above the trout. On the second cast I noticed a sidewise movement of his head at the time the fly should have been passing him. I struck, and the trout was hooked. He ran downstream. Fortunately I kept him out of the weeds and landed him. He weighed a little over two pounds.

The second trout took the fly on the first cast, but ran into the weeds and finally got off.

The third trout would not take the fly until he had seen it a number of times and it had been cast directly on his nose. He then rose and took it with a splash. After a stiff fight he was landed—another two-pound fish.

It took me a long time to raise the fourth fish. I thought I saw him turn for the fly several times, but I never seemed to feel anything. Finally he turned across about a foot and took the fly squarely, but he made for a lane in the weeds in the middle of the stream and I could not get him out before the fly tore away.

Here were four trout which could not be caught with the fly on a nine-foot leader and were easily caught with the same fly on a fourteen-foot leader. The water was very clear and still, and the sun was almost overhead—most difficult conditions. No doubt at some other time these fish could have been caught with the regular tackle.

In our streams we do not often have the chance to try these experiments, as rising fish are not so plentiful or so easily watched. We must fish our nymph flies where we know the trout are likely to be, and in the way the nymphs themselves behave in our waters. In rapid water they can be fished upstream and allowed to float down with the current, keeping the line just tight enough to strike readily on any indication of a fish. Or they may be fished across and downstream, being very slightly moved in small jerks but not rapidly pulled, as these insects do not swim steadily but in spurts.

The May-fly nymphs are likely to come out and swim in the water toward dark, and they all move about after dark. That is one reason why late fishing is so effective: trout do most of their feeding at this time. Nymphs are vastly more effective than surface flies after dark. In fact, I have often seen the water alive with trout moving at dark and been able to get very few rises on a dry fly at such a time, when a nymph fly of the right pattern and size would take trout as fast as wanted. The latter represented the type of food the trout were feeding on.

Last season gave me many instances of the great effectiveness of this kind of fishing as against the dry fly. On one occasion I fished one of my large pools with two separate dry flies just as carefully as I knew how. A friend had just fished the pool ahead of me with another dry fly. The net result of both our efforts was one trout and two rises.

I then put on one of my stone-fly nymphs tied on a No. 14 hook and began at the top of the pool, fishing downstream. Only a few casts were made before I had a trout. Standing in the same place without moving down, I took fifteen fish and did not bother to fish the rest of the pool, as I was getting them too fast for pleasure. Some of the fish taken were of good size, and none were seen with the dry fly.

A friend who is regarded as one of the very best fishermen in the country and who writes frequently for FIELD & STREAM was fishing my Gate House Pool, which is about six hundred feet long, in the middle of the day. I told him he would not do much with a dry fly in such water at that time, but he only smiled and went ahead. When I met him at the top of the pool, he reported that he had taken one small trout and raised two others. I persuaded him to put on one of my nymphs and to fish the same pool back again. He took five large trout and missed four others. At the lower end he was completely converted to nymph fly-fishing. I could give endless instances of similar experiences.

One day last May a considerable number of excellent anglers fished the lower Beaverkill where there was a very large hatch of small May-flies in progress. These flies were mostly in the air and a very sparse rise of trout occurred. Only a few trout were taken, and I asked if I might open them and see what they were feeding on. The stomachs were found to be crammed full of small dark May-fly nymphs. Only one larger stone-fly nymph was found and only a few adult winged flies. This showed clearly that the food of these fish on that day consisted almost entirely of small May-fly nymphs and that the fisherman had an extremely small chance to get many of these trout on any kind of dry fly or ordinary wet fly.

The following day I tied several nymphs close in size and color to those I had seen in the trouts' stomachs and went to a large pool on the Neversink. I fished the pool carefully with a dry fly and a small streamer, and a friend also fished it over with some good wet flies before I put on the nymphs. My friend got two trout on wet flies, and I got none on dry or streamer flies. Standing in one place at the top of the pool and using the small dark nymph I had tied, I then took fifteen trout without moving and could have taken more, as they were still biting well when I stopped. Of course, these fish were all put back, as this was only a test to show the value of the nymph fly properly fished when the conditions are just right for its use. I am sure I could have taken fifty trout at that time easily. In the afternoon of the same day on adjacent pools the nymph fly was not so taking as a small streamer or a wet fly or even a dry fly. This was probably because the nymphs were not so plentiful in the water, and the trout turned their attention to other kinds of food. The nymph is not a fly to be used at all times; but when it is clearly indicated by conditions, there is no fly which will catch so many fish.

Now as to the nymph flies to be used in our streams. Usually those dark in color are the most effective, because in gravelly rocky streams these are the commonest underwater forms. In some streams there are some greenish or dark yellowish forms, but I have never seen any bright-colored nymphs in this country as they have in England.

The size of the nymph is most important next to the color. This varies in different streams and at different times, and must be right for the stream fished if the best results are to be obtained. I carry an assortment of sizes, from those on No. 16 hooks to those on No. 10 long-shank hooks. As a general experience, nymphs on a No. 14 or No. 12 hook are the most effective. Those which imitate the actual nymphs of the stream are, of course, the best. I have spent several years in tying patterns and testing them out until I have nymphs which are really good in all streams I have fished of late years.

Anyone can make nymphs by trimming down wet flies or dry flies with scissors until they resemble the insects found in the stream and in the stomachs of the trout. You can do this in a few minutes if you wish to test out the nymph fly. While the results will not be so good as that with a more exact imitation, it is very easy to make a fly which will be far more effective than any dry fly most of the time.

While large trout are not readily caught on a dry fly, it is surprising how many will be taken on nymphs, even small size.

In fishing the nymph I have not had good results with short leaders or with those over .007 of an inch in diameter for the three feet next to the fly. It looks as if the fine, long leader were necessary to make the nymph swim naturally in the water, and it appears as if the shorter heavier leader made the nymph behave unnaturally. Perhaps others can get better results than I can with short leaders. I have failed with them in this fishing on every occasion.

Anyone who will spend some time in the study of fishing a nymph fly will soon get the tricks of it and be able to see every trout as it takes the fly, most of them breaking the surface as they do for a dry fly. I have found no advantage in fishing the nymph deep, as the trout will come to the surface for them if they will come at all. I myself enjoy this form of fishing just as much as that with a dry fly, and have had the greatest pleasure in learning a new technique and in shifting from one kind of fishing to the other. I do whichever gives me the most pleasure; but when I want to catch trout in any quantity, I always use a nymph.

Anyone who will master this technique will soon find that he is able to catch trout where others are liable to draw a blank.

The Kelly Rainbow

FRANK DUFRESNE

When a man stays nine years on one Alaska trout stream, you know it's something special. (June 1933)

The northbound train on the Government-owned Alaska Railroad hesitated briefly at the whistling station of Willow before puffing and groaning into the dusk on its way up through the white peaks of the Alaska Range toward its terminus at Fairbanks, 470 miles from the seaport of Seward. Momentary as was its stop at Willow, however, the train carried one passenger less when it creaked slowly across the high wooden trestle, one lone fisherman seeking the truth concerning one of the most highly touted trout streams in all of Alaska.

For years this particular fisherman had journeyed up and down the far, wild lengths of the Territory, wetting a line wherever and whenever opportunity allowed. In its time and place many a stream and lake had been labeled superlative, only to be checked off somewhat regretfully in favor of newer conquests. Was this to be the case again? Could Big Willow River, not far from the thriving, bustling city of Anchorage, compare with the remote silvery reaches of the Upper Kobuk, many miles north of the Arctic Circle; with Pilgrim River on the "pup-mobile" line from Nome; with certain icy-cold tributaries of the great Yukon, or with the scores of trout-filled creeks in the southeastern Alaska archipelago? Well, I had my doubts—in fact, plenty of them.

Up the steep, sandy siding strode a tallish individual of indeterminate age, cheery of eye, all whalebone and sinew. "The name's Kelly," said he briskly.

I introduced myself, supposing I was meeting one of the many transients, better known in Alaska as *cheechakos*, who visit this place. "When did you get here?" I asked.

Kelly laid two capable paws on my duffle and swung the heavy bag to his shoulder in a manner which betokened plenty of pack-board experience. "Nine years ago," he answered.

Nine years on one trout stream! My indifference did a right-about-face and raced quickly to respect, a reversal of opinion destined to be much heightened in the twenty-four hours which were to follow.

"Come on down to the shack, an' look at what I got sliced up for supper," invited Kelly. "Tomorrow we'll go out after 'em."

He led the way down to where a couple of abandoned railroad cars had been jacked up and fitted out as overnight camps for the accommodation of visiting fishermen.

I started slightly at the size of the rainbow trout slabs waiting to fulfill their fate in the skillet. Nothing less than a five-pound fish could have produced the like of them. However, one big fish does not make a trout stream by any means. I felt an urge to voice doubts on the matter. Things were looking entirely too good to be true. Numerous wild-goose chases have taught me the pessimistic lesson that rare are the occasions when a local guide cannot hide himself behind one or the other of these time-honored alibis.

"What about the water?" I asked. "Isn't it too low or too high, too cloudy, too clear, too—something?"

Instead of equivocating, Kelly leaped at the question. "Big Willow ain't too nothin'," he stated flatly. "She's just right. Mighty few times when she ain't. Now if you'll drag a box up to the table, we'll tear into this fish while it's still smokin' hot. Plenty of time tomorrow to settle that other question."

Afterward, when the dishes had been washed and stacked away, we sat outside in the cool night air and watched Big Willow put on its regular evening show. "Watched" is not the correct word, for the performance appealed mostly to the sense of hearing—the intermittent purr of the current and the chatter of fast water over the gravel, broken now and then by the splash and glistening flash of feeding trout in the big pool in front of our door, and the heavy spatterings of salmon fighting their way upriver over the shallows. It was restful, soul-satisfying.

While we smoked in silence a big old boss beaver came swimming out of the gloom of the far cottonwoods, furrowed a gleaming trail across the river and slid itself half out of water on the sand within five paces of us. Its small eyes glowed with an odd appearance of hostility, bright as the cigar ends in our hands, while it sized us up briefly before plunging into the water. Shortly afterward it popped to the surface well out on the bosom of the river and sounded an alarm to all night-roving wild folk by slapping its "nightstick" smartly on the water.

" 'Tis the traffic cop," said Kelly softly, digging his cigar butt into the damp earth. "He comes on shift about this hour every night. Now that he's on the job, we'll turn in and leave him run the river till sunup."

In the morning a slick o' frost covered the ground where the sun of late August had not already searched it out.

"She's a dinger for rainbows," mused Kelly as he leaned his spare frame in the door of the car and looked out upon the river over which a bower of golden and crimson leaves rattled faintly on their drying stems, while now and then a single leaf fluttered downward into the rushing water. "Yes, sir; a dinger! A mite late for flies mebbe, but spinners'll take 'em."

We struck out along a newly brushed-out tractor trail which led at right angles from the railroad, penetrating for many miles up Big Willow watershed to a recently developed gold mine. The weather was clear, the slightest bit tingly, and the air filled with the tiny twitterings of migrating songsters. Nearer at hand, magpies and gray jays flirted furtively about in the underbrush as though fearful of being caught in some mischief. Kelly appeared to know every foot of the country, pointing out spots here and there where he had set out his traps for fur-bearers during the winter. Here he had come off second best in a scuffle with a cub bear; there a wily wolverine had finally made the fatal step after weeks of trap robbing.

Where a punky, fallen birch had been ground to snuff-colored powder by the tread of passing caterpillars we surprised a brood of spruce grouse dusting themselves. Like exploding smoke bombs they took to the air, somewhat spoiling the effect of their picturesque getaway by crashing pellmell into the first trees, clucking like a bunch of idiots as we passed under them close enough to knock off their silly heads with our rods.

After an hour or more of brisk walking, Kelly led the way through a thicket of dead-ripe high-bush cranberries to the bank of the Big Willow just above where it poured its racing flood against a log jam and came swirling back in a deep, scud-flecked eddy.

"Go after 'em," said Kelly. " 'Tis an old story with me."

I dropped a line into the current. Scarcely had it straightened when I was fast to a fish. A living, iridescent rainbow leaped high out of the gray waters and danced halfway across the river on its tail, as though charged with lightning. In a few minutes I landed the trout, a beautifully colored specimen about eighteen inches long and looked to Kelly for approval. There was none.

" 'Tis no fish fit for a man to creel unless he's hungry, or wants to make a show of numbers. Turn it loose and try again. Cast well out and let your lure go with the current. The big ones lay deep."

Following Kelly's advice, I soon learned that it was easy to catch fish in Big Willow, but to take one worthy of his stamp of approval was quite another matter. Rapidly I hooked and landed five good-sized trout, all of which he shamed me into releasing, although one of them exceeded twenty inches in length. I began to wonder just how big a rainbow would have to be to suit him.

Suddenly I got a savage strike with plenty of weight behind it, and for a moment believed I had established connections with such a fish. Deep in the water an unseen force ripped yard after yard of line from the reel in sullen fury. Settling myself for a long fight, I was astonished to see the waters split, followed by a huge bolt of bright scarlet shooting into the air and scattering jeweled spray in all directions. Above the dull roar of the water I heard Kelly's shout, "Leaping Lena!"

This was his pet name for the coho salmon in its bright-red spawning colors, its "wedding dress," as it has been aptly termed.

Although it was not a fish I desired to keep, the "leaping Lena" put on a glorious, reckless battle. Like all of the salmon family I have encountered in Alaska, it fought with senseless ferocity, succumbing to the fly rod only after it had worn itself completely out by twenty minutes of maniacal leaping and gyrating. Its weight was about fifteen pounds.

Occasionally I have hooked this particular variety of salmon in other Territorial streams, but never with such regularity as on Big Willow that day. As they take no nourishment after leaving their home in the sea to spawn and die in the headwaters of the rivers and creeks, the strike appears to be delivered in pure anger. At least twenty of them hit my lure that day. Before night my rod tip was a sorry-looking affair.

Failing to secure a rainbow worthy of the Kelly trademark, we moved on downstream. Where a small, glass-clear side stream had its confluence with the main river I took a half dozen fine grayling with a Black Gnat—slim, graceful beauties which found their way into my basket without protest from my companion. It was at this same place that we came near to argument. An extraordinarily brilliant specimen of rainbow trout took the fly, and after a cautious, long-drawn-out struggle was led into the shallow water, where Kelly stretched a tape over it. I saw his thumb-nail slide up the tape to the figure 24, hesitate, then move along another half inch. My heart leaped.

"Is it a fit fish?" I asked.

Kelly shook his head. " 'Tis a fair trout, but if you're a fisherman you'll do better," he said, and batted not an eye when, half peeved, I twitched the hook from the trout's lip and allowed it to fan itself wearily back into the current.

This grand gesture gave me some cause for regret later on, for it seemed that I was not to take a better fish. More than once I thought the moment had come, but each time it turned out to be one of the vivid, hook-nosed "leaping Lenas" or a rainbow not quite up to the mark. Not that I could find fault with the fishing. It was comparable to the best I had ever experienced; of such caliber that I can honestly proclaim Big Willow to be one of the very finest trout streams in Alaska. Its accessibility is a decided point in its favor. One has but to step off the railroad car and commence fishing, whereas a great many of my favorite places are buried in the wilderness. During the course of my day astream with Kelly I hooked upward of a hundred fish varying from one foot to two feet in length. That's fishing!

Determined to stay with it until Lady Luck showered down, I trudged behind my long-legged host as he led me along game trails beside Big Willow, portaging a hundred yards or more at a stretch to reach his favorite pools, although as far as I was concerned one spot was as good as another. On this trend of thought I asked Kelly how much of Big Willow offered such wonderful fishing, as we were enjoying.

Said he, "From the headwaters of this river to the Susitna below the railroad it's above twenty-five miles, and I've taken fish in every mile of that. It ain't all so good, though, for in the upper six or seven miles they run pretty small. I figure it's about eighteen miles of first-class fishing.

"Another thing that'll surprise you," he added. "Big Willow is purely a migratory stream. During the winter months there ain't a fish in it. They've all gone down into the Susitna, and mebbe into the salt water of Cook's Inlet, for all I know. But in the spring they come back thicker'n hair on a dog's back. If I was to name the best month of the year for you to come back here and try Big Willow, I'd say May; that's when the king salmon run. Rainbows is good fishin', sure enough; but if you never had a forty- or fifty-pound king on a trout rod, you just ain't had fun—that's all. Takes me from two to four hours to land one under the best of conditions. Mostly, though, I don't land 'em."

I looked sorrowfully at the tip of my rod, twisted like a corkscrew by mere 12- and 15-pounders of the "Leaping Lena" variety, and I made a mental resolve to bring along several extra tips if fortunate enough to pass this way during the May run of the giants.

By midafternoon it became evident that Kelly had given me too much river to work in one day at the rate we were going; so again and again we took to portaging the bends, racing against the lowering sun, even now casting long shadows through the cottonwoods and birches. On the last of these cut-offs we traversed a series of beaver dams and sunken brush piles in the center of which stood an enormous beaver house which showed several years' work in the making.

Kelly noticed my interest. "The traffic cop's home," he commented briefly, and pushed on a few yards farther to reach an open gravel bar not far above and across the river from the railroad cars we had left in the morning. The shadows of the trestlework actually darkened the waters as I made my last and most eventful cast of the day.

So swift was the water at this point that my spinner, though weighted, danced and strained at the surface like a thing alive while I stripped off sixty or seventy feet of line. When the strike came, there was nothing about it to indicate a large fish; the spinner simply disappeared. When I set the hook, the line cut slowly and diagonally across stream with but little strain on it. Thinking to test the size of the fish, I began pumping. Then I felt the first smashing, unleashed force telegraphed along the line and rod, and knew I was fast to a real fish. It was not another scarlet coho. Indirect testimony of this came to me through Kelly's low admonition: "Steady, man! Watch your slack!"

Suddenly, far downstream, a rainbow trout of magnificent dimensions rolled to the surface and began such a vicious, breath-taking battle that I was almost sure it would end in a limp line. More and more line was yielded from the reel as the great fish catapulted itself into the air, one leap following another in rapid succession, while the red jaws wrenched angrily at the stinging bit of steel which held it captive. Combined with the rushing force of the water, the fish was straining my tackle to the limit; and now, at the end of the day, I felt none too secure about any part of it. For a while I played the game safe by giving out line, until all at once I found myself staring at a very nearly emptied reel.

Already it had been demonstrated quite to my satisfaction that my equipment was far too frail to lead that whopper back against the current. This left but one procedure open. I floundered downstream in the wake of the fish, wet to the waist, until it swung back under the influence of a wide, strong eddy. Now the battle became more localized, although it was fully twenty minutes before I got a close-up view of the trout.

Thrilled by its great size and gorgeous coloration, and believing the fight won, something akin to horror struck me when I noticed the tiny hook dangling loosely in the torn lip, ready to fall out at the first slack in the line. The battle was not over. The trout had plenty of strength, for like a bolt it dove back into the deep water, boring, boring, boring until I just about decided it would never stop.

Luckily it indulged in no more acrobatics. Some time later—I have no recollection of minutes involved—the big fellow showed up again and allowed himself to be led, unresisting, over Kelly's booted feet as he stood knee-deep in the water. It was without question the largest rainbow I had ever seen—close to thirty inches in length, perfect in proportions.

This time Kelly produced no tape measure, but slid a practiced hand under the gleaming gill plates. The game was won, I knew, but vanity demanded verbal acknowledgment.

"Don't pull that fish out of the water until you answer me one question. Is it a Kelly rainbow?"

Kelly gained a secure grip with both hands and heaved himself upright. "Aye," he answered gravely, " 'tis a fit fish."

Selective Trout

RAY BERGMAN

The author of the all-time best-seller, Trout, *gives classic pointers on how to cut down on those splashy, "refusal" rises and how to come up with what the fish are really looking for.* (May 1934)

Sometimes trout take any fly eagerly, rising easily and with assurance, so that it seems almost impossible to miss them. But on the whole these times are few. As a rule, one will be more likely to find the trout selective in some special way, if not to the point of desiring a certain pattern of fly, at least to the degree of being particular as to the general coloration, the size or the shape.

Often the selectiveness of a trout pertains to bottom rather than to surface food, to some nymph or grub which is floating just under the surface, to small minnows which scatter in all directions as the trout try to catch them. At such times the fish make surface disturbances which lead many anglers to believe they are rising. Frequently, when selective in any of these degrees, they will rise to a dry fly which is not in any way representative of the thing they are feeding on. At other times they appear to rise to the angler's faulty offering, but in reality they simply splash at it, causing the fisherman to believe that he has missed the fish by ill-timed striking.

I have spent a lot of time and effort striving to solve the secret of selectively feeding trout. Sometimes I have succeeded in my efforts; at other times I have failed miserably. But during the last few years I have been steadily increasing my percentage of successes. The causes leading to this have been infinitesimal, often elusive; some have escaped me entirely, but several very pertinent facts have asserted themselves, and these I will endeavor to isolate and describe.

There was a time when I bitterly and wholly blamed myself if a trout splashed at my fly and I missed him. Always I thought that I was off on the timing of my strike. I also had the idea that whenever a trout came to my fly and refused at the last instant, the faulty floating of the fly was always the cause of such refusals. As a matter of fact, both splash rises and refusals may be caused by the fly itself—because it does not match the conditions perfectly. While refusals are often caused by drag, the fly is not always refused because of this reason.

In recent years I have come to realize that the right fly or lure for the prevalent condition will usually stop splash rises and investigating refusals. In experimenting with various flies I found that the way they floated on the water had a lot to do with the way the trout rose to them.

The first time this conclusion forced itself upon me I was fishing a brown-trout stream in northern New York. Here and there were scattered hatches of whirling duns. As I seldom use double-winged dry flies, I matched the natural with a Dark Cahill. I got plenty of rises, most of them splashy ones, but couldn't hook a fish. After I had tried slow striking, medium striking and fast striking without bettering the condition, I decided that the trout were refusing my fly because it did not suit them. What could be the trouble? The No. 10 size seemed to match the naturals well enough, and surely the fact that I was using a buzz wing instead of a solid wing couldn't be the cause.

On looking closely at the floating naturals I noted that they rode low, while my artificial rode high. The naturals also had the appearance of being glued down on the water; they hugged it tightly, while my fly sort of bounced along the surface. I had no other Cahills with me; so I went back to camp and tied one which I thought might work. On a No. 10 hook I tied a fly with hackles that would ordinarily have been tied on a No. 12. I also spread the hackles as much as possible, so that they would cover a larger expanse of water. Besides this, I followed Dr. Edgar Burke's method of construction and carried the entire fly down the hook, farther away from the eye. These differences in construction made the fly sit lower and also overcame its tendency to wabble—the very two things I was striving for.

On my first cast with the new fly I rose a trout. Instead of splashing he dimpled, and I had no trouble hooking him. For the balance of the day I was no longer bothered with refusing trout.

From that time on I never wasted much time fishing with a fly which continually brought splash rises. As soon as such rises occurred repeatedly with resulting misses, I immediately changed flies. This is what I discovered. At times the trout wanted high floating flies, but at other times they wanted low floaters.

When high floaters were wanted, nothing could beat flies of the spider type, and the more spidery they looked the better they worked. When they wanted low floaters, three flies stood out from the rest. They were: Ginger Cahill, Dark Cahill and a small gray fly with delicate hackle wings. The best size, striking a general average, was a No. 14, with No. 12 running second. They were tied as small as possible for the hook size.

During these experiments I proved conclusively that properly balanced flies were taken by the trout far better than those of improper balance—even though the patterns were identical. Perfect balance caused the flies to grasp the water securely, and this simulated the appearance of many natural insects.

Always a keen admirer and strong advocate of the fan-wing Royal Coachman, I now tied some with spread hackles and balanced according to Dr. Burke's ideas. I found that this improved their effectiveness. I also discovered that if the wings were flattened out away from the upright they were still better. A ginger fan-wing Royal tied with a buff-colored body served to interest many fish that would not rise to a regular, and always I found that when a fly had a tendency to hug the water tightly it was taken more frequently and with less fuss than when it rode too high and was uncertain in its equilibrium.

It was in color selectiveness that I had the greatest difficulty. There were times when the slightest variation in the shade of a hackle made all the difference in the world. But of course it would be quite impossible to carry an assortment of flies made up of all the color shades. To simplify matters I worked out the following hackle color chart. It was not perfect by any means, but flies tied from it were very satisfactory except when I ran into extremely selective hatches.

I used six basic hackle colors. They were reddish brown, ginger, honey, blue-gray, black and olive. Brown and ginger were most generally used for clear days. The honey took care of the sulphur, pale yellow and light buff hatches. On some streams a preponderance of blue-gray hatches made flies tied of this color the most effective. The black and olive were not used much, but when they were needed nothing else compared with them for killing effectiveness. In addition to this I added fan-wings and spiders for those times when the trout were not visibly rising to naturals or when no naturals were on the water. I consider an assortment of this kind, when sizes from No. 10 to No. 18 are included, very close to ideal.

The wrong color or the wrong size of fly for any particular rise was sure to bring one of three things: a flat disregard of my offering, a refusal after investigation of the artificial or a splash rise. The flat refusal is one which the angler immediately recognizes as a signal to change patterns. The investigating refusal soon makes the angler realize the same thing. But the splash rise is one which many anglers fail to recognize as a refusal. They are usually inclined to blame themselves rather than the fly. I could cite many incidents supporting the fact that splash rises are not sure rises. Let me give you an example.

Last year in August, Vic Coty and I were fishing a stream where the fan-wing Royal was supposed to be the only fly worth using. Naturally, we followed the general rule and fished with this popular fly. During the first hour we received some fifteen splash rises, but hooked only one fish—a small one.

On this day there weren't any visible rises to natural flies, so that it seemed useless to try a different pattern of fly, but Coty, acting on a hunch, decided to try a Paulinskill, a pattern of honey color, because it was a fly which had often brought him good results during the late season. It worked like a charm. Within the next hour he had risen and hooked four nice trout, while I, persisting in the use of the fan-wing Royal for experimental reasons, could do nothing better than get splash rises which I missed. Darkness precluded any further experiments on this day, but to me the two hours proved conclusively that if you do not have the right fly your chances of success are poor, even though you are getting rises.

Another incident quite striking in detail was the following. It was a day of apparent inaction. Very few flies were on the water, and those that were did not interest the trout. I started fishing with the Brown Spider. In two hours I rose and missed ten fish—all good ones. I then tried the fan-wing Royal. This the trout did not want at all. Switching back to the hackle type, I tried a Ginger Spider with a tapered white body. This proved to be the fly which they wanted. The difference between the two spiders was considerable. The Brown was tied palmer without any body and the hackles were dull. The Ginger had a well-defined tapered body and the hackles were glossy.

On the following day, fishing the same stream, conditions proved quite different. Because of the experience of the preceding day, I started out with the Ginger Spider, but could not get a business rise with it. I then tried various other spiders and variants, but obviously they were not what the fish wanted. In these trials I noted one thing: the Ginger Spider brought the most rises, even though they were splashes. From this I concluded that the color was right but the size wrong. Putting on a No. 14 Ginger Cahill tied with short hackles turned the tide at once. It proved to be just the color, size and shape they wanted.

These are only a few examples. During the past ten years I have had scores of similar experiences, and the selectivity has taken many different angles. Besides size, shape and color of the fly, other things had a bearing on the problem. Always the fly had to be presented in the right way and, unless one were a past master at the art of throwing a loop cast, a long leader was very necessary.

So different were the needs of different days that it was impossible to formulate anything but the most general rules to cover them. But taking percentages showed up the following facts.

On bright days between the hours of 10:00 A.M. and 6:30 P.M. during the months of June, July and August the ginger and honey flies were most likely to produce, and small sizes were most effective. Before 10:00 A.M. and from 6:30 P.M. until dark and after, the larger flies, such as spiders and fan-wings, were the best, with ginger and red brown being the best colors. On dark days a gray fly seemed to bring best results, although here I found that a low-floating ginger fan-wing showed up fine in certain waters.

Different parts of the same stream often revealed different conditions prevalent. Fast waters were likely to be more productive when sizes 12 and 10 were used, while still waters called for 14's and smaller, with the exception of the spiders, which worked best when they were tied with a large spread of hackle. But the spiders only worked well when the trout were a bit off feed and did not respond to a low floater.

It was a game of complications and contradictions, and I could not begin to formulate the results into an infallible semblance of order. Unless I knew the waters well and was aware of the general fly characteristics throughout an entire season, it was a matter of blindly experimenting until I arrived at a workable solution. Knowing a stream well, however, simplified things greatly. For instance: on one stream I knew, the hatches ran about 75 per cent gray to 25 per cent any other color. Here gray flies, either spiders or the natural type, proved best four-fifths of the time. On several streams I found a prevalence of black hatches. There a small black fly always proved the best, taking a general average. Olives I found useful and necessary only on occasion, but when they were needed nothing else would produce. The following table I composed from 80 days of fishing when selectivity was apparent in some very noticeable degree.

From 10:00 A.M. until 6:30 P.M.

25 days—Ginger, small
7 days—Ginger, medium and large
15 days—Brown, small
5 days—Brown, large and medium
10 days—Gray, small
2 days—Gray, medium
8 days—Honey, small
2 days—Honey, medium
4 days—Black, small
2 days—Olive, medium

Morning and Evening

28 days—Ginger, medium and large
3 days—Ginger, small
19 days—Brown, large and medium
3 days—Brown, small
22 days—Gray, medium
5 days—Olive, medium

These figures were arrived at after real experimentation and are taken from records covering the last ten years. I did not blindly try one pattern on any single day and adhere to its use regardless. I carefully gave every color its chance, and the colors and sizes which brought best results earned their places in the list from merit and not from favoritism. The streams wherein the experiments took place covered a wide range of Eastern waters, and weather conditions ran from bright to heavy rain.

So far in my discussion about selective trout I have confined my remarks to the dry fly. Often the best solution to selectiveness is the nymph. Here we run into a specialized art which is really nothing more than wet-fly fishing developed to a high degree. Unfortunately, many of the anglers who attempted nymph fishing in the past few years had the erroneous idea that the nymph was a sure cure for failure; that it was only necessary to tie one on a leader, and the trout immediately jumped in the creel. Nothing could be farther from the truth. The nymph, while extremely effective and the certain means whereby many a good trout may be taken which would otherwise remain uncaught, must be fished in the right way, or else it is no better than any other fly or lure.

To help those who wish to become proficient in the art of nymph fishing I am going to narrate a few of my experiences of the past year, giving the conditions and the methods of fishing. Understand, I do not use nymphs regularly—that is, I never start fishing with one and use it consistently the entire day. Rather do I use them for unusual cases when nothing else will do: for located trout which repeatedly refuse other offerings, for second chances at fish which slap at the dry fly, for days when worthwhile trout refuse to rise under any circumstances.

On the whole, I do not find the nymph particularly effective until the streams become clear. It will not take the place of bait when fishing swollen, muddy streams. I consider May and August the two best months, although July runs a close second, and I have used nymphs successfully in June. The best fishing I have ever had with them was in August, at which time I consider them very valuable indeed, especially on low, extremely clear water.

My first need for nymphs became apparent the latter part of April in the

Poconos. The day was very bright with a temperature of 31 in the early morning which, however, rose steadily as day advanced until it reached a high of 78 at 2:30 P.M. The stream seemed quite dead, but we managed to pick up an odd trout or two with wet flies in the first three hours of fishing. They ran very small.

Now we knew there were plenty of fair-sized natives in the stream. Conditions were ideal. The water was clear and of medium height. The trouble was clearly with us, and not the trout.

I finally reached a deep stillwater. It was impossible to fish it without getting right in it. A heavy stand of brush completely covering the stream below and a similar barrier on either side made anything but a short cast a hazardous proposition at best.

Getting in the water cautiously, I found that it was nearly waist-deep. Once in position, I stood motionless for some time, carefully watching the water for signs of active fish. While I was standing there the sun reached a point where it disclosed the bottom of the stillwater to my eager eyes. What I saw made my pulse beat wildly. At least fifty trout were congregated close to the bottom, not over ten feet from me! They appeared to be moving about in a limited area, and darted here and there a few inches at a time.

I tied on a nymph of somber coloration. Casting it directly upstream, I let it float down with the slight current. It did not sink deep, and the trout ignored it. The second time I cast it farther upstream, so that it would have a longer time to sink, and this time it floated well down, within six inches of the fish. One trout, a small one, became interested and took. After that I couldn't get another touch, although I did get several approaches and refusals. Clearly this nymph wouldn't do.

I then tried one of a rust color with silver ribbing. Because it was hard to follow the course of the nymph as it floated down, I also tied a Coachman at the top of the leader to serve as an indicator. The first time this nymph reached the location of the trout, action began. I saw several flashes, the Coachman gave a sudden dart, and I was soon in possession of an 11-inch native. I took twelve trout as fast as I could make a cast, hook and play them. Then, for some reason, the fish suddenly decided to move upstream. I finally located them about half-way up the stillwater, and here I repeated the performance of below.

There wasn't any trick to the fishing. The nymph was allowed to follow the current the same as a dry fly, except, of course, that it was sunken instead of on the surface. As it floated down I stripped in line just fast enough to take in the slack without exerting any pull on the fly. If I saw a flash or if the Coachman made any untoward motion, I immediately struck.

On this day the trout took the nymph seriously. There were very few misses, and in most instances the No. 10 fly was completely in the mouth of the fish.

My partner, fishing wet flies in the same manner, had no luck at all. But when he put on one of the rust-color nymphs, he was soon taking as many fish as I.

The second incident has to do with one trout—a 2¼-pound brown. The time was August, the weather mild and clear, the stream very low. While walking along the brook we saw this fish break water. At first we thought it was a rise, but close investigation proved that the surface disturbance was made by either his tail or his dorsal fin. It was evident that he was feeding on nymphs. His method of procedure was very interesting. First he would go to the head of his range—at the tail of the riffle leading into the pool. Here he would take a perpendicular position, his broad tail breaking the surface of the water, and start rooting among the loose rocks. After a minute or two of this he would then move downstream about fifteen feet, turn about and work up slowly, picking up the nymph life he had dislodged from the rocks.

I was fishing dry and decided not to change immediately. For fifteen minutes I cast over this fish, trying several patterns which were good on this particular water. Sometimes the fly floated so close that it touched his dorsal fin, which was above the water most of the time. But he refused to have anything to do with my offerings.

Then I tried a buff black-ribbed nymph with guinea-fowl feelers. I waited until the trout was on one of his upstream cruises and then cast the nymph so that it alighted in the riffle just above the place where he rooted in the rocks. I was on the left-hand side of the stream looking up, and the trout was against the right bank. In making the cast I threw a loop so that when the nymph floated over him there wouldn't be any chance of making him leader shy. As the lure floated near him he saw it and immediately sucked it in without the least bit of commotion. He took it so deep that I had to use a disgorger to remove it from his throat. When I related the incident to a friend, he told me that he had seen this trout acting the same way when he had fished the stream in June and that he had failed to interest him in a dry fly.

The third incident shows another valuable use for nymphs: that of getting the most out of any pool you might consider good. On a certain stream in northern New York there is one pool which contains a large number of trout, most of them of good size. On this particular evening I had decided to stay with it from 6 P.M. until dark.

When I first arrived, I saw two trout rising and promptly took them with a No. 14 Dark Cahill. After that I fished dry for an hour without getting a rise or seeing a fish move, and then I teased one up with a Ginger Coachman. That seemed to end the fun as far as dry flies were concerned. I tried them off and on until dark without getting a rise. But the buff black-ribbed nymph, fished sunken on a slack line, produced six strikes and three hooked fish. These three were much larger than those taken with the dry fly, so that I felt amply repaid for the effort.

The fourth incident covers the most common use of the nymph. Fishing wasn't any too good. It was 4 P.M., and since 9 A.M. we had been diligently fishing with dry flies. During that time I had not seen a fish larger than 10 inches, and very few of those. Then I came to a likely-looking spot. An old stump on the left-hand side of the stream, as one looked up, was undermined by the current, which swept down upon it at a 45-degree angle. After swirling under the stump the current then turned and swept outward again, the two currents thus forming a V.

The first cast with my fan-wing brought a rise in the current above the stump. The fish splashed and showed himself plainly. As it was a trout well over a pound, I decided he was worth trying for. Twelve different patterns of dry flies failed to bring a response. Several naturals which floated over him during this time were also refused.

Clearly the trout was feeding under the surface. His rise to my fan-wing had been a curiosity jump rather than a business rise. I decided to try the buff black-ribbed nymph. In fishing it I cast about three feet above the location where the trout had jumped. I let it float down on an absolutely slack line. When I figured that it had reached the stump, I brought the line taut. I felt the fish, but did not connect. Although I thought my chance was gone, I tried again. This time I waited an instant longer before bringing the line taut, and when I did I was fast to the fish. He had taken it the second time, and when a brown trout does that it means both the lure and the method of fishing it were right.

Nine times out of ten I find that the trout which splash at the dry fly are susceptible to the nymph. You can usually get a second chance at such trout if you will only give the lure a try. Inasmuch as you use the same leader and handle the cast the same as when fishing dry, it is a simple matter to do so.

There are a few things to remember about this nymph fishing. First, be sure the lure is wet, so that it sinks readily when you use it. Second, never give it any motion when fishing upstream in moving water. Just let it float along naturally, the same as a dry fly. A good way to fish upstream in fast water is to tie a dry fly on the leader about seven feet above the nymph. Choose a good floater for the purpose. Usually the indication of a strike will be simply a pause in the movement of the dry fly. When you see this, you must strike at once. As a rule, the indication showing the strike is so slight that you hardly notice it, but you must be keyed up to the game and be ready to set the hook at the slightest untoward motion of the dry fly.

For early and late season or whenever you run into minnow-feeding trout, nothing can compare with a bucktail fly. There are many varieties of these in existence, but the more minnow-like they appear the better they appeal to the fish. For the large streams, sizes 4 and 6 have been my best bets, but on small streams, even if the trout run large, I prefer a lightly-tied affair not larger than 12.

Usually it is best to fish the bucktail across and down the stream. At times I find that holding it in the current directly downstream over a likely-looking spot brings very good results. It should always be jerked slightly, so that it simulates the action of a crippled minnow. My best trout on a bucktail last year weighed 4 pounds. He was taken the last day of the season on an all-white fly.

Selective trout! It is a large subject and a deep one. It is a topic calling for wide and spirited discussion. Every rising trout that refuses your offerings is an interesting problem. When you fail to interest such a fish, something is wrong —either with your fly, your method of fishing it, or your delivery generally. Instead of quitting trout that refuse you, experiment with them. If you keep everlastingly at it, you are bound to add new tricks to your stock of stream lore.

Deep Nymphs for Stubborn Trout

JAMES R. WEBB

Add a third dimension—depth—to the newly introduced nymph and you've got the greatest invention since the worm. (July 1935)

It was the opening day of the trout season back in 1930 in New York State, where the season opens on the first Saturday in April. The water was cold and murky, but I imagined I had seen some sort of insect awakened by the early spring sunshine, and was making a vain attempt to take a trout or two without benefit of worms. I knew better, but persisted stubbornly. The one trout I had encountered all day caught me off guard and departed derisively with my best bucktail fly.

Of course, there were battalions of fishermen afoot, few of whom seemed to have any foolish prejudices as to the use of bait, yet none of them was having much success. Then along came a fellow fishing with some "bugs" of his own contriving, tied to represent aquatic nymphs, or immature insects, on which he had taken the best creel of trout I had seen that day.

Nymph fishing was pioneering in those days. Some such lures had, of course, been in use for years by a very small number of the trout-fishing fraternity but, in this country at least, had been given very little publicity. After the above demonstration I began to hold post-mortems on the trout I caught, to find what they'd had for breakfast. Try it yourself, and you'll find that these early-season trout certainly do go in for nymphs.

The artificial nymphs then on the market were crude affairs, mostly of English extraction, and had little resemblance to the creatures consumed by the trout. So I hunted up a fly-tying vise, and prowled around for materials with which to imitate these trout tidbits. Even the first crude lures proved surprisingly successful; and as the lures developed into more lifelike imitations, and a sort of technique developed in their use, the results became more and more gratifying.

A great deal of popularity was assured for nymph fishing when, in 1933, there appeared in FIELD & STREAM a series of notable articles which dwelt very glowingly upon the great effectiveness of these lures. New methods develop rather slowly, for we fishermen cling to our prejudices and are really very reluctant to change our style of fishing. We buy new lures eagerly, but seldom give them a thorough trial. Unless they deliver immediate results, back we go with renewed faith to those devices and methods which have proved successful for us in the past.

Gradually the new methods take hold, however. Dry-fly fishing was slow in gaining favor in this country; yet now it has very largely replaced the use of wet flies here in the East. But while the dry flies have gained this popularity, the proportion of bait fishermen hasn't seemed to decline one bit.

I would like to see among the converts to nymph fishing some of those who now persistently use worms—some of those skeptics who scoff at the use of light tackle and regard a trout fly merely as a vain article of millinery. What a lot of fun such fellows miss!

Most of the literature on fishing with these nymph flies has very naturally stressed their use near the surface, at times when trout are feeding on living nymphs coming up to the surface to "hatch" into mature winged insects. Obviously, it is at such times that artificial nymphs should prove most effective; and when trout are feeding at or near the surface, there is no reason whatever for fishing the flies deep.

There are times, however, when there are no hatches of insects; when the trout find all their food down around the bottom of the stream, and cannot readily be attracted toward the surface. Such conditions are the rule rather than the exception early in the season, and also prevail at times later on. At such times most fishermen resort to the use of bait. Doubtless many of them would prefer to use a more sporting lure if they could feel that it had a reasonable chance of success. For such conditions I prescribe a nymph fished deep.

As trout become larger and their jaws more formidable they feed less and less at the surface. But nymphs fished deep still interest these old fellows.

Many writers on trout fishing persist in reiterating, year after year, that if one expects any tangible results at the start of the season he must resort to the use of the "garden hackle." I used to believe this. Now I know it to be utter hokum. I do not mean that nymphs are infallible, or as effective in early April as they are later on. Yet I have taken trout in April more consistently—better fish, too—in the last few seasons with nymphs than in the preceding seasons, when I used worms for this early-season fishing in the same waters.

Of course, worms are more effective at times. One day last April I was fishing some fast water containing some splendid trout—mostly rainbows. Another fisherman, using night-crawlers very skillfully, took six very beautiful trout weighing from one to three pounds each. Using nymphs, I had to content myself with a pair. However, three other rainbows were insecurely hooked and lost, as I was unable to hold them in that fast water on the somewhat small hooks I happened to be using.

Many times, even in April, the nymph flies have seemed more effective than bait. And a little later on, with insect life becoming more active, the nymph fisherman need ask no odds of anyone. I believe the trout taken on nymphs will average larger in size than those taken on any other type of fly except the bucktail or streamer type, which should hardly be called a fly, as it imitates a minnow rather than any form of insect.

This nymph fishing is, of course, just a specialized form of wet-fly fishing. Its technique is very different from the traditional method of using wet flies, but is not very difficult to acquire. One day last season I gave one of my boys a nymph and a few brief instructions, and turned him loose on a much over-fished stream. Very soon I found him playing a 16-inch rainbow.

Suppose we take a little imaginary trip to one of your favorite trout streams, shortly before the season opens. Just as you're becoming very much bored with the account of the big brown I lost last year, we pull up at our destination and climb stiffly from the car. Hurriedly we don our fishing togs and assemble our rods. There's a bit of chill in the air still, but the song sparrows are singing cheerily—and isn't it great to be out again!

We clamber down over the hill to the stream, coming out on that riffle where you caught those browns last summer. But the water is higher now and has a cold, dark look. Misgivings assail you, though you try not to show it. It would have been such a simple matter to stow away a can of worms in the back of the car somewhere.

But these riffles must be full of insect life, even though there is no evidence of it at the surface. Attached to rocks on the bottom must be lots of little cylindrical caddis "cases," sheltering their grub-like tenants. Clinging to other rocks may be great mossy masses made up of myriads of tiny black-fly larvae. And in the crevices and under the stones, where the trout can't get at them, flat-bodied stone-fly nymphs are skulking. You will try to make your nymph fly behave like one of these larger creatures that has been dislodged from its hiding place and is being swept off downstream.

Somewhat dubiously you attach a 9-foot leader tapering to 3X size, and tie on a likely-looking lure, selecting for this heavy water a large one tied on say a No. 8 hook. Standing near the shore opposite a promising stretch of water, you cast across and somewhat upstream. Since you wish your fly to travel deep and are not weighting your leader with split shot, you must take advantage of whatever downward currents there may be.

You cast to where the surface curves downward as it passes over a submerged boulder, or where a backwash circles around and reunites with the main current, forming tiny whirlpools. As the lure drifts off downstream, its course is followed with the rod tip, since this tends to prevent the line from exerting a sidewise drag upon the lure. When the line straightens out and starts to pull the lure unnaturally, you recover and again cast diagonally upstream.

Where conditions permit, you walk downstream with the drift of your lure, as this permits it to travel farther before the objectionable side drag develops. Particular attention is devoted to large submerged rocks, in the shadow of which trout are apt to lie. Without pulling on the lure, the line must always be kept tight enough to detect a strike instantly. This requires constant alertness and considerable practice.

After you have stowed one or two goodly trout away in your creel, the air seems more balmy and the bird songs ring with good cheer. There is something to this method of fishing after all. You forget that you ever were skeptical.

When you come to a large still pool, you find it necessary to vary somewhat the methods that you used for fishing the fast, broken water. For this still water you tie several feet of 3X gut to your 9-foot leader, but use the same fly, or one almost as large. Usually such pools must be fished from above; so you take a position at the side of the stream above the pool.

Casting out to midstream with lots of slack in the line, you allow your lure to drift naturally down into the deeper water. If it is not taken, you work it over to one side, slowly recover, and cast again. The lure is most apt to be taken about as the line straightens out. Keep the tip of your rod up and school yourself to strike ever so gently; for when one drifts a lure downstream in this way, the trout seem to have an uncanny way of nipping the fly from the leader.

Such are the methods of fishing a nymph deep. I have never found any advantage in retrieving the lure in a series of jerks, or in imparting any other unnatural motions. However, a very slight twitch on the line will sometimes make the critter appear to kick its legs as if very much alive.

I recall such a case last season. A trout could plainly be seen cruising around close to the bottom, near the head of a large pool. Again and again I drifted my nymph past him, without his showing the slightest interest. Finally I tried a tiny twitch on the line. "Insect!" the trout seemed to exclaim, and how he did hit that nymph! He was a chunky brown trout weighing a pound and three-quarters.

For this deep-nymph fishing, I have had most success with lures tied on Nos. 8 and 10 hooks, the model used having rather a long shank but a free-standing point. Much success may be had with very crude, impressionistic lures that merely have a sort of nymphy look, provided they are skillfully handled. But fished with the same degree of skill, the more realistic imitations will take more and better fish. A sub-surface lure is seen much more clearly by the trout than is any fly on the surface; and the larger the lure, the more its defects are accentuated. So I try to imitate some specific insect, such as a caddis larva or a May-fly nymph, as closely as my fly-tying limitations will permit.

To date, my most effective pattern has been a representation of a stone-fly nymph. This creation has a flat body, so finished with very thin rubber as to give it a light gray belly and a darker brown back. These heavy-bodied lures have a tendency to ride in the water with the shank of the hook down and the point up; so the fly is tied with the back toward the point of the hook.

Two fibers from a pheasant tail feather represent the tail setae, and two shorter ones the antennae. Three single fibers of guinea-hen feather are made to project from each side of the critter's thorax, at the proper positions and angles to represent legs. Sometimes a pair of tiny dark hackle points is added on the back, as wing pads. This fly may be unconventional—but it is very deadly.

When conditions are at all favorable for it, I personally prefer dry-fly fishing to all other methods. And I certainly do not advocate this method of fishing nymphs deep at times when trout may be attracted to the surface. But when one must resort to deep fishing of some sort, isn't this nymph fly-fishing more appealing than the use of bait? Surely the most real enjoyment may be had out of fishing when the skill of the angler is most fairly pitted against the wariness, strength and agility of the fish. All of these elements become greater factors when one uses light tackle and an artificial lure which must be made to appear like a living creature.

When a worm is used, the trout very often swallows the bait and is hooked away down in the gullet, where he cannot possibly dislodge the hook. In this case, the only way he can escape is by breaking the line or heavy leader—usually impossible, no matter how clumsy the angler may be. Worm fishing is poor conservation in that many under-sized trout are fatally injured when they swallow the hook. And I suspect that many big trout, which do somehow succeed in breaking away, die a slow death from that bait hook lodged in their interior.

Nymph fishing has none of these objections—and it's a lot of fun. Try it out; and if the trout are stubborn and won't come to the surface, fish your nymph deep.

The Diver Does His Stuff

JOHN TAINTOR FOOTE

America's greatest writer of fishing fiction tells one on himself.
(May 1939)

Now that concrete roads beribbon the country in all directions and motorcars are filled with a smooth determination to sneak up to seventy while you tell your fishing pal the latest non-parlor story, the natives, along even the more remote trouting waters, regard a dry-fly angler, fully panoplied for the chase, with a lack of interest that amounts to complete apathy. In these later times the countryside has become aware that the first spring blossoms will bring a migration of such creatures to each wadable trout stream in the wake of the state hatchery fish truck; that, despite their appalling appearance, they are as harmless as the shitepoke and the teeter snipe whose haunts they invade, and that they will depart, as mysteriously as they came, with the last of the mosquitoes, leaving behind them only the raucous chuckle of the more persistent kingfisher to rise above the gurgle of the river.

There was a day, however—alas, it will never come again—when fish trucks were as unnecessary as they were unknown. In that delightful era children fled screaming into the schoolhouse, the cheeks of country maidens blanched with dread, farmers reached for the old double-barrel standing behind the door at the sight of a strange figure, apparently in the last stages of dropsy, shod in a pair of average-sized canal boots, making ponderously for the nearest creek.

Somewhat later, suspicion of a pair of animated elephantine waders and what-not changed to amusement as the word went around that these were not demented, deep-sea divers stalking inland, but only honest citizens of somewhat larger communities "got up for fishin'." Later still, particularly among the younger males of the hinterland, derision gave place to a certain amount of curiosity as to how anybody rigged out like that conducted himself on a trout stream.

It being well known that a pair of rubber boots, a pole, a line, a hook and some night-crawlers were all that were needed to secure an ample panful, why did anyone get into such duds and go swinging an elongated buggy-whip up-and down-stream to catch trout? Was it just a city notion or was there something in it? Maybe, with those funny-looking clothes and shoes and gadgets, you could catch bigger fish.

In those days, one could be sure of a half-skeptical, wholly absorbed gallery if one fished a bit of water which allowed the boys of the neighborhood an uninterrupted view of the proceedings. Also, I must add, with a sigh, one could be reasonably certain of producing for the edification of the spectators, the rise and capture of several fat, butter-yellow brownies or the less wary, olive-and-black, scarlet-spotted brookies to be slipped, without too much ostentation, into one's creel.

And now let me say that there are experiences in the life of every angler so tragic, so bitter, so filled with regret that for years and years recollections of them will set him to tossing in his bed and muttering in his sleep. I propose herewith to record, as best I can, such an experience. I do so with pain and anguish.

In a year long since past, along the lower stretches of a Sullivan County river, my fishing companion and I parked our car at the edge of the state road and slid with some difficulty down a shale embankment to the water's edge. We had read, not long since, LaBranche's *The Dry Fly on Fast Water*, and profited thereby. Mr. LaBranche had not succeeded in making purists of us, however. If they were rising, we fished upstream with the floating fly; if no trout were breaking, we fished downstream with the sunken variety. Many years, on many trout streams, have not caused me to alter this procedure.

We were, accordingly, fully accoutered with all the clothing and accessories for both wet and dry fishing. We wore waders and wading socks and shoes, of course. Our fishing jackets were cut to meet the tops of the waders, a hand's breadth or so below our armpits. Abbreviated as these garments were, their designer had still contrived to endow them with an unbelievable number of pockets. They contained front pockets, side pockets, back pockets, outer and inner pockets, pockets within pockets. Somehow we had discovered and managed to make use of them all.

In consequence, from a point well above the waist down to our gargantuan wading shoes, we presented an appearance of alarming obesity. Thanks to fly boxes, leader boxes, an oilskin raincoat, etc., which stuffed our precious pockets to the bursting, we jutted and bulged from this point upward in an unexpected, not to say startling manner, until, at last, the whole was crowned with a disreputable hat that served at once as a head-gear and a sort of pincushion for variously colored used flies.

Other details of the ensemble were fishing scissors, dangling on a string which went around the neck. A leather-bound bottle of fly oil with brush fastened to the breast of the jacket. A metal rod holder sewed to the bottom of same. There was, in addition, a 20-inch creel, the size made necessary by the fact that we didn't want to bend the big one that we hoped and prayed, each time we entered a stream, would rise and be taken.

To the creel was tied a heavy metal "priest" to put out of business the long-looked-for monster, together with lesser fry which came our way in the meantime. Our nets—small, easily handled affairs—were snapped to a ring sewed in the back of the jacket between the shoulder-blades. They were also fastened to the ring by a stout cord, lest they be dropped into some hurrying river when unsnapped and in action.

As to my fishing companion of those days. He was noteworthy for two things: an extraordinary ability to take trout and an apparent lack of balance while doing so. This latter characteristic was accounted for by the fact that the intensity with which he fished caused him to forget all else, including where and how he set his feet on slippery or rocky stream beds. As a result, he was apt to advance between casts in a series of alarming gyrations that, now and then, were the forerunners of appalling and complete immersions.

I called him, in consequence, "The Pelican, or Great Diver," shortening his full title to "The Diver" on less formal occasions. As for him, he addressed me by a wide variety of dubious given names, none of which was ever, by any chance, my own.

Having arrived at the river's brim, dressed as above, on the day I am describing, we were confronted by a rush of foam-flecked water smoothing out as it became the green depths of a pool. The shadow of an iron bridge lay across this pool. Beyond the bridge, on the far side of the stream, a small hamlet clung to a plateau from which rose abruptly a high, cloud-piercing, wooded hill.

I should perhaps mention here that a somewhat bitter, though concealed, rivalry existed between The Diver and me as to whose creel would prove the heavier when night came on. It was our habit to make a show of giving the other fellow the best pool or rift, wish him all the luck in the world, and then sneak off, find better water if possible, and, as The Diver put it, "Try to make a sucker out of him."

With the above precedent in mind, The Diver, on that far day, addressed me as follows: "Well, Oswald, pick out what you think is good—above, or below, or this stretch here. Take your choice."

Adhering to our formula, I promptly declined the offer.

"I had a better day on the Broadhead than you did," I reminded him gently. "You take what your want."

A faint cloud passed across The Diver's face.

"You sure tied into 'em over there," he said with forced admiration. "But listen, Elmer, it was coming to you after what I did to you—I mean after your tough luck up on the Ausable." The Diver's eyes roamed up and down the stream, noting its character and possibilities. "This is a swell pool, Mortimer, and that rift looks good. Suppose you take a crack at it here, and I'll go above and see what it's like up there."

I had crowded an ordinary day's work into the morning, and had driven the car all the way up from New York that afternoon. The sun would not be long dropping behind the hills, I noted. It seemed best to start fishing at once and where I stood, rather than to go searching laboriously for more promising water.

"All right," I decided. "If it's all the same to you, I'll start in here."

"Suits me, Egbert. I'm on my way." The Diver waved a courteous rod. "Hope you get 'em, Gus." He strode off up-stream.

I took a coiled dry-fly leader from between the moist pads of a leader box and placed it for a more thorough soaking in a miniature bay at my feet. As I straightened up, a voice shrilled out above me.

"Pete! Oh, Pete! Lookit!"

A boy's face was staring down upon me over the railing of the bridge. It was joined by another and another. Presently there were four young faces in a row, observing me with a mixture of scorn and amazement.

"Lookit them pants and them shoes."

"Them's to git in the creek with."

"Must be figgerin' to git in up to his neck."

There was a general suppressed titter.

"Hello, boys," I called.

"H'lo," said one.

The rest said nothing. They simply continued to take in my bloated and bulging person in rapt silence.

Suddenly the faces disappeared, and I heard high crescendos of mirth coming from somewhere above. I was greasing my line when the faces reappeared to watch the process with the same wondering attention that previously they had bestowed upon me.

They watched me finish my line-greasing and put the line-greaser back in my coat. They watched me tie on the leader and tie a dry fly to that. They watched me take the brush from the oil-bottle and carefully coat the fly. They watched me cleanse the leader of any possible oil or grease by drawing it through a cake of leader-soap.

They watched all this in round-eyed silence save for an occasional breathless "Lookit." Now and then it was too much for them. The faces would disappear like one, and shrieks of laughter would come to me to mingle with the chuckle of the more rapid water at the top of the pool.

At last, all being ready, I waded in. Conscious of the critical eyes staring down upon me, I must admit to shooting out an unnecessarily long line on my first cast and dropping that dry fly like a languid bit of thistledown well up the pool. I had elected to fish dry because I had seen the splash of a rising trout out of the tail of my eye while making my preparations. Now, for the benefit of my gallery, I proceeded to give an exhibition of what I regarded as expert casting.

I worked slowly up the pool, shooting out a long dexterous line with hardly a ripple marking where it fell. There was no longer any laughter on the bridge. My rod-wielding was being accorded a close and, I think, respectful attention.

But nothing came of it. I forgot the gallery in my efforts to raise a fish. I worked to the top of the pool, then on up into the rapid water, using shorter, less dwelling casts. A half hour passed, and I was still fishless. Then I saw The Diver execute a deft three-quarter turn-and-stagger just at the head of the rift. He was coming down-stream, fishing wet. Since the ridge above the hamlet had already taken a jagged bite out of the blood-red sun, it was time I followed a good example.

In changing to a looped wet leader, with one tail fly and a dropper, I became aware that my gallery had not deserted me. They had kept me under observation by following along the state road as I had worked up-stream. They seemed undaunted by my failure to produce results. Their attention was as swerveless as heretofore. Now and then I could see lips move, but the roar of the fast water in which I stood drowned their comments, whatever they might have been.

These faithful followers were blotted out of existence, so far as I was concerned, a moment later. On my second cast down-stream there rolled up from the very middle of a deep slick between two froth-rimmed boulders the biggest brown trout I had ever seen. He engulfed the dropper fly.

Years have passed since then, as I have said, but I can still visualize that great head and the huge unhurried roll of him as he turned and went down with my Wickham's Fancy. How he contrived to seem leisurely about it in the press of that fast water is beyond me, but he seemed to dwell for seconds on the surface of that slick. It was as though he had risen in a pond.

The whole thing had the unreality of a dream. I had fished a good stretch of water with a variety of dry flies without a sign of a rise. I had fished this particular slick not five minutes before, and then waded along its edge—enough to put even a callow fingerling on his guard. The dropper fly was, to all intents and purposes, on the surface, and yet this wise old grandfather who had scorned the previous offerings I had floated over him had seen fit to come up and take it. Such is the nature of trout, and of such are woven the uncertainties, disappointments and unexpected rewards that go to form the inimitable pattern of an angler's day on a trout stream.

I tightened instinctively, mentally bracing myself for the shocking violence of granddad when he felt the hook. Strange to say, his resentment was so mild as to be negligible. He simply sank unhurriedly down to the bottom to become as moveless as the two boulders that caused the slick in which he lay.

For perhaps fifteen minutes there he stayed, quite oblivious to all the pressure I dared use, the light snell of that Wickham's Fancy and its No. 12 hook considered. Meanwhile the sun had definitely abandoned Sullivan County, New York, for a 12-hour period, and the rushing water all about me was taking on unbelievable lavenders and pinks and purples at which one could only strain one's bedazzled eyes. It was already a bad light in which to net even a 12-incher and, so far as I could tell, granddad seemed prepared to continue resolutely doing nothing until midnight or beyond.

In my extremity I thought of The Pelican, or Great Diver. I glanced upstream and saw him about a hundred yards above me, making his perilous way down the rift, casting as he came. I let out an old-fashioned hog-calling welkin-ringer, and he responded with a banshee's top note signifying that he would be with me shortly.

A lot of water ran—not over the dam but between and past my legs before he at last came near enough for me to make myself heard above the splash-gurgle-roar that made up the song of the rift. He was spattering casts to right and left of him between side-slips, skids and some steps from a chorus routine.

"Quit that damcasting," I yelled, "and get here quick."

"Whas-a-matter, Filbert?" he yelled back. "Are you snagged?"

"Listen, fool, I've got the God-awfullest trout on that you or I or anybody else ever saw. Hurry!"

As I waited for him to cover the yards, which seemed like miles, to where I stood I saw my gallery, still in attendance, watching me from the road with a strained attention that showed their interest in the situation to be supreme.

Another of their kind appeared on the bridge and observed the absorbed group on the state road.

"First bat for one ole cat," he shrilled.

The gallery remained entirely loyal to me and my affair of the moment.

"Forget it," one of them screeched back. "This guy's hooked a terrible big fish."

The newcomer hastily abandoned all thoughts of light diversion. Emitting a wild rebel yell, followed by a series of Indian war-whoops, he galloped to the scene and became as immersed in watchful waiting as the rest.

The Diver having arrived at my side, we now went into conference. It was decided that he should get below granddad and sneak up on him from the rear. He laid his rod on the bank and proceeded to execute this maneuver, net in hand, squinting down into the slick at the point where my rigid leader disappeared into the water.

"Can you see him?" I yelled.

"I can see something. It looks like a—"

The Diver never finished that sentence. In leaning forward and down in an effort to pierce the multicolored surface with his gaze his equilibrium forsook him. He waved both arms and the net rapidly in the air for an instant ere he executed a combination jack-knife and full-twist into the middle of the slick.

I am of the opinion that a purple knob on his forehead which he later displayed was not, as he claimed, the result of a collision with a stone embedded in the river's bottom. I have ever maintained that either his head crashed into the broad and stubborn back of the indignant granddad, or, as I explained to The Diver, "He may have slapped you with his tail."

The moments immediately following The Diver's exhibition of his art were, like The Diver's waders, filled to overflowing. He floundered to his feet, but long before he was once more erect, net still in hand, I had seen the leader cut through the water as it passed up and around one of the boulders. The remorseless strain on my rod was gone.

Speechless, hopeless, undone, I stared mournfully at the emerging Diver. And then—oh, joy! oh, rapture!—I felt the vibration along the rod that only a swimming fish imparts. I frantically stripped in slack. My heart surged as the rod tip bowed again toward the surface of the stream.

"He's still on!" I yelled. "There—just ahead of you. Net him!"

Once more The Diver peered dutifully into the slick with water from his hat brim running into his eyes. He passed a dripping sleeve across his face and peered again, then plunged his net below the surface. He brought it up with an eight-inch chub, fast to my tail fly, writhing in its folds.

I stared stupidly at the bewildered Diver holding that pitiful minnow up for my inspection. There was a thunderous silence. At last he spoke.

"K-k-k-kidding me," he said as the temperature of trout-stream water in early May reached for his bones. "K-k-k-kidding me. Just a g-g-grade A louse."

And now there arose, well above the noise of the rift, the most abandoned shrieks of laughter that I had ever heard. My gallery, no longer able to stand, were rolling in paroxysms on the state road. I have heard boys made helpless through the hysteria that seizes a class of youngsters after some hours of too-rigid schoolroom discipline; but that was nothing compared to what the appearance of that despised chub in The Diver's net did to those Sullivan County urchins. They took this to be the antagonist that had held me for twenty minutes in the rift and forced me to call wildly for aid. This was what all the clothes and gadgets and preparations at the bridge had led to—an eight-inch chub. It all but slayed them.

Retreating to the car, I showed The Diver the snapped snell of my dropper fly that had parted at granddad's first rush like a single strand from a fine-haired maiden. I explained to him that the chub must have taken the tail fly as it swung in the current at the stern of the stationary leviathan. At last he was disposed to admit that he had not been the victim of a foul and repulsive deception.

"Didn't you see him at all?" I asked.

"No, P-P-Percival. I saw something down there that l-l-looked like a log, but it was as long as my l-l-leg."

"That was him," I assured The Diver. "He was longer than your leg."

As we drove sadly away from that fatal stretch of river, beginning now to reflect here and there the pale fires of the first stars of evening, my erstwhile gallery were still pawing weakly at one another and emitting exhausted cackles along the edge of the state road.

Wait a Minute!

FRED EVERETT

Why your approach to, and positioning on, the stream may be far more important than your pattern of fly. (June 1937)

Have you the soul of a fisherman? If you haven't, please don't read any farther. If you have, you will understand. Yesterday the sun came out, and as I drove down an ice-covered road I came to a southern slope, and there was a spot where the snow was melting and a tiny trickle was beginning to sparkle its way down the hill. Sunshine, melting snow, running water—need I say more?

And so my thoughts took possession of me and I jumped ahead to the coming season. I pictured in fancy a favorite hole and the trout I raised and missed last season. Would he be there? Next time he wouldn't fool me. In our dreaming, how we fool those wily old granddaddies! We never dream of small ones.

As I visioned that beloved stretch of water and many, many spots where success and failure had played their part last season one question kept recurring in my mind: why couldn't I fool those big fish which I knew were there? And right on the heels of that question came the realization that I did, once in a while. But, to be honest, did I? Did I, with full intent of purpose aforethought, fool those fish, or was it not true that the strikes came when I least expected them and often when I was least prepared to meet them? In other words, weren't they accidents or a hand-out from fate?

116

Take, for example, one of my most thrilling experiences last year, which was also one of my bitterest. It was in the middle of July, a hot day full of sunshine. The Willowemoc was low, and the trout were not inclined to come out and play. Doc Gardenier and I were lackadaisically casting side by side, up a long, shallow pool. I had grown careless in my casting, and of a sudden there my fly was, high up in a branch.

When you are using a 3¾-ounce rod and a 12-foot 4X leader, don't try to yank a tree over. I have tried it and seen it tried with no apparent effect on either the fly or the tree, which always stay just where they were while you hunt for a new leader and fly or try to figure out how best you can mend your rod.

So I waded over to the bank, stripping in line as I went, until I got where I could give a steady pull on my leader and tear the fly out of the leaf in which it had caught. In doing this, I stepped through a loop in the line. I couldn't go on until I had stepped out again; so I flicked my fly up ahead to get it out of the way while I untangled myself from the line.

While I had one foot in the air and was uncertainly balanced on the other, bent over to slip the line from under my raised foot, I heard a noise about where my fly was floating, not more than ten feet away. I looked up just in time to see a million-dollar trout flop back into the water with my fly. At the time it happened, that fish weighed about three pounds. Now, as I think back, it would have gone at least five pounds.

It seemed like half a day before I got hold of myself, rod and line and answered that strike. I'm sure, under the circumstances, I didn't strike too soon; I must have been too late.

Now, I had been casting over that water with that same fly before I hung up in the tree. I had been out in the stream, using from twenty-five to thirty feet of line and leader. Yet I hadn't raised a thing. Then I walked almost on top of that fish, fussed around getting my fly loose and, with no thought of technique or anything else except to get my fly out of my way, raised the biggest trout of the season right under my nose.

Isn't that something to make a fellow stop and think? I did. I waited more than a minute on that one, for I spent all the rest of the afternoon and evening trying to bring that fish up again. And, believe it or not, I raised him seven times! But don't get too excited, for every time he came up it was only to cheer me on. That fish must have thought, "Well, he's only an amateur, and I'll encourage the boy." Each time he came up, it was not to take the fly, but to drown it or slap it with his tail. Twice he knocked it clear out of his private domain.

In the hours I spent on that fish I have gleaned, in retrospect, one choice bit of information. I used my complete assortment of flies, both wet and dry, and also nymphs. I cast from above, below and to the side. And every time I raised the fish, I did it from exactly the same spot where I stood for the first rise, and each time on a different fly. In the light of other experiences, that now means a great deal to me.

I have experienced many other unexpected rises, many of which brought good-sized fish to the net. And, no doubt, so have you. What is the answer?

Well, for one thing, when we are not expecting a rise, we cast carelessly and freely—we act naturally, forgetting this and that which we have been reading and trying out. Also, what is even more important, we happen to be standing in the right place from which to cast to that particular spot, and we get results, regardless of the fly or the way we cast it. And that is the thought for the day —or at least for this article.

When I reach a trout stream, a strange malady takes possession of me, and I have the delusion that the most urgent and vital thing in this world is to get into that water and start casting my fly. And that is exactly what I do. I just can't wait a minute. There is no cure for it, but there is a method that will turn the fever of enthusiasm to good use. I enter the stream below where I want to start fishing and cast to my heart's content, or until the fever subsides. In this way I get the kinks out of my system, line and leader.

By that time I have reached the good water and am sane enough to wait a minute before I approach and fish each spot. That minute is spent in figuring out, to the best of my ability, the right spot from which to fish the hole. It has nothing to do with the size or the pattern of the fly, the leader, the line, or any theories. Only one thing—where should I stand to fish this particular spot?

You may have all the theories, fancy flies and clever technique; just give me the correct answer to that question, and I ask no more. Except under rare conditions, any fly, even crudely presented, will do the trick if it goes to the right place from the right angle. I believe that this simple rule is all one needs to become a successful angler. But oh, how hard it is to follow that rule!

Without question, one of the really fine places to expect a brown trout is at the foot of a pool where the water just begins to fall over rocks or dam. Yet how can such a spot be fished? If you stand below the falls, the fly is dragged back by the rushing water. If you stand above and cast down, a fairly good idea, you must be expert in casting a long, slack line; and then the odds are against you, even if you get a strike. So it behooves you to stop and figure.

Can you work your way up close enough to fish off the end of your rod, holding it high, so that only the fly rides the water? Can you do it and keep low enough not to be seen? Or can you fish the spot from the side with a short line, maybe leaving the water entirely and fishing from the bank? In doing so, can you approach from the side of the rock opposite that where the trout is hiding—if you know which side? And if you can approach from that side, will you be able to cast into a current that will treat you right?

That is only one example of the many conditions which one meets with on the stream, but it will demonstrate what I mean by waiting a minute before starting to fish a spot. It is my belief that over 90 per cent of the anglers fail because they fish from the wrong spot. I do it so often that I lose all faith in my own ability to become even moderately expert.

It seems to me that most of us put too much faith in methods and theories. We read this and that, get new lures and depend on them to procure fish, expecting that they will do the work for us. And we are always disappointed and curse the lure or the theory, instead of putting the blame where it belongs—right on our own heads. The lures are good, because they produce for others. The methods are good, for the same reason. They would produce for us if we could bring ourselves to wait a minute and use our fish sense, instead of expecting the new lure or theory to do it for us.

It's a fine thing to read the new theories, to buy new lures and to know how the other fellow goes about filling his creel. But we mortals who have only a short time on the stream can simplify our problem into two main issues. First, where can we reasonably expect to locate a good trout in the water we are going to fish? Second, where should we stand to present our lure to the best advantage?

The fly doesn't make such a great deal of difference. If it did, why is it that a check-up almost any day on any stream will show trout being taken on as many different flies as there are anglers on a stream? Nor does it matter so much whether you cast like George LaBranche or a beginner at the game. Don't let such things bother you after you have reached the stream, for they are all of secondary importance and should have been taken care of beforehand. Your reason for being on the stream, aside from drinking in the glories of nature about you, is to locate and catch fish.

Naturally, one must first locate a fish before he can cast for it intelligently. How can that best be done? Sometimes easily; at other times, I wish I knew.

Many anglers sit down and look a stream over and wait until they see a rise. Others have studied the fish's habits and know just about where to find them. Some use the hit-and-miss type of fishing and cast over all water until they discover which type of water the trout are using that day. And sometimes fish are located by accident.

Of course, some people are fortunate enough to know a stream so well as to be on speaking terms with all the best trout and know their hiding places. Common sense will usually tell an experienced angler where enough trout are apt to be, even in new waters, to give him reasonable success.

Last summer I fished a stream I had known for years. I thought I knew pretty well where to locate the best fish. Then I went out with a native boy who, to my surprise, took me to a stretch that I had long before given up as no good. And that young mountaineer pointed out some of the craziest spots that one could imagine, locations in the pools where I had stood to do my fishing or where I should never have dreamed of casting.

At first I thought I was being kidded, but after raising seven big trout in seven successive pools I looked at the boy with respect. Each time he told me I must creep or sneak up to a certain spot to cast from in order to float my fly where it would bring up the trout. And he never even looked to see what fly I was using!

After that experience I approached this stream with a great deal of diffidence. Here, almost in my front yard, was a trout stream worthy of anybody's mettle. It is notorious for being fished out—even I have thought so except on opening day. Now I go back often, and each time I come away satisfied that I still have much to learn.

But I am locating the fish, often by accident. I remember one hole where I hooked and lost a beauty. In fishing the hole, I had cast up to the head of the pool where the current swept between two rocks, a spot that looked ideal. But there was not a stir to all my offerings.

I decided to go on; so I cast my fly off to one side of the stream into shallow still water, near a big rock that helped form the shore-line. Then I let go my line in order to reel in the slack, and *sock-o*! A streak cut out from under that rock, through water so shallow that his dorsal fin broke the surface in a straight line to my fly, splashed as he turned and dived back under the rock.

I answered his strike as soon as I could, but by the time I had let go of the reel and lifted my rod he was deep in his retreat. For one moment I felt him vibrating on my line, and then the leader sawed in two against the rock. Never would I have expected a trout in such a place—but there he was and maybe is to this day, although I raised and missed him a week or so later. It is a difficult place to fish, and I have yet to find the correct spot to stand in order to do the job perfectly.

Up on the Beaverkill, in the Lew Borden waters, I located a big trout one day when it seemed that all the trout had gone visiting. Fishing had been so bad that, as a last resort, when I came to a spot where heavy fast water rushed into the head of the pool, I put on a bucktail and a spinner, casting down and working the line back up through the current.

Off to one side, in the eddy, was a big rock, quite some distance from where I was fishing. As I pulled my bucktail up the current, some eight or ten feet from the rock, out rushed the big trout, over into the current, smashing my bucktail hard.

Now this experience is not unique, but this time I was in a position to see the trout coming. Most big trout do this very thing. From a deep hiding place they watch certain currents; and when food comes along, out they flash and back again, so fast that one sees only a streak of light. In order to fish for these trout, one must carefully approach a spot where he will not be seen by the trout and at the same time be able to present his fly naturally. If he will wait a minute and figure this out before trying to cast, his chances are increased many fold.

Once in a while we meet a fish that has chosen wisely and uses a place where it seems impossible to reach him without giving ourselves away. I know such a trout—we are friends of two years' standing. Every time I am on the Beaverkill, I visit this trout and pay my compliments. Each time I do it from some different angle, but to date he has scorned me. Yet I know he can be approached if I will persist, even if I have to get down on my hands and knees and crawl upstream to him. I often kneel in a stream, for one should keep as low as possible at all times when in the water.

The question is often asked, how should one approach a pool to fish it and where should it be fished from? There is no one answer to such a question, because every pool has its own answer. But in broad terms, I believe most anglers spend entirely too much time in the water. The best place to fish from is the shore, if possible, for then one can keep down out of sight and will not alarm the fish by sending out telltale ripples or crunching the gravel. Always remember that the best place from which to fish is the nearest possible spot where one can keep out of sight and cast where the trout can see the lure.

To emphasize this, let me pass on to you an experience I had some years ago. I was going fishing in a near-by stream, and I stopped to see a mountaineer friend nicknamed Zeke. He is by far the best fisherman on that stream, and I had been anxious to see him fish it. Well, he went with me, but, to my disappointment, picked out a place for me to fish and then went on upstream for his fishing.

However, I was not to be denied. I wanted to watch Zeke fish, and watch him I did from behind some rocks. And what I saw seemed unbelievable. Zeke was using wet flies, two tied close together. These he kept dry and fished on a 7½-foot leader, the knot to the line being just beyond the tip of his rod. He carefully approached each hole, knowing just where to stand, flipped the flies on the water and dragged them across the surface so that they looked like two flies, one chasing the other.

After catching a few trout that way, he put on a sinker and would walk right up to a rock so that he could just reach over it with his rod. He would let the flies sink and then drag them up and around the rock so that the flies would pass directly under or very near it. Any trout hiding there could not help but see these flies, and did they hit them! That experience taught me, more than anything else, the value of a short line and how important it is to stand where your fly can be presented so that the fish will see it.

I repeat: when you get on the stream, work out your first nervous energy, if need be; forget all your theories and concentrate on locating a trout, and then try to figure out the best place to stand to present your fly properly. Don't be in a hurry, but wait a minute at each new pool, and at the end of the day you'll have more and bigger stories to tell.

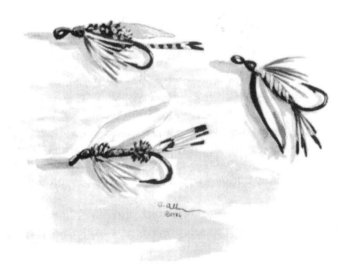

That Forgotten Wet Fly

LARRY KOLLER

How an ingenious variation on the ancient team-of-wet-flies technique murders big, smart browns. (February 1938)

Old things are often best. An old pipe, mellowed by age, caked and blackened by years of smoking enjoyment, still brings us the greatest pleasure. Our old rods hold cherished memories of enjoyable days on the stream. Maybe this year we will land the big one that we couldn't hold a few seasons back, if the old rod will do its part—and we don't doubt that. We have confidence and pride in all our equipment, although it is seasoned by years of outdoor use. Strange it is, then, that our methods of angling don't follow suit.

In recent years the Eastern fly-fisherman has clung rather tenaciously to the dry fly as the most reliable method of taking trout. There is no doubt of its effectiveness when conditions are right on the proper stream, but it is far from infallible. The old-time fly-casters took their fish by other methods, and certainly these methods still produce results.

I have always been a dry-fly man. Ever since I was big enough to wade a stream without being washed away, my trout have been taken mainly on the surface fly. Wet flies and bucktails were just something else to clutter up the fly-box and were seldom used. The younger generation of fly-fishermen usually make expert use of the dry fly their goal and spend very little time learning other methods. Most of these boys have never received any instruction on the proper method of handling the wet fly and seldom give it much thought.

In this class of modern anglers I can easily include myself. Every day on the stream found me loaded down with the supposed necessities of dry-fly fishing: bottles of fly oil, cans of line dope, tapered leaders from 9 to 18 feet in length and varying in weight from 3X to 5X. My pockets were stuffed with an assortment of dry flies, nymphs, special creations and what-nots. Always I hoped for a big trout, and after months of preparation to raise him my leader would seldom stand the strain of holding him.

But I never gave up hope. Many nights were spent in tying just the right pattern of dry fly on a tiny hook; leaders were tinted to the proper color and carefully tapered; fly oil of unquestionable merit was formulated, so that the artificial could do the job of raising the big ones to the surface. On the whole, my blank days were not many, neither did I creel many big trout.

After many seasons of this I began to feel that something was lacking. I took trout when the other boys did and sometimes when they didn't, but on some streams and on those days when the wind or something else was wrong my basket smelled only of the fish taken on the last trip. It took a certain day on a famous stream to change my methods.

On the southern slope of the highest peak in the Catskills lies the source of a noted trout stream. Throughout the seventy-odd miles of its length it offers every type of water known to the fly angler. The headwater tributaries are filled with native trout eager to take any bright fly.

Deep pools and runs in the valley below give dry-fly casters cause for excitement. White-water rapids farther along its boulder-bottomed course make bucktails and streamers worth while and the wet fly a good bet. In the past decade I have taken trout on the dry fly from its clear waters without too much trouble, but my success, for the most part, has been limited to the upper half of its length.

The lower reaches of this stream have always intrigued me, partly because here I have taken my worst lickings as far as trout are concerned. Here the Builder of all things has laid foaming water heavily on Mother Earth's rocky bosom. The valley slopes are entirely wooded even as at the beginning of time and peopled with its native wild creatures. Many miles of the banks are without roads of any kind and unscathed by habitations of man, the destroyer. Below, the river swells in volume and loses its speed in a broad valley until it is claimed by the Delaware.

Season after season I had fished this stream with dry flies, streamers, bucktails and even bait, but success was not mine. Very occasionally—not more than once a year—I would take a nice catch of brown trout on a bucktail when conditions were right: water above normal level and slightly colored. In lower clear water, when vision was good, the fish seemed to sense the deception of the bucktail, with the result that I found that my efforts with this lure under normally good fly conditions were wasted.

Dry flies were simply something to amuse the chubs, which are numerous in this part of the river. Nothing annoyed me more than to drop a new, freshly oiled fan-wing Royal on a nice riffle, only to have it sucked under by a big lazy chub. This member of the dace family seems always ready to take any and all dry flies throughout the day, whether the sun shines or no. And after washing slime off a dozen or so dry flies and nursing each back into presentable shape, I was quite ready to change methods or call it a day. The trout never seemed to get a chance to inspect the fly, even if they were of a mind to accept it.

With bait I had similar results. The small-mouth bass, plentiful here and with closed-season voracity, simply could not resist any two-inch shiner, live or dead, and kept me busy releasing fish and rebaiting. Sometimes I would take a nice trout on bait, but it was far from satisfying. Wet flies, following the accepted modern method of using small, sparsely tied patterns on the end of a tapered leader and floated across and down, also enticed only the chubs and bass.

Five years of this kind of angling found me pretty well resigned to never taking a decent catch of trout from this stretch but nevertheless willing to die trying. The trout that I did kill were large enough to show me the possibility of great sport when I finally found out what they wanted and how they wanted it.

During these fruitless years of angling, tales reached me now and then about a seasoned fly-caster of legendary accomplishment. Many a day the natives along the river had seen him come down to the bridge with "the tails stickin' right out the top of the basket." Old John they called him, and he used nothing but wet flies. A deep mystery involved his methods and his special patterns, but there was no mystery about his creel. It was the biggest he could buy, they told me, and always full at the end of the day. His trout were not small either, seldom under a foot long and usually averaging better than a pound. His only angling difficulty, apparently, was to keep the boys from finding out how he got them.

As is usual with gossip about the unknown, conflicting accounts assailed my ears. He used big flies; he used small flies. He tied his own on the stream bank after catching a natural; he bought flies at Jake's, even as you and I.

The old fellow's method of handling his flies was also just as clear. He never fished downstream; he cast across the stream, and always sank his flies. Maybe he kept them on the surface; who knew?

I felt that this individual certainly had something that none of us knew about, but the problem was how to get it away from him. He always fished alone, and rumor had it that he stopped casting as soon as anyone came in sight. But on this everyone agreed: he was a hard worker, earning every fish that he took. That meant nothing to me, for I worked plenty hard and seldom had much to show for it.

Many fishing days passed, and yet I had not met this fisherman. From many descriptions that had been given me, I felt that I would certainly know him. It all came about rather unexpectedly, but quite favorably, much more so than I had hoped.

Five o'clock on a Sunday morning in mid-May found me trekking up the Oakland Valley to Eton Falls, where the river breaks over a stratum of rock to form a pool several hundred feet long, boulder-lined, deep and fast, with froth-flecked whirlpools on each side. Big browns lie here in the fast run, safe in the deep crevices that cannot be seen from the bank.

I had left my car in the woods after driving as far as possible, but I still had a two-mile walk ahead of me. Grouse roared wildly out from beneath my feet; two deer bounced up the hillside, crashing over blow-downs, and with a clattering of loose rocks disappeared into the laurels. A grandpa porky, puffing and grunting from his long climb up the hillside, stopped in the middle of the trail to eye me suspiciously before shuffling away, his quills bristling aggressively.

The day seemed perfect. I had waited until the river and weather were right. Plenty of fly hatches were in the air, and the water was clear and of normal height. The warm sun beat down through the new foliage, bringing out little wisps of steam from the damp leaf-mold.

My hopes were high—today I could not fail, even though days past had been fruitless. My kit held every kind of lure that had ever taken a trout for me since the very first. All kinds of bait, every useful pattern of fly—each should have its chance.

The pool at my feet was deep in shadow. I threaded on a minnow, hoping to attract a big fellow still on the early-morning feed. Carefully I cast across the run, manipulating the rod tip to effect a swimming motion to the bait. Soon a quick flash, a sharp tug, and I had my first strike! Letting the fish mouth the bait for a moment, I set the hook. After a short run there broke from the surface a beautiful—bass!

Throughout the morning the performance was much the same. Only two trout graced my basket, natives and rather small, both taken on the bait. Flies were definitely a flop with me, and failed to bring a single brown trout to creel.

By mid-afternoon, with two miles of stream behind me, I was ravenously hungry. Picking a flat rock, I stretched out for a few minutes, perhaps longer. When next I looked downstream, there was a fisherman working toward me, whipping the water rapidly. A greenhorn, I thought, wearing out his arm. But no, somehow he seemed familiar. Old John, sure as shootin'. As I watched, immediately interested, there was a splash, a vicious tug at his rod tip, and then he leaned far back, arching his rod to set the hook.

Wild with excitement, I dashed down and netted the fish, a 16-inch brown. Slowly and with great care I extricated the fly: a common Gordon, though about twice as large as any I ordinarily used. My greatest surprise was his leader. It was about 6 feet long, mounted with three flies, but of unusual thickness, probably about 10-pound-test, untinted.

Naturally, I asked him if that was his first fish.

"Gosh no, son. Feel that basket."

I did, and nearly dropped it. I took out every one, each an elusive brown trout, straightening those that were too long for the bottom of his ample creel. Eleven fish I had side by side, not one less than a foot long, and two over 17 inches. A limit catch, if I ever saw one.

With his famous reticence, he reeled up his line and leader, preparing to quit.

"Had tough luck downstream," he told me. "Lost my fly-book. Kinda hungry, too. Forgot my lunch this mornin'."

What an opportunity! Plenty of eats in my coat pocket, and the Lord only knows how many flies!

Food loosened up his tongue a little after I had explained my problems and failure to catch these darned trout for so many years, but he looked at my flies with evident disgust.

"Son," he poked at me, "you're one of these newfangled fishermen who uses all the doo-dads that are meant to ketch mebbe a 10-incher. You don't even know how to fly-fish to raise a decent trout in this river, or to hold him if you do. I've fished this river for thirty years or more, and never needed all that stuff to ketch me a mess of fish. Now jest use that head of yours for a minute.

"These trout are mostly all good-sized browns and plenty wise. They feed all day long in this fast water, but you never will see a raise. You boys all fish the glassy water where a fly will float good but doesn't interest any fish. The trout that do lie there are only resting.

"When fish are feeding, they move up into the fast water right on the edge of the break from the rapid. Then when something comes along in the line of eats, it has to be big enough to make it worth their while to dash after it. Once they start, they don't have much time to look it over—it's now or never.

"That's one reason why I use a heavy leader. Tisn't often that a fish in this fast water can inspect the leader. And I use one that's strong enough to land 'em. No use to go to all the trouble of hooking 'em and let 'em break off with a fly in their mouths."

"But there must be more to it than that," I argued. "I've used big flies and only caught chubs and bass."

"Well, there's a little more that you didn't give me a chance to tell about, son. You've been fishing the wrong places, and, too, the flies have to be handled right. I cast across and bring 'em back with my rod held high, so the flies will skip on the top. That's the way these here water crickets swim, and that's what the trout feed on mostly.

"Now about that leader again—you have to use a heavy one to support the three big flies when you're skipping 'em on the surface and to straighten out the cast. With the flies on top, there isn't much of the leader that's on the water anyway. But no matter what kind of leader you get, don't use one with dropper loops. It makes foam on the surface, and the trout can see that. I loop my snell around the leader above a knot, where it won't slip."

I still wasn't quite satisfied, though plenty interested. It didn't seem possible that such simplicity in angling could be the key to success on this hard-hearted stream. There must be something about his flies.

"Nope, nothin' special, except that I can't get big enough flies at the stores. It seems that everybody else uses a lot smaller sizes than when I first started fly-fishing; so I have a young feller tie 'em up for me. The Gordon is my best bet, 'cause it looks something like the water crickets. Any ordinary fly will do, though—female Beaverkill, Light Cahill or Mallard Quill—as long as it's large. Big without being bulky—sparse, I guess you'd call it.

"Now there's another little trick that I can't tell you about, but I'll show you. Come along."

He led me upstream to a long run, broken by big boulders and very fast. Casting directly across, he retrieved rapidly, rod tip high and his hand shaking in a sort of palsy motion. That must have been what he meant to show me. It gave the flies a darting, erratic motion as though struggling across the current.

No raises were forthcoming from this run, but I wasn't in the least dis-couraged. Farther upstream I tried my hand at it, and soon became absorbed in the novel departure from my usual style—so much so, in fact, that I missed the rise of a brown that would easily have weighed a pound. Excitement so claimed me in the next few hours that I failed to land a single fish, though I raised many.

I left the stream that day with an empty creel. My excitement and inexperience in this type of fly-fishing had been responsible for that, but I had no regrets. Failure of that day was lost in anticipation of better days to come, now that knowledge was mine. Subsequent trips have proved the old-timer's logic. Very few are the lickings that the stream hands me now, thanks to these wet flies and his not-too-modern method of handling them. The dry fly has never given me as consistently large fish in any waters, nor an even chance of landing a heavy trout.

* * *

Of course, it isn't logical that I should confine this discovery to one stream. Our smaller mountain streams, narrow and heavily overhung with foliage, offer great possibilities for wet-fly fishing. As an initial experiment, I spent one Sunday during the first week in May on the west branch of a well-known Sullivan County stream, famous for its dry-fly fishing. A rain the night before had raised the water slightly and should have started the fish feeding.

Partner began with worms, and I with No. 8 wet flies. After the morning mists had cleared away, fly hatches began to come out, and I started to creel some nice fish. The worm didn't seem to deliver the goods for Partner; so he switched to a dry fly. Following him upstream, I took nearly a limit catch on a cast of Gordon and female Beaverkill, size eight, to his one fish on the floater. I really couldn't account for this, as flies were hatching, although we didn't note any rises. The trout were probably taking the nymphs as they rose to the surface before hatching.

Many times dry-fly fishermen encounter streams known to have an abundance of brown trout but which fail to measure up to their appearances as far as taking fish goes. I have such a stream in mind. A feeder of a large river, it broadens out to many fine pools and pocket holes where browns often lie. The water is of an amber hue, reminiscent of a popular beverage, and is well shaded. It's an ideal early bait stream in high water, heavy catches of nice trout being taken there at the beginning of each season.

When fly-time comes along and the water drops to normal level, I have not been very successful with the dry fly. For several seasons I experimented, with almost total failure, until last year, when I began to work on the likely places with big wet flies. Now I consistently take fair catches from the same waters that a floating artificial will ride untouched and perhaps unnoticed.

It may be that, on this type of stream, shade and dark water affect vision to such an extent that the fish take no interest in surface food. My flies are cast repeatedly to the same spot and skipped on the surface over a hiding place until I either raise a trout or realize that none are feeding.

On these smaller streams dry-fly casters who switch to wet flies are often surprised to find bigger fish coming to their offerings than ever before. The largest trout in the stream usually will take the right wet fly, properly handled, even though steadfastly refusing the best dry-fly presentation.

In addition, wet-fly fishing should have a great deal of appeal to the beginner. Flies and leaders are more serviceable and less expensive than conventional dry-fly equipment; patterns and fancy gadgets—oil bottles, line dressers, tweezers, and other accoutrements—need not be so numerous. Methods may be a bit more complicated, but are certainly worth the effort.

It is my good fortune to be able to tie my own flies and leaders, and by this means I have added a bit to the knowledge that Old John gave me. Wet flies for the big river seem to be more effective when tied with noticeably long tails, of a length similar to those adorning the ever-present stone-fly nymph. Wings can be longer and slimmer than the type found on standard patterns, and hackles quite short and very soft.

My leaders are tied with short lengths of gut projecting from some of the knots at equal distances along its length, so that I may use two or three flies. Eyed flies without gut are more dependable in holding qualities and are easier to carry. They are attached directly to the tags on the leader, eliminating the snell.

The snelled-fly book usually looks like a whisk broom at each end after a few flies have gone astray from their fasteners, and requires a pretty big pocket to handle it. Eyed flies on a tagged leader make a very neat cast and create less fuss on the surface than the dropper loop and snelled-fly arrangement. This is more important in taking wary trout than the weight of the leader in use.

For many seasons the dry fly had been my first and only angling love. Wet-fly fishing now has opened up a new vista of enjoyment and increased results for me. The veteran fly-fishermen that haunt many of our popular streams today still cling to these original artificials for filling the creel. Certainly a more intimate knowledge of this style of angling will add much more pleasure to any sportsman's day on the stream and probably mean a heavier basket at the day's end.

Since my acquaintance with Old John I have found that every one of my fishing trips has held new interest and pleasure for me, even on those famous dry-fly streams—the Beaverkill, the Willowemoc and the East Branch of the Delaware. Surely this seasoned old-timer, with years of fly-fishing experience behind him, cannot be very far wrong.

Telling on a Trout Fisherman

ARTHUR J. NEU

Big-fish adventures told with zest and color by an early national fly-casting champion. (April 1938)

Fortunate is the trout angler whose excursions take him where the fishing is generally lean, sometimes fair and occasionally good. One day he will "hit into 'em," and the memory of that day will live with him always.

The day which I am likely never to forget was June 14, 1916. That was before they carried the water of the Schoharie miles through a tunnel in the Catskills and dumped it into the Esopus, which until then was one of the finest trout rivers I ever hope to see. Our party had been on the Esopus a week. The water was high, the fishing indifferent.

On that morning Lou Darling and I chose to go downstream into the reservation, just above the Ashokan Reservoir. I went down to the last pool, known then as the Miller Pool. For a reason that I do not now recall I was using a Great Dun dry. I had seldom used it before, and do not remember ever having caught a fish on it before or since.

Having taken a few small trout, which I had released, I was resting beside the stream. I noted what seemed to me the rise of a good fish in the tail of the pool. For a while I watched him feed in leisurely fashion before deciding to try him. As I stepped into the stream I saw other rises. From then on, for more than an hour, it was my good fortune to be in the middle of a concentrated, purposeful rise of worth-while fish.

At one o'clock we returned to camp. Darling had had only fair fishing in the pools he had selected. The other men, having had poor luck elsewhere on the stream, were waiting for us.

I hope I may be pardoned the childlike vanity that I exhibited. To their queries of "What luck?" I answered nothing. Instead I put my creel on the grass and drew forth a 15-inch brownie. As they exclaimed loudly I drew forth as silently as before one of 17 inches—followed by one of 19 and then one of 21 prodigious inches.

By that time one or two of the party, unable to restrain themselves longer, came over and looked into the basket to see whether it was bottomless. Satisfied that there were no more monsters, they turned loose all the adjectives they knew. When they had exhausted their ability to express astonishment, I unrolled the rainshirt I had carelessly carried on my arm and displayed a brown trout measuring 24 inches and weighing 4 pounds.

I had the big fellow mounted—a reminder that there was such a day and that there may be another. Often I look at him and live again the fight that brought him to the net.

I had seen him rising in an almost impossible spot, just above where the heavy water rushed into the pool. The Miller Pool, looking upstream, was the shape of the letter d. The top of the letter represents the stream, rushing in. It formed a whirlpool, with a backwater in the loop of the d. To wade into the stream in a position to cast to the rise necessitated getting from one submerged rock to another, maintaining balance against the rush of the water. A false step meant being carried into the perhaps fatally dangerous waters of the pool. Foolish! Sure it is, but we all do it—or did in 1916.

On the very first cast the trout rose to the Dun, was hooked and tore downstream. Before I had time to think, he had reached the limit of the pool and nearly the limit of my line. If he reached the rapids, he was gone! So I held the line firmly against the grip and gave him the rod. I say "rod," but that 2½-ounce bit of bamboo seemed more like a toothpick at the instant.

For some seconds I stood there, my balance far from secure, playing tug of war with that big brownie. I expected to see either the rod or the leader break. But I was resigned to the risk, since it was the only method that had any chance of success.

The little rod held. So did the leader. The trout turned and headed into the backwater.

Then I was faced with the task of retracing my tortuous way out of the stream, at the same time keeping a taut line. How I did it I don't know. Somehow I sloshed out of the stream and stumbled along the rock-strewn bank to a better fighting position.

The big fish seemed lost in the backwater. His home was in the fast current, and apparently he did not know how to conduct himself to advantage in the pool. He circled interminably, and at each round of the backwater would attempt to get into the current. I turned him with difficulty at first, but with more ease each succeeding time.

I tried to bring him to the net too soon, and all but lost him. He made a quick dive that carried line and leader under a submerged log. Fortune favored me, however. The log was fast only at one end, and by running the rod under it I was able to free the line.

At long last he came to the top. I put the inadequate net under him, scooped him up, hugged him to my breast and, looking no doubt like Eliza crossing the ice with her child, ran twenty feet up the bank.

At this point Darling, who had come down the opposite bank and watched the end of the fight, yelled: "Get up the bank further, you boob, or you'll lose him yet!"

Another day sticks in my mind. It was May 16, 1931. The Newark Bait and Fly-Casting Club had arranged its annual outing for that day on the Musconetcong in New Jersey. During two days prior to the outing seven hundred fish, running up to 18 inches, had been stocked—the easily caught hatchery trout of which we've all heard so much.

I arrived at the stream at 9 A.M. From then until dark I stopped only for a short lunch. I fished the fast water and the slack stretches, the runs and the pools, the banks and the rock pockets. I exercised every wile I knew. I did not take a single trout!

Later that year I took a novice, to whom I had given some instruction in dry-fly casting, on a trip to the waters of the Trout Valley Association on the upper Beaverkill. Having recently won the national dry-fly title, I was considered somewhat of a he-caster even by the experienced members of the party, let alone the novices.

One day during the trip, the trout being indifferent, I was trying some trick casting to get under the branches of an overhanging hemlock and got hung up. The fly, a beautiful floater, was securely hooked in a branch well above my head. While I was using what methods I could to get it free I heard a snort of mirth.

My novice friend had been watching the whole performance from the opposite bank and was laughing at me. He came over and helped me recover the fly.

Annoyed a little, I decided to show him some "casting as was casting." A tricky upstream wind was blowing in puffs, with short lulls between. I remarked that I would demonstrate the practicality of some of the things I had been teaching him. Pointing out a run over a submerged rock, I put the fly in just the right position above it. As it floated over the dark, dimpling surface a nice trout rose eagerly. I missed him clean.

I grinned sheepishly, remarked that my mind had been on casting and not fishing, then hurried into my next act. I told him I would demonstrate how to counteract the wind by keeping the fly low at all points of the operation. On the first attempt I hooked myself squarely in the middle of the back. The barb went clean through my coat and outer shirt. My novice friend had to cut the hook out with his knife. He said nothing—and he said it eloquently.

The late Charles T. Champion, a pretty tournament caster and an officer of the bank where I was then employed, taught me to cast a fly in tournaments and to fish for trout with a worm. I caught my first trout in the Hackensack River (imagine that!) while trying for suckers. In 1908, with a trip to the Neversink in prospect, I took considerable pains in preparing my bait. When I set out, I was equipped with a two-quart can of worms. These were not ordinary garden hackles, but worms that had been bedded down for a week in moss and fed on sour milk—a treatment supposed to make them irresistible to trout.

I was to stay in the village of Neversink with John Mercer, whose place had been recommended to me. I found him on the stream, casting a feathered lure across a still pool. In answer to my surprised inquiry as to what he was doing, he said, "Fishing for trout."

I was incredulous. Here was a man apparently practicing for a tournament, and he told me he was fishing for trout. Of course, I knew that in England trout were supposedly caught on a fly. But I had had doubts about the veracity of persons who said they practiced the art thus and small faith in its success under any circumstances in American streams. I looked upon it as a fad not to be mentioned in the same breath with milk-fed worms.

Mercer was stripping a wet fly. Even as the aforementioned thoughts flitted through my mind I saw a flash of silver close to the fly. The tiny bunch of feathers disappeared as if by magic. The rod bent double. Soon he brought a nice native trout to his net.

I had no flies with me, of course. I borrowed one from Mercer. With trembling fingers I put my rod together. Before I left the stream I had taken a trout which gave me the greatest fishing thrill I had ever experienced until that time—greater than the combined thrills of filling a basket by the old method. Not one of my luscious worms was used on that trip, and only on one or two rare occasions have I used a worm since.

One such occasion was during a flood on the Esopus. The creek was over its banks and the color of well-creamed coffee. The trip was ruined. Those who didn't like pinochle were free to enjoy themselves by watching others play pinochle. Squire Hasbrouck, our host, who never was happier than when he was stirring up people to action, looked out at the leaden sky and opined that if anyone really wanted to catch trout, and wasn't a purist, he could do it.

"Ridiculous!" we said.

The old boy had made us believe some strange things in the past, but not this. Catch trout in that discolored torrent? He was just trying to get someone wet.

The Squire offered to show us, and we, a jeering crew, followed him to the river. He waded through the water-covered meadow and close to what was, in normal times, the willow-bordered bank of the stream. Carefully he reached over and lowered an immense night-crawler into the top of a submerged willow. In less than three minutes he had caught a trout. He continued to catch trout and to throw good-natured gibes at us. The trout were out in the edge of the overflow for the double purpose of getting away from the current and to feed on insects that clung to the willows. We all caught trout by the Squire's methods.

The greatest rise of trout I have seen was on that same Esopus, below Coldbrook Station. There was a good hatch on, and for more than an hour the fish fed steadily on the flies. More big fish were coming to the surface than I have ever seen at one time. There were three of us on the stretch. Our flies so exactly matched the insects on the water that we frequently mistook a natural for our female March Brown. We did not take a single fish! Explain it? I wish I could.

Nor can I explain this: I was on a public stream in New Jersey with a party of five. Many others were also fishing the stretch. The water was higher than normal and slightly discolored. Four of the five in our party had had much experience as fly-fishermen. The fifth had just adopted the method. The consensus was for use of a spinner or a bucktail, but we tried all artificial methods. We were at it five hours.

The four experienced fly-fishermen did not take a fish worth putting in their baskets. The novice returned to the car with six trout averaging a pound each, all taken on dry flies in the same waters we had fished. Luck? Maybe. But I think that on that day he was a better trout fisherman than the rest of us.

Two experiences on the Firehole, in Yellowstone National Park, stick in my memory. The trout were Loch Levens, much like our Eastern brown trout in habit, I supposed. It was a murky, cool day in September. The fish were breaking the surface frequently.

* * *

I cast several patterns of dry flies until my arm ached. Not a rise! I had noticed that my guide was fishing downstream and landing trout on wet flies. So I changed to wet and tried several patterns, still without success. I went to the guide, who was not the kind to vouchsafe information unless asked for it. He showed me his tie, and since I had none of the pattern he let me have some. I resumed fishing, but still could not get a single strike.

There was as much pride in me as there was secretiveness in my guide. I disdained to ask further information. Instead I went down and got behind him. I watched him while he caught two trout, one of them a nice two-pounder. Then I went back to my fishing and caught all I wished without difficulty. While I had been sinking the wet flies and allowing them to float downstream naturally, in the best accepted method for most of the Eastern fishing, the guide had been stripping the fly hard across stream in a way that no natural insect on earth or in the waters on top of or under the earth ever acted.

Incidentally, I saw the reverse happen to an angler in the Catskills. For years he had been using the stripping method on the brook trout in the Adirondacks with great success. He knew no other method. He spent ten days on the Esopus in its prime and he didn't take a fish. Then he asked a question or two of his brother fishermen.

The other experience on the Firehole came a few years later, following participation in the national tournament at Denver. A number of the boys, particularly some of those from Chicago, were itching for their first crack at the firehole. My memory may trick me, but it seems to me they told what they were going to do to those Loch Levens.

On the previous trip I had established more friendly relations with the guide before leaving, and he had told me of a little-used freight trail that led to some good stretches of the river. On this later trip the fishing was reported poor, and a number of us decided to see what lay along the freight trail. Experience bore out the report. Although we tried all manner of wet flies and every method of using them, success was very limited. Almost nil.

In desperation I resorted to a spinner. At a spot where the stream converged into a heavy run something grabbed the lure. I struck, but there was not the slightest give. I knew I had a very large fish.

It was one of those rare times when an angler is able to anticipate every move of his quarry. The fish tore downstream, and I followed him. He alternated with short rushes upstream and across. I followed him about three hundred yards and caught glimpses of him but twice in the space of a half hour.

At this juncture Fred Peet of Chicago came along, and after watching my antics for a while he grunted: "Bring him up! Let's see what you've got."

I could tell the fish was tiring, though he still struggled deep. Wishing to give Fred a look, I exerted all the pressure I dared on the four-ounce rod.

"Good Lord!" exclaimed Fred. "You must be hooked to the bottom of the stream."

It seemed even to me as though I must be hauling up a water-logged mattress. The fish came to the surface ever so slowly. He was not struggling, only resisting with his weight. Upon seeing him, Fred became more excited than I was.

"Bring him in, man! Bring him in!" he shouted.

But I was not to be hurried. When the trout spied us, he turned downstream. For another fifteen minutes or so I played him. Finally he came to the top, like a brown and gold submarine. Just as I was on the point of working him toward shore and my net, with no effort on the part of the fish the line snaked toward me and the fish was free.

For what seemed ten seconds he lay suspended, unaware that he was loose. For the same ten seconds I stood slack-jawed in amazement. Then my big trout sank silently into the depths.

As I rule I do not attempt to guess the weight or inches of the one that got away. This one was as long as my leg.

Investigation showed that I had been the victim of a broken split-ring in the spinner. When the openings came together at the swivel, the spinner simply parted. It could have been split when I put it on, or might have broken during the fight. So went the largest trout I ever hooked.

A number of years ago a companion and I made a hurried trip to a stream that, for a certain reason, shall be nameless. Upon arriving at our hostelry, we found the most disgruntled bunch of fishermen I have ever seen. They had come for their accustomed week or ten days on the stream at that season, but conditions were against them. They had been there several days, and none had taken a trout.

The morning following our arrival the weather was frigid and the stream still high and discolored, although it had receded somewhat from its peak. No one thought of fishing except my companion and me. However, since we were to be there only a day, we determined to give it a try. With little thought of success we started using spinners—and began taking trout at once. Thereafter we took them as we pleased, when we were not on the bank trying to get our blood in circulation. We kept only the best, which filled both baskets.

When we returned to the hotel in the middle of the afternoon, our host, who was noted the length of the stream for his penuriousness, was so overjoyed at our catch that he wanted us to stay on as his guests free of charge. Of course, we did not accept. I often wonder what he'd have done if we had. Nevertheless we fed the hotel. And throughout the evening we heard him going about telling the other anglers that it was plain there were plenty of fish in the stream if they were men enough to catch them. He did not wish his patrons to pick up and leave, as they had been threatening to.

Since the transformation (for the worse) of the Esopus, many of my companions, who used to go there regularly, transferred their activities to the Beaverkill. On an occasion that I well remember a party of us went there to spend the first two weeks of June. We found the water unexpectedly low and the weather warm. So we agreed that if there was nothing doing within two or three days we would go on to the Ausable.

The first day the fishing was poor. The next day it was worse. The third day, without warning, without change in conditions, three of us took thirty-six trout measuring thirty-six feet. The two others were Ken Lockwood and Jack Schwinn, and the stretch was that rough one below the acid factory.

Did we go to the Ausable? Emphatically we did not. We fished on, hoping for a repetition of that glorious day. Not only was there no repetition of such fishing, but the bottom practically dropped out of the stream. Not a fish worth mentioning was taken the rest of the trip.

But next June—!

The Dry Fly—Its Origin and Development

PRESTON J. JENNINGS

The author of America's first major fishing entomology, A Book of Trout Flies, *produces evidence that the dry fly may be far more of an antique than we think.* (June 1938)

The advantages of using an artificial fly, tied of light, buoyant materials which do not readily soak up water, run through the angling literature from time immemorial. Practically all of the ancient writers on the subject of fly-tying and fly-fishing referred to such materials as hogs' wool, hair from Devon cattle, mohair, seals' fur, and other water-resisting materials for the bodies of their flies.

Up to the beginning of the nineteenth century, fly-fishing was done in a manner known as wet-fly fishing. In other words, the fly was allowed to sink below the surface of the stream, but the buoyant body materials prevented it from sinking too rapidly or deeply.

Soon after the turn of the nineteenth century, the need for a fly that would float in an upright position with the wings erect became apparent, and one of the first to recognize and record this was one George C. Bainbridge, author of that fascinating and still useful book *The Fly Fisher's Guide*, published in Liverpool in 1816.

Just what or who Bainbridge was is of little consequence, but one paragraph in the preface of his book has always fascinated the writer and it will give an insight into his character. With the reader's permission, it runs as follows: "In order to explain the motives which directed the intrusion of the following pages upon the public, it may be necessary to premise that desire of fame, or expectation of profit, was not amongst the number." Surely, here is a man worthy of credence and, let us say, admiration as well. Now let us look at what Bainbridge has to say about the floating fly. In speaking of the Grey Drake, he gives first the suggested dressing of the artificial fly, and then he says, "This fly should be thrown directly over the fish, and so managed, if possible, that the wings may not touch the water." And that, in the writer's opinion, is the first record of the necessity for a dry fly.

It was the earnest desire of Bainbridge that his book become an incentive, as he puts it, "to some one more competent" to write a complete work on water insects. Some years later, in 1836, Alfred Ronalds published his instructive book *The Fly-fisher's Entomology*, but apparently Ronalds overlooked Bainbridge's suggestion with reference to fishing the Grey Drake as a dry fly, because Ronalds does not mention it or any other floating fly.

A few years after Ronalds' book was published, it appears that flies tied with upright wings and designed to float were in use by certain professional fly-tiers and fishers. One of these was James Ogden, author of that rare and interesting little book called *Ogden On Fly-tying* published many years later, viz., 1879. In this book Ogden says, "I have made this fly (Green Drake) my especial study from a lad. . . . When a lad I commenced tying them buzz. . . . I used this as a sunk fly for many years with great success. . . . I continued using the sunk fly till I could not take another fish on it, when I introduced my floaters, and I am confident I am the originator of floating flies, having introduced them forty years ago." This statement, if correct, and incidentally Major J. W. Hills in his book *A History of Fly-fishing for Trout* states that Ogden's book "bears every mark of truth and accuracy," puts the date of the first floating flies, or flies tied with the specific idea of floating, as the year 1839.

In the much-prized and unique book, *A Quaint Treatise on Flies and Fly Making* by an old fisherman, and edited by W. H. Aldam in 1876, are two specimens of floating Mayflies beautifully tied. These have been attributed to the hand of James Ogden, the first man to tie a floating fly.

From 1839 to 1851, the year of the publishing of the third edition of Pulman's *Vade Mecum of Fly-fishing*, little bearing on the subject was recorded, but in this instructive book the author says, "Let a dry fly be substituted for the wet one, the line switched a few times through the air to throw off its superabundant moisture, a judicious cast made just above the rising fish, and the fly allowed to float toward and over them, and the chances are 10 to 1 that it will be seized as readily as a living insect. This dry fly, we must remark, should be an imitation of the natural fly on which the fish are feeding." There is the dry fly, as well as instructions for keeping it dry by false casting between regular casts.

Fishing with floating flies appears to have enjoyed an increasing popularity in England, until the great apostle of the dry fly, F. M. Halford, collected 100 patterns of floating flies currently in use and incorporated them in the first and probably the best of his seven books on trout and trout fishing, *Floating Flies and How to Dress Them*. This book appeared in 1886 and is a valuable addition to the fly-fisher's library. From that time on, dry-fly fishing was the thing, and the humble wielders of the wet fly were practically relegated to the same class as poachers and worm-dunkers, especially as far as the chalk streams in the south of England were concerned. That condition has been corrected to a large extent, due to the efforts of Mr. G. E. M. Skues, who found that a tiny hackled fly tied in the imitation of a small nymph and fished as a wet fly would, under certain conditions, take fish that could not be taken with a strictly dry fly.

In America the dry fly made its appearance around the early 90's; in fact, a plate of 15 dry flies appears in the book *Favorite Flies* by Mary Orvis Marbury, published in 1892.

It appears that Thaddeus Norris recognized the advantages of using a dry fly as early as 1864, as he writes in the *American Angler's Book* as follows, "If it could be accomplished, the great desideratum would be to keep the line wet and the flies dry." The heavy oiled-silk casting lines were not then in use, so it was necessary to wet the line in order to give it sufficient weight to cast against a breeze. Norris then goes on to say that once when fishing the Willowemoc his companion was able to take several dozen fish because of the fact that he was using a fine leader and fresh flies; and by cracking the moisture from them between throws could lay them gently on the surface of the pool where the flies would be seized by a brace of trout before the flies would sink or could be drawn away. He says, "Here was an exemplification of the advantage of keeping one's flies dry and the fallacy of the theory of not allowing the line to fall on the water, for in this instance I noticed that a fourth or a third of it touched the surface at every cast. Here was dry-fly fishing full-grown."

After Marbury, little, if any, mention was made of the floating fly in any of the American books on trout fishing until there appeared in the July 1909 issue of the magazine "Recreation" an article called *The Evolution of a Dry Fly Fisherman*, by G. M. L. LaBranche, in which the author gives a vivid account of his conversion from a "chuck and chance" wet-fly fisherman to the mastery of the fine art of fishing with a floating fly. This article is the forerunner of that delightfully written book by the same author *Dry Fly and Fast Water* published in 1914.

In 1912 Emlyn Gill published his book *Practical Dry Fly Fishing*, which book has the honor of being the first one published in America devoted exclusively to the dry fly and dry-fly fishing.

Theodore Gordon did much to popularize the dry fly in America, and it is to be regretted that he did not leave for the future generations of fly-fishers a book on his findings. He was a close student of the natural fly, and many of his flies were tied to represent naturals on which trout feed. The Gordon Quill dry fly, when tied according to Gordon's specifications, is a fine pattern of general fly and is one that closely resembles a number of the ephemeral flies occurring in the Catskill and Adirondack regions.

In late years the trend seems to be toward the impressionistic in fly-tying, and many of the current patterns known as variants and spiders bear little resemblance to the natural fly found on the water—at least as far as human vision is concerned—but they must look good to the fish, as they are killing flies.

The increasing wariness of the trout, and the resulting necessity for using long, thin leaders have contributed to the popularity of these flies, as they can be handled on a light leader without causing snarls. They float high and are not easily water-logged.

Tastes change, and time alone will tell whether these impressionistic flies will find a permanent place in the fly-fisher's kit, or whether history will repeat itself and we will again have to turn to a closer representation of the natural fly in order to take fish on the dry fly.

The Wet Dry Fly

SID W. GORDON

As knowledge of aquatic insect behavior advances, an expert presents a new series of artificials to imitate the many adult flies that swim down underwater to lay their eggs. (August 1939)

Every fly fisherman is familiar with the wet fly, many use the dry fly, and some know how to fish the nymph; but in our two thousand years of fly-fishing history there is something which has been overlooked. That is, the wet dry fly. I believe that I have found the answer to why flies like the gold-ribbed Hare's Ear, the Slim Jim, the Orange, the gold-ribbed muskrat-belly fly and others enable us to coax a trout many feet from its home.

For years we fishermen have been arguing that a certain fly is taken because it resembles a hatching nymph, another fly is effective because it resembles a minnow, and yet another kills fish because it is taken for a fairy shrimp. When we can give no sound reason why the trout take a particular fly, we smugly condemn it as a lure. I propose to add a new angle for argument around the fireside, but I shall leave it to your own observations upon the stream to accept or reject this new angle, which may open a different slant on fly-fishing and flies.

We all know that the nymph, the underwater bug from which the fly hatches, lives from six months to three years in the nymphal stage before it comes out of the water to become the living fly. When it mates and deposits its eggs upon the

water, we fishermen call it the dry fly. When the dry fly comes floating downstream toward us, it often becomes drenched and drowned. For a great many
years trout fishermen have imitated it in this drowned stage and called it the wet
fly.

But there is a fourth stage—to me, a most important phase, because there is
so large a proportion of flies on our trout streams which do not deposit their eggs
upon the water. They always deposit their eggs under water!

When these "dry flies" descend under water, you cannot call them wet flies.
They are not drowned flies, for they can be seen crawling on the rocks or sticks,
depositing their eggs under water. When they go down beneath the surface, they
have a flash and a movement such as no drowned fly ever has.

In order to judge the great difference in the action, place a live sedge-fly in
a pint bottle. Fill with water and up-end the bottle very quickly until the sedge
is submerged. You will never forget the under-water action of that sedge with
its silvery airy envelope, nor the speed with which its legs and feelers move the
shiny body without breaking the envelope of air.

These flies are not waterlogged or dead, inert objects drifting where the current
may take them, for their little legs are working rapidly as they swim to the
bottom. There are air bubbles around their bodies, and these give them the flash
and movement which the trout can readily detect. Until some better classification
is found, I know of no better or more appropriate name for a fly under such
conditions than the wet dry fly.

Why shouldn't the trout take such a fly in preference to a wet fly? A wet fly
has deposited its eggs. It is an empty shell compared to the female wet dry fly
that carries sometimes a thousand unlaid eggs, a swollen mass that means food
to the trout which sees it under water.

You reject the withered peach at the fruit store, immediately selecting the
full, luscious fruit. Surely a trout which lives to eat has the same discrimination
to some degree.

When you get into a medium hard-water stream or a hard-water stream,
you will find that such a stream of good lime content will harbor well over a
million insects in eighty rods. Pick up a stick or a rock and look for caddis
houses. Practically every other house will have a female caddis nymph (larva)
which hatches into the caddis-fly, or sedge-fly, as we fishermen call it. When we
imitate them in the artificial fly, they are called the Silver Sedge, the Brown
Sedge, Welshman's Button, Caddis and a great many others too numerous to
list here.

I am sure that there will be at least a half million cases, or houses, in this good
stretch of stream. If half of them are females, you are fairly safe in assuming that
125,000 will be under-water egg-layers or wet dry flies, for about half of the

caddis females in that stretch of eighty rods will deposit their eggs under water. Figures like these cannot be overlooked when a man decides whether or not to imitate something which occurs in great numbers in his waters.

The entomologist groups the caddis-flies into one large family and calls them the *Trichoptera*. You will notice that they have roof-like wings over their bodies.

Getting back to the statement that there are a million insects, or nymphs, in a stretch of eighty rods of good water, there is another species which has the under-water egg-laying habit. We fishermen call them the duns, or May-flies. We ask the tackle salesman for the Iron Blue Dun, the Pale Watery Dun, the Olive Dun and the Orange Dun. All these imitate the living dun *Baetis*, family of the *Ephemeridae*, and only *Baetis* of this family has the under-water or wet dry fly habit as far as I know. If you examine the sticks and stones and see this nymph crawling around, I think you will agree that there are at least another 20,000 insects in that stretch which lay their eggs under water.

This nymph is a fast swimmer. When it hatches into the dry fly and goes beneath the surface to deposit its eggs, it does not have as much of a flash as the caddis-fly, but is very much worth while imitating.

The May-fly, or dun, has upstanding wings, not roof-like over the body like the caddis-fly. When it goes under the water, its wings sort of fold around its body, probably by water pressure, and carry smaller bubbles. It does not have the flash of the caddis-fly, but even so, with its smooth body, it does have a flash and a movement far superior to any wet fly.

The caddis-flies have four good-sized wings, sometimes much longer than their bodies. Their wings are rougher, scaly and hairy, as you will see under the microscope, and their bodies are much rougher than those of the May-flies.

The caddis-flies, or sedges, roll and tumble down to the bottom of the stream to deposit their eggs. Their rough bodies and scaly and hairy wings, usually longer than the body, hold and trap more air than do the May-flies.

The stone-flies, the flies of the riffles and the fast water, are very numerous too, and many of them lay their eggs under water. While they are clumsy flies to imitate, the nymphs and the flies are nevertheless a large item of trout food and should be imitated by the fly-tier.

Before I describe some of the imitations upon which I am working, let me caution you a bit about fishing them properly. Very few fishermen take the time to observe the action of the nymph, the dry fly or the wet fly as they behave naturally in the water. Take a little time off from your fishing and watch the action of these wet dry flies as they go beneath the water, and offer them to the fish in the same natural way in which the fish are accustomed to take them.

When deer hunting, you wouldn't think of hunting down-wind for deer; your scent would be carried ahead of you, and the deer would run long before you sighted him. All wild things run first and look afterward when anything frightens them.

If you throw that wet dry fly downstream ahead of you and drag it upstream toward you, a good-sized trout will be put down. He'll swim away fast and look afterward. He knows that a small fly cannot swim upstream, and your common sense will tell you that not even the nymph, let alone the dry fly or the wet fly, can swim upstream against a current. It is true that the wet dry fly will struggle more, actually swimming against the current, but even so he can make no headway and must work down and with the current.

So present your fly to the fish with normal, natural action. In the early season the light leader and the tapered line will not carry your gold-ribbed fly down close enough to the trout. Use a level line or a quick-tapered line too heavy to float, so that line, leader and fly will sink quickly. Cast upstream or up and across the stream and drift the fly along much closer to the bottom than to the surface. Place the fly ten feet above the spot you think the trout may be; your heavy line will drag it down and tumble the fly to the trout just as the rolling, tumbling natural insect would come to him.

While I never fish for meat, I do insist upon catching every fish in a stretch of stream, if I can. Carry two lines with you—a level, quick-sinking line and a tapered line. The man who fishes with only the tapered line seldom gets down to the big ones which the heavy, level line will often enable him to take, and he misses a great deal of sport.

A spare drum for a reel costs so very little extra, and takes so little time to change, that I can never understand why an all-round fisherman neglects this most important item. He will clutter himself with gadgets until he looks like a Christmas tree, but he won't throw an extra drum, wrapped in oiled silk, in his creel.

As the season advances use that light tapered line; and when you come to a good pool, change to the spare and go down and get them where they are. I can coax a brook trout away across a stream with a wet dry fly and make him take it at your feet if you will stand perfectly still. A rainbow will almost always make a smashing attack if it is presented to him naturally.

But a brown trout is different. The brown does not like the daylight; he is an evening feeder. If there are ten trout in a pool, the brook trout will be more in the daylight, but the brown seeks the coolest, darkest spot in the pool. I do not believe the daytime vision of the brown trout is nearly as keen as that of the brook or the rainbow. Both the brook and the rainbow will follow a fly, but a brown wants it about two feet from him at the outside.

In the evening the brown feeds on or near the surface. Then only the tapered line will take him; but in the daytime you must drift it right past his nose, and usually some small trout will take it before he does, which puts him down. I have found more than fifty snails in a brown trout's stomach, which shows that when he feeds in the daytime he is a bottom feeder in our Wisconsin and Michigan waters.

Let us now look at the list of flies available on the market that more closely resemble the duns and sedges which have the under-water egg-laying habit. After you investigate the living flies in the water, I think your own observations will confirm their naturalness.

I believe that six patterns of the caddis, or sedges, three of the duns, or May-flies, and two of the stone-flies, in various hook sizes from 16 to 8, can be worked out which will apply all over this country. These patterns should be secured from the commercial fly-tying concerns at very little increase in cost, if any, over the regular wet flies.

The gold-ribbed Hare's Ear is probably the best commercially tied wet dry fly in its resemblance to the egg-depositing sedge, or caddis-fly, in the water. Use sizes 16 and 14 for brooks and browns and size 10 for rainbows. For evening fishing use sizes 8 and 10. But all should be tied with about three turns of gold below the body to represent the full egg sac of the female.

In my opinion, there is no "best" fly on the market which represents the dun in its wet dry state. The gold-ribbed Hare's Ear and many flies with rough body and gold ribbing, fished wet or dry, are sold as imitations of the duns. In no way do they resemble the dun in any of its phases, wet or dry!

To forestall any criticism or controversy, I trust that you will settle this to your own satisfaction by looking at the bodies of all the dun flies, from the 3-inch *Hexagenia*, one of the largest of the May-flies, down to the tiniest duns which we imitate on No. 20 hooks. None has a hairy body!

Looking at the caddis-flies, or sedges, practically all have hairy or rough bodies, and the fur from the hare's ear is a good imitation. The light fur from the muskrat belly is much easier to obtain and is equal, if not superior, to the hare's ear. Either must be ribbed with gold to give it the flash of a live sedge going down to deposit its eggs. If you are a stickler for exact imitation, tie the wings more along the hook like the Welshman's Button fly, and you will have a perfect Hare's Ear.

Greenwell's Glory and Wickham's Fancy should take trout, as they are fair imitations of the egg-depositing dun, but I believe that only a smooth body of such material as moose mane, quill and porcupine is a true imitation of the dun which goes under water. The quill body is shiny to a certain extent, but a quill body with very fine gold ribbing and about three turns down and back at the bend will give it the necessary flash. Some of these duns have as many as three thousand eggs in their bodies just at egg-depositing time, and the gold or silver tinsel is still the best material we have to imitate their transparency. Slim Jim, the smooth-bodied fly with its narrow silver ribbing and Plymouth Rock hackle points for wings, slanted in the hackle, is probably the trout's conception of a wet dry dun.

Any good squirrel-tail fly, with a gold or silver rib and not too much hackle to represent the six legs and two horns, is a very good imitation of the largest of the sedges, or caddis-flies. Tie it on an 8 or 10 hook and leave off the tail, for only the duns and the stone-flies have tails. Substitute turkey wing-feather or bucktail if you wish, but dress it lightly, and you will have a good imitation of many of the large sedges.

Why be one of the rushing, driving fishermen? Sit down on a rock or a log or stand perfectly still in the water for a few moments and carefully observe what is going on at your feet. The trout themselves will teach you how to fish. Quit the continual driving of the fly, and I am sure that you will agree with me that any good commercial fly whose body shines and holds air like the dun or the sedge will take many fish if you drift it down to them.

Below are the dressings of four of my flies which seem to take exceptionally well and which I think imitate, to a fair degree, some of the flies I saw under water. I trust your own observations will bring forth many better patterns than these I have tied, for the wet dry fly is only in its infancy.

As these insects all have but six legs and two or three tails, nine strands of hackle give an exact imitation. If the bodies are too long or the hackle too thick, you have an overdressed fly which will never drift down to the trout.

SMALL SEDGE (*Rhyacophila*)

Hook. Model perfect, size 14.
Body. Pahmi fur spun on light-colored silk. Egg sac and ribbing, narrow silver tinsel.
Tail. None.
Legs. Gold whisks from golden pheasant crest. The legs of the small sedges range from yellow, green, brown to black.
Wings. Mallard, canvasback or wood duck. Tie like the big sedge, described below. Many species have wings of white, gray, brown, black or mixtures.

LARGE STONE (*Perla*)

Hook. Sproat, size 8, or long shank, size 10.
Body. Slightly soil your lemon yarn on the outside windowsill. Rib with very finest black silk to imitate the segments of the body. Wrap with stripped outer covering of white goose quill. Now rib with silver tinsel.
Tails. Two short strands of the ends of dark moose mane.
Hackle. Sparse and down-tied of Rhode Island Red hen feather.

Wings. Mallard, wood duck or canvasback mottled breast feather. Tie very flat over the body. The new wing-vein material, cut to fit, is perfect.

Large Sedge (*Phryganea*)

Hook. Sproat, size 8 or 10.

Body. Muskrat belly, spun on light-colored silk thread. Rib narrow gold or silver, five turns for egg sac at bend of hook. Stop body at point of hook.

Tail. None.

Legs. Some have yellow, some orange and some brown legs. Use these colors, down-tied hackle and very sparse.

Wings. Turkey wing-feather well down over the body. One wing loose, the other caught in the gold ribbing at the hook bend, to hold the air.

May-Fly (The dun, *Baetis*)

Hook. Model perfect, size 14.

Body. Soft orange quill. Gold-ribbed with egg sac.

Tail. Three whisks of golden pheasant crest, the orange and black feather.

Legs. Red (brown) game and white game cock. Stiff hackles. One turn of white hackle behind the eye. Three turns of red game hackle behind the white. Tie off behind the hackles. This stiffens them and exposes the body to the fish, as in the living fly.

On some of my sedges I use the neck feathers of the Hungarian partridge, the ruffed grouse, the prairie chicken and the sharptail. These soft feathers, partly tied down over the body, the rest left free, are good imitations of the rolling sedges.

You are going to be very much surprised at the different colors you will find on the bodies, wings, legs and "horns" of the various insects, as well as the variation in size. You will use hooks from size 16 to 8, but I use mostly 14 and 10. I use model perfect hooks up to 10, and sproat hooks in sizes 8 and 10. Good luck!

PART THREE

THE MODERN TEMPER

A Silver Rainbow

RAY P. HOLLAND

Movie stars are notoriously temperamental. But when you cast Silver Creek's legendary rainbows in the leading role—watch out!
(January 1940)

The saying that distant pastures are always greener fits a fisherman better than any other type of individual. I never knew a fellow who liked rods and reels and lines and flies who didn't have some pet spot picked out where he hoped to fish when and if old opportunity offered.

All of us have many times made trips to far-away streams and backwoods lakes, and learned to our grief that we could have had better fishing right close to the old home town. But we will keep on going and seeking and trying out new streams because that urge for those greener pastures is inherent in most of us.

And that's the reason for it all. When the Pathé Company asked, "Where is the best place in the United States to make a trout-fishing picture?" I said promptly, "Silver Creek." I could have said the Ausable, or the Beaverkill, or the Brule, or the Madison, or the Neversink, or the Yellowstone, or any one of a dozen or more famous trout streams that I had fished and knew intimately.

But I didn't. I said, "Silver Creek," a stream that I had never seen. And I'm

153

going to go all the way and admit that I didn't even know where it was. All I knew was that Silver Creek was in Idaho and that H. L. Betten had once told me it was the greatest piece of dry-fly trout water he had ever seen.

That started it. Then one summer when the youngest son was fishing the Madison of Montana, he met Ben Davis of Pocatello, Idaho.

"Did you ever fish Silver Creek?" asked Davis.

"No," said Dan, "but I hope to some day. I've heard about it."

One sultry noon I was having lunch in New York City with an artist-fisherman, and he said, "Perhaps there are more big fish feeding on the surface in Silver Creek than in any stream in the world; but hell, you can't catch them. They're too smart."

And so this Silver Creek thing built up over the years until I was prepared to state glibly to the Pathé representative that Silver Creek was the place to which they must go if they wanted to make a real trout-fishing picture. This project had been under discussion since the Pathé Sportscopes, "Bird Dogs" and "On the Wing," had been made the fall before, and Dan and I were to do the fishing.

And it came to pass that all arrangements were made. The first thing we had to do was find out where Silver Creek was located. Idaho is a big state. But the creek called Silver wasn't hard to find, in spite of the fact that the army of dry-fly fishermen that crowd Eastern trout streams had apparently never heard of it or its rainbow trout.

In late June, Dan and the Director, the camera-man, the sound expert, and numerous and sundry assistants, with enough equipment to fill a couple of trucks, arrived on location. I was to show up later, after much of the preliminary work had been done. The boys had been on the job four days when I got there. This business of taking a motion picture that will stand the test of a critical public is a long-drawn-out, tedious affair.

"How are you getting along?" I asked the Director.

"Swell," he replied.

And Dan winked at me. Later, when I asked him why, he said: "You'll find out. We're not fishing Silver Creek. We're fishing in Wood River."

The next morning we roared away from the town of Ketcham for Wood River. Two truck loads, filled with men and cameras.

I think our boss man must have read Horace Lytle's story of the director who told him to bring his dog down parallel with some heavy pine woods and have him stand a covey of quail in a little patch of broom-sedge that lay just off the point of the woods. Anyway, our Director took me to the edge of the stream, a beautiful mountain river that rolled and tumbled and eddied. Perfect trout water.

"See that glassy spot," he pointed. "I want a fish caught right there."

That was an order to ponder over.

* * *

We had a local guide working for us, and I got him off to one side.

"Where is Silver Creek?" I asked.

"Sixty miles to the south of us," he answered.

"Is it full of rainbows?" was my next question.

"Sure, and big ones, but it's no place for a dub to fool around. It takes a fisherman to catch them."

I let that pass.

"Do you think I could catch one?" I asked him.

"Maybe," he answered, "but you won't catch one with four or five men walking up to the bank and setting up cameras and falling in, because those trout in Silver Creek aren't that kind of fish."

Just then another truck drove up with a load of lumber, and a couple of sons of the saw and hammer began erecting a trylon.

"What's that for?" somebody asked.

The Director told us how little we knew about motion pictures. "To get a real shot of a rising fish, we have to take him from above, and the camera-man will shoot from the top of this when it is completed."

Then we went into executive session, and we explained to the Director and the camera-man that fish can only be caught where fish are, and that there weren't any fish right under that slick spot. But that didn't bother him in the least.

"We'll put fish there," he replied.

"But they won't hit a fly," I answered.

"We'll make them hit it. We've already arranged for the whole thing. The fish will be here in a few minutes."

From a distant hatchery came our motion-picture stars in aerated tanks. Forty-three of them—beautiful rainbow trout weighing from 3½ to 5 pounds each.

I then discovered that other workmen had previously fenced off Wood River. There was a wire screening upstream fifty yards and another wire screening downstream. Into Wood River went the fish, and into the stream went Dan to catch one of them. He tried all sorts of lures, and not a hatchery fish cocked an eye skyward.

"We'll let them rest until morning," said the Director. "It's 3:30 now, and we'll knock off for the day."

I looked at Dan, and Dan looked at me, and the Sound Man, who was a fisherman, looked at both of us and whispered something to the guide. In less time than it takes to tell it, we were rolling away for Silver Creek.

I have never seen an English chalk stream. Maybe they have trout waters over there equal to Silver Creek, but I doubt it. She's a meadow stream, lying in a fertile valley. Where we first stopped, the creek was probably sixty feet wide.

The pasture grass went right up to the bank. In some places there were a few rushes.

"Be careful when you go in," said the guide. "It's deep right up to the edge."

"How deep?" I asked.

"Oh, maybe three feet, or maybe four."

I sat down on the edge of the bank and slipped off into the stream, almost to the top of my waders. A hen mallard with seven or eight youngsters objected seriously, and I thought for a minute she was going to attack me.

That water was cold. So cold through the waders that it made me gasp. The source of this deep, slow-moving stream was less than ten miles from where we fished. A series of big springs bubble out of the earth and run together to make Silver Creek bank-full of ice-water.

The wind was blowing a little, and I could see no sign of feeding fish. I started casting as I moved upstream. The guide squatted on the bank.

"Tough wind," I remarked. "Think I'd better hunt a little quieter spot where I can lay a fly down easier."

I thought of that remark of his—that it was no place for a dub to fool around—for when the fly wasn't blowing back or the leader dropping in a coil, I was slapping it down like a hawser.

"Is this considered a particularly good spot?" I asked him.

He never got around to answering. A young stick of dynamite exploded under that brown bivisible, and I left it fastened in the face of the first Silver Creek trout that came to my fly.

That evening I took three fish weighing from 1½ to 3 pounds. Dan and the Sound Man each took fish, and we pulled into headquarters about 11 P.M., ready for something to eat.

The next morning we again went to Wood River. Dan fished over those hatchery fish most of the day, and some of them actually came up and took a look at the fly; but, as it didn't look like or smell like sheep plucks or beef scraps on which they had been raised, they refused to play ball.

"We'll get 'em tomorrow. We've got to make them strike," said the Director when he told us good-by at four o'clock as we headed for Silver Creek and fishing.

That evening there was no wind, and at the end of one hour's fishing I was willing to go on record that it was no place for a dub to fish. I hadn't as much as raised a single trout. Fish were feeding everywhere. The water was being dimpled and ringed as far as we could see upstream, and no matter how carefully I laid that fly the feeding in its vicinity stopped when it hit the water.

Climbing out of the stream, I cut across a bend to see what luck Dan and the Sound Man were having. They were nowhere in sight; so I went to work again, first soaking a 12-foot leader tapered to 5x. There was a hatch of light yellow caddis-flies on the water, and the nearest I could come to matching them was with a Light Cahill with a white body tied on a No. 16 hook.

I had only four of these flies. I left all of them in heavy fish, and not because I was a dub, either. I hooked the fish without losing the fly. That's usually half the battle, but these roaring, ripping rainbows refused to stay hooked. They came out of the water on their tails and thrashed along the surface like sailfish. They jumped high in somersaults and fell on the leader, and after trying these tactics for a while they would dive under a moss-bed at the edge of the stream, and that was that.

After losing two, I took off the 5x tippet. I lost the third fly, and I took off the 4x tippet. I lost the fourth fly and I cut off another foot of leader and was down to 2x. And then they didn't rise so well.

Upstream a way I located a bend where I could spot six big fish feeding. I could fish it from the bank without getting into the stream. I took off my creel, spit on my hands and went to work. The Sound Man came along and asked, "What luck?"

I had taken two rainbows, one a 3-pounder, but I told him, "Old Grampa is lying right out there, and he has been rising steadily, but every time I offer him something to eat he gets mad and sulks."

I had marked this big fish by my creel on the bank. I would go away and leave him and catch smaller fry; and when he went to feeding again, I would slip back and offer him a choice morsel. It began to get dark, and he had refused to show interest in anything I had used.

Among my flies was a brown hackle nondescript with a tuft of deer hair, in place of wings, and a red tag. Harry Betten had given it to me and told me it would work on Silver Creek. I laid it out, and Grampa took it. He came into the air a full three feet, a gorgeous 4-pound rainbow with a stripe the full length of him. He took line downstream clear to the backing, and then into the air he went again and roared back, angry at the thing that held him. Seven times he came out of the water, and every time he came out I yelled and the Sound Man yelled. At last he began to tire, and before I could stop him he dived under a moss-bed.

"Get out of there!" I yelled.

As though he had heard me, he raced thirty yards upstream with a last glorious leap. As I worked him back he was rolling from side to side, and I knew the battle was about over. But not quite. Into that moss-bed he went a second time, and this time he rolled on his side, and I could see him lying there gasping. I started to slip off the bank into the water.

"You can't wade that," said the Sound Man.

"But it's got to be waded," I answered.

As I eased the net down and under him he never moved a fin. He had fought a good fight, but he was licked.

Old Grampa was a grand fish, and I held him right side up in the water until he got his wind. When I took my hands away, he slowly moved across stream and down under his moss-bed. And I've got the Sound Man to prove it.

The next morning we were back at Wood River, and the Director said, "Give those fish a worm, and we'll take the fight and the jumps and cut them into a fly-fishing scene."

So worms we dug and hooks we baited, but those hatchery trout wouldn't touch them. They would smell the worm-baited hook and probably say, "That's not hamburger. We'd better leave it alone."

"Get hamburger!" ordered the Director.

We got hamburger, and we put some on the hook. Immediately a great big hatchery rainbow loafed up and sucked it in. And Dan set the hook.

Did he jump? Did he fight? Not that fish. He was all worn out from holding his own in that current. He just rolled on his side and said, "This is part of a fish's life, and I'm caught."

"Cut!" yelled the Director. "That'll never do. Make him jump."

But you couldn't make a plow horse win the Derby. We knew it, and by this time the Director knew it; but he still had in mind that beautiful spot, and he said a fish had to be caught there.

At this particular point we began to hold out a little encouragement. In the lower end of this pool, out of the current, some fifteen or twenty rainbows lay like cordwood. Up at the head of the pool, more virile fish cruised around in the eddy. I had noticed something when we arrived that morning. So had Dan.

Alongside those black leviathans in the eddy lay a long, slim, gray fish that was hard to see. When he moved from place to place, he just disappeared and was over there. You didn't see him go. Apparently he had gone upstream or come downstream to visit with the boys from the hatchery. He was almost invisible against the sandy bottom where the hatchery fish stood out in bold relief.

The camera-man got up on his decapitated trylon. Dan got out in the stream. The Director manned a portable camera from another angle, and Dan started to fish. I was observer.

A streamer fly hit in the eddy, swung out in the current and hung there for a second before it was twitched back upstream to be cast again. The gray fish moved nervously. Again and again the fly came down, and each time the fish darted out toward it. He would only go a little way, and then he would swing back to his original position beside his new-found friends from the State Hatchery.

The lure was changed to a Coachman, and at the first cast the big gray fellow shot out in the current, came up behind the fly, hung there a few minutes and then returned to the edge of the eddy.

"O.K.," I called, and the Director said, "Turn her over!"

The Coachman shot down, hit at the edge of the eddy and started out into the current. But the old boy nailed it. It couldn't fool him any longer, and into the air he came. Then he headed for a rock near where Dan was standing; and that worthy forgot picture-taking for some time, because this Wood River rover foamed the water white in his efforts to get in and get under.

The little light bamboo was too much for him, although at times it was bent far more than a good rod should ever be bent. Away from the rock the rod would swing him; downstream he'd go, and then back for the rock he'd head. But he was up against a game he couldn't beat, and as he was lifted out, a good heavy netful, the Director shouted, "Cut!"

"Now," he said, "I'll go to Silver Creek with you fellows. We'll go tomorrow and try to catch some of those touchy fish that get scared if you peek over the bank at them."

For fear we might still want to use the Wood River set-up, with the high tower and other paraphernalia, the Director hired as a "creek watch" a nice old gentleman who was living in a trailer near our scene of activity. He said he was a Government rodent eradicator. In plain words, he poisoned ground-squirrels. We asked him why anybody would want to poison ground-squirrels up in that mountain country where agriculture and grazing were impossible.

"They are hard on the roots of pine trees," he replied.

Explaining further, he told us that they dug holes down around the roots of the trees, which dried out the roots. Therefore he was employed by a paternal government to poke strychnine down all the squirrel holes he could find.

We told him we would be back in a day or two and to watch the fish and make everybody obey the signs which the Fish and Game Department of Idaho had erected to forbid fishing in that section of the stream. He assured us that he would take good care of our fish while we were away.

When we had gone down the road a few miles, it occurred to the Director that we had carried away the hamburger which we had bought to feed these fish in order to keep them healthy and happy. So we returned. When we drove up to the camp and called, our creek watch came around from behind, and he had a spade in one hand and a can of angleworms in the other. When we returned later in the week for a few shots to fill in, the vermin eradicator had broken camp and departed, and apparently most of our fish had gone with him.

Wood River is a fine fishing stream, and it has plenty of fish in it, although we were able to take only the one big fish. It is fished heavily by visitors from the near-by resorts. But Silver Creek is hardly fished at all. The guide said that visitors all make one trip to Silver Creek and then give it up as a bad job, because it's no place for a beginner. I was glad he didn't say "dub."

But some of the dubs do stray down there occasionally. I met a young fellow one evening who was fishing Silver Creek for all he was worth. He was sitting on the bank. He had on so many Western clothes that you knew the minute you looked at him that he came from the East. He wore a ten-gallon hat that would have done justice to Texas. He had on cowboy boots and blue overalls and a knotted bandanna, and he was still-fishing, I supposed with a worm.

"Any luck?" I asked him.

"I don't think there are any fish in this river," he answered.

Just then he pulled up his line and cast it out a little farther, and I saw that he was still-fishing with a big brass spinner! Now, one of the pledges of the Square Circle is to help youth along the paths that lead to successful hunting and fishing, and with that in mind I said: "You'll never catch anything fishing a spinner that way. You must cast it out and work it back through the water."

Without moving his head, he raised his eyelids and looked me square in the eye.

"Who asked you?" was his comment.

He had me there.

The first morning our trucks pulled into Silver Creek to get down to serious business, there were at least forty trout feeding in sight. We kept the crew back away from the shore while they got the cameras set. Dan and I went downstream and eased into the water and started working back toward the cameras.

"Turn her over!" yelled the Director. "Fish!"

And we fished. At about the third cast Dan hooked a fish, and out it came. Before it could make the second leap I had tied into another, and it looked as though we were going to make a picture.

"Cut!" yelled the Director.

"What's the matter?" I asked.

"Fish aren't big enough," he replied.

They weighed only about a pound and a half or two pounds apiece. I looked at the Sound Man, and the Sound Man looked at me.

"Maybe we can find you a marlin somewhere," he called.

And talk about dumb fish! After we caught those two, there wasn't another fish feeding within sight of us. The word went around that there was dirty work at the crossroads, and the boys went into the moss-beds, of which Silver Creek has plenty.

I couldn't help but think of those poor, benighted people who contend that fish are dumb. I thought of John Taintor Foote's story of his experiences on the Big Sturgeon in Michigan. Dozens of big rainbows lay in plain sight under a bridge. John tried them with everything he had, but they would pay no attention to any lure. Then he caught some grasshoppers. He would drop in a grasshopper, and slowly a fish would rise up and take it. After feeding them three or four, he put a very small hook in the next grasshopper and dropped it in just the same way. And a fish rose up, looked at the grasshopper carefully, and went back where he came from.

Never will I forget the evenings on Silver Creek. I'm going back there some time when there are no camera-men to yell and shout, "Turn her over! Cut!"

As we fished flocks of young ducks swam ahead of us. Blue-winged teal, mergansers and mallards were everywhere. They argued with us as to the water rights, and a pair of coots almost put me off the stream. If you have never seen a pair of mud-hens defending their family against a two-legged man armed with a trout rod, you have something to look forward to. They turn all their feathers forward until they look like nothing I have ever seen before. Then they swim straight toward you; and when about ten feet from you, they make a sudden lunge and belch at you. That's the only word that describes it.

There was a constant stream of mourning doves whipping up and down the river. Marsh hawks and an occasional prairie falcon pestered the ducks. It is always interesting to see how quickly the little ducks can get into the rushes and out of sight when the old hen sees a hawk and gives the word. Apparently the ducks have never learned that marsh hawks are beneficial.

For several days we fished and photographed. One afternoon we located a bunch of big fish feeding where there was a clump of cattail rushes growing out in the stream. In places there was mud in Silver Creek, and this was one of them. Usually you could wade through it without too much trouble to a gravel bottom. These fish looked as though they would furnish plenty of action for the cameras.

"Take the slow-motion camera out in the center of the stream," said the Director.

It was my understanding that this camera complete cost about $14,000, and it weighed over a hundred pounds. The boys all got into their boots, and they started taking her out, a piece at a time. When they got the tripod out and the camera in place, the river was less than a foot beneath the camera.

"Get in position," said the camera-man, and I started through the mud, up ahead of the camera.

"A little more to the right," said somebody. "That's too far; come back a ways."

"Turn her over," said the Director.

"Fish," said the camera-man.

I worked out line and sent a little brown spider 'way up near the clump of cattails. There was a dimple on the water, and the spider went under. I twitched my wrist, and the river exploded. About three pounds of rainbow shot out and then headed straight for me.

Now, under ordinary circumstances, I have a fair amount of that thing called "form" when I am fishing. I would particularly exercise any ability in this respect that I might have when fishing before a slow-motion camera, but this was different. I had to get in slack. I usually carry slack line coiled nicely in my left hand. But in this particular case I threw it behind me somewhere, and it mattered not where. On came the fish. I got a flash of him as he passed me; or to be more exact, as he went underneath me, because he went between my legs and on past the camera, where he jumped again.

"Cut!" yelled the Director.

I could hardly blame him this time. The only thing I hadn't done wrong was put my foot through my net. I was so tangled up in tackle that there was nothing left to do but wade over to the bank, reel in and start over again.

We went over Galena to get some pack-train shots in the Sawtooths. We camped on Redfish Lake. May I add that if ever there's a beautiful spot on earth it's the sight you see when you come over Galena and look down on the valleys of the Salmon, fenced in by Idaho's Sawtooth Mountains.

Dan went into the famous Middle Fork, where he caught cutthroats. It was a section designated as a wilderness area, but twenty-four miles from an auto road he found fishermen everywhere, and there was a CCC camp alongside Redfish. I talked to two of the boys.

One of the boys said that they were cleaning up the dead wood in the forest. The other said, "It's a racket. We don't do nuttin'." And from this unpopulated wilderness we went back to Silver Creek, where there was no one to bother us but the wild ducks and the doves and the trout.

Perhaps the high spot of the whole trip happened one morning when Dan and I were waiting in a beautiful stretch of river for the word to fish. Each of us had a good fish spotted, and we were all ready to go when we heard the words, "Turn her over. Fish."

We worked out line together and cast together, and two rainbows raised together and both were hooked and both of those dumb fish started downstream toward us, jumping as they came.

"Cut!" yelled the Director.

My fish had wrapped himself around Dan twice. Dan's fish had passed to the far side of me, and his line was around my neck.

Silver Creek is no place for a dub to fish!

Spare the Rod and Prove
a Point

LEE WULFF

*A top fly fisherman casts to—and lands—a salmon using no rod at
all. Not a trout-fishing piece, as you may point out, but surely one
that gave ultralight trout tackle a huge boost.* (January 1946)

What I wanted to get was absolute proof as to how essential the rod is in playing
a fish, especially a fish on a fly. I've sat in on sessions with other anglers before
the fire in fishing camps and doodled on angling banquet tables while the subject
of how light a rod should or should not be has come up for the full round of
discussion. Like most other factors in angling, this one is a thoroughly debatable
issue and one that gets its share of debating. And, as is usually the case, there
is much more debating than actual research. So I've gone a distance in making
up for that lack, leading me to an interesting experiment and some final conclusions.

Fishing for bass, muskie, trout and the rest of the American fresh-water game
fish has contributed to the experience on which I base my conclusions in regard
to the use of light rods; and light tackle for the big fish of the sea has given me
an understanding of the playing of all fish that I could never have attained without
it. For this article, however, I'm going to use the Atlantic salmon to illustrate.

The Atlantic salmon, when fresh-run from the sea, is not surpassed by any other fish in fresh water as a tester of tackle and angling skill. The length of their runs, due to their life in the sea, is attested by the amount of line required on the reels of the anglers who seek them, beginning around 150 yards and going upward. They are fish of the open water that depend upon their speed and strength for freedom. Weeds and snags are seldom encountered, and the battle is one of open water and constant motion. The final factor is their stored-up energy, sufficient strength to see them through almost a year of starvation.

In playing the fish the rod acts as a cushion to soften the shocks of the fish's movement on the weakest part of the tackle, which is usually the delicate leader or the grip of the hook in the fish's jaw. In a secondary measure it acts as a lever with which to guide the fish or move him in a given direction. In considering the length of the rod in comparison with the hundreds of yards of line out when playing a marlin, for example, the length of the rod becomes insignificant.

Long ago, when I began fishing for Atlantic salmon, I used a 9-foot 5-ounce fly-rod. All around me were two-handed weapons, wielded almost exclusively by men who firmly believed that salmon couldn't be played successfully on rods like mine. My experience with the 5-ounce rod led to the eventual use for salmon of my lightest trout rod—a two-piece, 7-foot, 2½-ounce rod. In those firelight and banquet-table discussions many experienced salmon fishermen still held that the 2½-ounce rod, even more than the 5-ounce rod, was incapable of handling a determined salmon and that a good "sulker" would leave me helpless.

But in 1940, the first year I used the 2½-ounce rod, none of my fish gave me special trouble and they came in at about the same speed as on the 5-ounce rod. An 18-pounder was my largest fish of that season, which still left room for the doubters to say: "You're just catching small ones. A 30-pounder will show up your small rod."

Then, in 1942, a 30-pounder clamped down on my fly and was landed in twenty-six minutes without difficulty. More than a dozen salmon of over 23 pounds came in on the light fly rod without trouble in that season and the season that followed. I still felt that anglers placed too much emphasis on the rod's importance in the playing of a fish and that the use of a light rod depends more on the angler's skill than on the fish's toughness. So I determined to make a test that would prove my point beyond the shadow of a doubt.

I decided to land a salmon with standard fly-fishing tackle except that I would use no rod at all. To do this I might have trolled a fly behind a canoe, which should have made the hooking of a salmon a relatively simple thing. But I wanted to do it by fly-casting, and to do that I needed a certain type of pool to work in. Last fall I found one that suited me.

A tall man with a good long casting arm can cast a fly for some distance without a rod. When you stand on a smooth floor, it's simple enough to cast a standard fly line thirty feet or more by hand. The pick-up is easy from a polished floor, but not nearly so easy from the water. What I needed was a salmon pool with a rock at its head on which I could stand to cast and salmon lying near that rock. In addition I needed a steady flow to straighten the line out quickly and hold it near the surface for an easy pick-up. Those conditions were all met by the Seal Pool on Newfoundland's Southwest River.

The water bends in close to a big rock at the head of the pool and grows deeper as the stream bed hollows out with the slowing down of the flow. There, in the deepening water, the salmon lie. My tackle consisted of a No. 8 low-water-type Dark Cahill, a six-foot leader of about 2½-pound breaking strain, an HCH nylon fly line and 120 yards of braided nylon backing on my 3⅛-inch fly reel. That was all. The short leader was a concession to the need for keeping the fly near the surface; a longer leader was more difficult to cast. The pool had not been fished before that season, and I hoped the fish wouldn't be too wary.

I took a long time in getting out to my position on the rock. My movements were slow and deliberate, and I remained motionless on the rock for a little while before I made the first cast. Then, holding the reel in my left hand and using my right arm for a rod, I began to cast while Pfc. Carl Lowe of a U.S. Army Search and Rescue Unit manned my camera and Charlie Bennett, guide extraordinary, looked on.

My first cast took the fly out about twenty-five feet, and it swung in a good arc on the retrieve. On about the third cast a fish swirled behind the fly and took a good look at it. He must have seen me in my exposed position on the rock, too, because he failed to rise again, and eventually I lengthened the line and fished the water below his position. After a dozen more casts another salmon rose, taking the fly in his mouth just far enough to be pricked, but not hooked solidly, as the line tightened.

Reeling in, I slid down from the rock to wade ashore and give the water a rest before trying again. Near the shore I slipped and went to my knees on a jagged rock, tearing my fragile pre-war waders at the knee.

By the time I had taken off my waders and hung them up to dry it was time to try again; so I waded out to the rock, this time without the benefit of waders, to make a second try. The rise was not long in coming, and I found myself fast to a flashing, leaping salmon that was off on a good run down the pool to the deep, slow water. My reel went over to my right hand, and I let the fish take line freely. He wound up the run that carried him well into the backing with a couple of tumbling leaps as a final flourish and swung into the current again to work upstream toward me.

Then my left hand moved up to where my right hand was held high in imitation of a fly rod, and the fingers picked up the reel handle. I took in line. It was almost as if I'd been using a light rod as far as the effect of the fish was considered. I moved my arm forward and back to help take up slack or give line speedily. The nylon line, resilient and springy, helped my arm and body movements in absorbing the sudden shocks at the salmon's end of our connection. Slowly the backing came back onto the reel, and the fly-casting line began to pile up on top of it. The salmon's first wild run and his sudden rushes had been safely met, and from there on his movements would be more predictable.

I took in line when I could, gave it when I had to and dropped my playing arm when the salmon broke water in his spray-scattering leaps. There was, as I had anticipated, little difference in playing a fish in this manner and playing one with my light fly rod. From long experience I sensed when his runs would start and when they'd end and when he'd roll and go into a sort of underwater head-shaking dance. Each time I was ready with the move to neutralize his action. In seven minutes he had unwound his bag of tricks and found none that worked. He was in close and groggy.

In this sport of catching fish I like to do the entire job myself. A fish is often tricked into coming within reach of another individual who snags him with a gaff, which does not give a true picture of the ability of one man to take one fish on certain tackle in a certain amount of time. I wanted to leave no loopholes; so I decided to land this one the hard way—by myself and by hand-tailing without the benefit of gaff, tailer or sandy beach.

Charlie had been making grunts of satisfaction on the bank. Carl, who had alternated between taking pictures of me on the rock and trying to get the fish in the air on one of his leaps, moved in closer as the range of action narrowed down.

The salmon was visibly weary. He had run and leaped himself out, just as any other fish does when properly played, tiring himself with his own efforts; not being killed by the leverage of the rod. He headed in under the rock, and I leaned far out over the edge to put on the pressure required to make him angle off into the open water again. The current picked him up and swung him sideways, the long silvery line of his belly flashing in the dull light of approaching evening. He came in again, and I held his head higher so that he slid against the rock on a slant that led him to the surface. The solid rock jarred him when he struck it and he whirled away, half leaping. When he stopped, I put the pressure on and led him in again.

All the line and part of the leader had passed in through the line guard of the reel when I shifted it from my right hand to my left and went down to one knee. With my right hand I reached out to let my fingers get into position to close on the narrow point at the base of his tail. At the right moment I clamped down in a hard grip and held.

Some salmon anglers claim that this tail grip has a paralyzing effect on the fish's spine. Whether that's true or not, I know that most fish properly hand-tailed offer little resistance and don't begin to kick up much of a fuss until the grip is released and they drop to the earth or to the bottom of the canoe. This fish was like that, quiet until I dropped him on the sandy shore.

He weighed almost ten pounds, and the time it took to bring him in was just shy of ten minutes. This is, I believe, the first time this feat has ever been performed, and it leads to inescapable conclusions. The first of them is that a rod is not essential to the proper playing of a fish. Instead, the rod is more nearly essential to casting the fly within reach of the fish. Few of the thousands of salmon I've hooked could have been hooked without the aid of a rod, but the big majority of them could have been landed as that one was, without a rod. Therefore, in choosing the rod the skilled angler should make his choice on the basis of the casting distance required rather than the size of the fish that must be handled on it.

As for a fair evaluation of the rod's position in fly-fishing, it depends upon the stream to be fished and the individual who is doing the fishing. The rod must be capable of getting the fly out to the water in which fish are lying. One man may need a much longer rod than another who is a better caster. A tall man has an advantage over a short one in the use of short, light rods.

The rod is of great aid in taking up slack quickly when playing a fish and in absorbing the shock of the fish's sudden starts or in giving adequate slack for his leaps. The less capable the angler is in sensing these maneuvers of the fish in advance and the poorer are his powers of coordination in making the necessary adjustments, the longer the rod he will need to make up for that lack.

To be able to fish with a very light rod or no rod at all is an achievement, but it doesn't prove that the use of the very lightest possible rod or no rod at all is a sensible way to fish. The rod to choose is one that balances the individual's skill, his need for long casts, and the amount of fatigue he wants to put up with in his fishing day. If he casts hour after hour through the long days of June, a light rod with line to balance it is a blessing. He can wind up at twilight with his arm as fresh as when he started. His sacrifice will have been in passing up the chance of reaching fish that the extra distance of a longer rod would have reached or the slight advantage he'd have gained in leverage to guide the fish or keep the line free from obstructions while being played.

The ability to get around in the stream to the proper playing position deter-mines to a large extent what sort of tackle the angler needs. Those tough sulkers become just ordinary fish when the fisherman keeps downstream of them and keeps the pressure on them to a point where they're using up energy rapidly, whether they stay in one spot or move off. For the angler whose canoeman doesn't want to bother to move him to the right position or to the man whose legs and wading ability won't get him around the stream in good shape a rod of fair length and tackle of fair strength is a necessity if many fish are to be saved.

It all boils down to individual ability, and even in the case of the most gifted individuals there is a limit to the lightness of the rod, which is dictated by the casting distance required and wind that must be bucked or other casting difficulties. If an angler insists on fishing with a rod that is too weak to give him an opportunity to reach a number of fish equal to that reached by his neighbors, he's handicapping himself, with his only possible gain lying in being able to cast for a longer time. If he wants to prove he can perform a certain light-rod feat, the thing to do is to accomplish that feat enough times to satisfy himself as to his ability and then settle back to using the tackle that will give him the greatest pleasure yet won't penalize his chances of hooking fish. And these conclusions, I believe, hold for all types of angling.

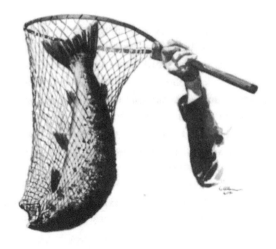

Underrated Cutthroat

RODERICK L. HAIG-BROWN

The Northwest's most eloquent spokesman raised his voice in praise of our least-known, least-appreciated species of trout. (April 1951)

Of the three true trouts, the cutthroat is the least regarded. The rainbow is a knight in shining armor, spread from his native Pacific slope to the four corners of the world, known to anglers everywhere as a bold, bright, gallant performer. The brown trout has the whole of angling tradition behind him. He is a shade conservative, perhaps, but very handsome, very wise and cunning in his ways, quick of eye and carefully selective in his feeding.

The cutthroat, however, seems to be thought of as a backwoods roughneck, somewhat unpredictable and vaguely undesirable. I think Western fishermen have always tended to underrate their fish. There is the old story of the British officer's report on Oregon Territory: "Country not worth a damn. Salmon won't take the fly." Even today many fishermen perversely cling to the belief that steelhead can be caught only on salmon roe, and there was a long reluctance of Western fishermen to believe that their trout would rise to the dry fly.

The cutthroat is the most widely varying trout I know and, at his best, the most beautiful. Although not as dependable a surface feeder as the brown trout, nor as brilliant a fighter as the rainbow, he is a very good fly fisherman's trout, with qualities of his own that make him just as worth while.

In most Pacific Coast streams open to salt water, the cutthroat is primarily a sea-run fish. He seems to make only a partial migration, usually afer a year or more in the river, and can be caught at almost any time of the year in the river's estuary or off its mouth. He ascends his river again not merely to spawn but to feed, taking quick advantage of times of plenty—the spring run of salmon fry, the summer abundance of caddis larvae, the wasted eggs of spawning salmon in the fall. In this sea-run form the cutthroat is a magnificent trout, thick and full-bodied and very strong, weighing up to four pounds and sometimes more than that—a powerful fighter and a free riser.

The sea-runs give such varied fishing, all the way from the use of No. 16 dry flies in the rivers to silver-bodied No. 6's in the estuaries, that I am never sure where I enjoy them most. I have found some of my keenest pleasure off the mouths of tiny unknown streams up the coast, beyond the reach of automobile roads. One never knows just what to expect.

I recall a late evening, when the tide was far out, the creek a narrow trickle across the tide-flats. Two or three casts without a fish, then a long cast to the head of a sodden, seaweed-covered log. A sudden bulge in smooth, shining water not six inches deep, the humped ripple following the fly, the boil and the pull. One knows then that they are around, and fishing really means something.

Offhand, I would say that the lake cutthroats mean less to me. Then I remember a catch of half a dozen green-backed two-pounders from the shallow, sandy slough at the head of Mace Lake. I remember sunny April days with a breeze making white-caps on Tierce Lake and clean ¼-pounders taking hold at every cast. I remember big fish, really big fish, almost impossible to move to the fly, seen cruising along the shores of the big lakes. I remember a difficult cast along a heavy-limbed log and the savage rise of 24-inch fish in a lake of half-pounders.

There is the other side of the picture. Pleasant lakes hopelessly overcrowded with poor, dark, little fish. Lakes too warm in summer with logy, half-starved, wormy fish. But it is the water, not the fish, that is at fault here. Too many coast lakes are low producers with good spawning areas; the cutthroat does at least as well in them as any other trout, probably somewhat better. The good lakes show clearly enough how well he can fill the angler's needs if he is given a chance.

Still moving up the watershed, away from salt water, we find the cutthroat in the mountain streams that feed the larger coast lakes. They are quite big, some of these streams, very clear and very cold. If the loggers haven't arrived there yet, their banks are heavily timbered and their bottoms are fine gravel, making for shallow pools and long swift glides close under the banks. May-flies and sedges hatch well, and the cutthroat is at his best there, clean and bright and firm, a free yet by no means suicidal surface feeder.

Most of the cutthroats in these good streams are fairly small—a 12-inch fish is normal, but one can always set a voluntary limit of 14 inches and still have something to show for it, and most days will yield at least one 16-incher. There is the possibility, especially near the lake, that some 5- or 10-pound monster will have wandered in for a spell of sunlight—a remote possibility, but real enough for the wise angler to keep it always in mind.

I remember a short afternoon on such a stream last summer. It was a very wet day, with a hard wind thrashing the tops of the firs and cedars high above the water, but the stream itself lay across the storm and it was almost quiet there. As I waded cautiously upstream May-flies were hatching freely, drifting down in steady procession to show where fish should be lying; but no fish showed. I stopped on a gravel bar to watch a smooth, swift glide tight against the far bank. Cedar and alder limbs dropped over it every five or ten feet of its length, and the May-flies swept swiftly by, far under the trailing branches.

For half an hour nothing showed. Then there was a quiet rise under the upstream alder. It was repeated, and in a little while I saw that two fish were rising right under the cedar branches, another just above them, and another under the downstream alder. It was the perfect challenge to any dry-fly fisherman, and I accepted it willingly. I got the fish, all five of them, but it took me two hours and an incredible number of casts to do it. Never have I enjoyed two hours of fishing more thoroughly!

The Coachman

JOHN ALDEN KNIGHT

A famous angler (and the originator of the Solunar Tables) explores the genealogy of, and the countless variations on, the world's best-known fly. (September 1952)

It was a warm June evening, slightly on the sultry side, and the trout in the long, deep pool were rising to drifting insects of four or five different varieties. Perhaps I had best amend that statement. The insects were drifting and the trout were rising, evidently feeding at the surface. It was up to me to discover, if I could, what variety of the many that were available appealed to the fancy of those fussy fish, to the complete exclusion of all others.

We had chosen this particular pool with a purpose. For two years it had been the home of a monster brown trout. This particular fish had been seen by many anglers, hooked and lost by several, and his probable weight was a matter of interesting conjecture. Estimates varied, ranging from 8 pounds to 11 or 12 pounds. My son Dick, who had played this fish for an hour and a half, only to lose him when the small hook pulled free as the big trout lay on his side not six feet from the net, placed his guess at between 10 and 11 pounds. For two seasons I had watched the pool, hoping against hope that I would have the good fortune to find the big fellow feeding to a surface hatch.

Up at the foot of the riffle, handy to the source of supply, at least twenty fish were feeding actively, and my companion took his position there to start operations for the evening. By force of habit, I suppose, I waded out into the deeper, quieter water opposite a jumble of large rocks along the far shore. There weren't so many trout rising here, but this is where the big boy lived, and I wanted to be on hand just in case.

I settled my wading brogues in comfortable positions on the rocky bed of the stream and gave my attention to watching a couple of active feeders, trying to learn something of their selection. Just as I had decided on a size 14 Cahill Quill and was reaching for my fly box, about thirty feet away the surface was broken as a huge snout engulfed a drifting fly. Glory be! The big fellow, after two years of patient waiting, was actually feeding to a drifting hatch.

Carefully, with fingers that trembled slightly, I tied on my best Dark Cahill Quill and tested the knot, the leader and the line end, making sure that all was in sound working order. Then I cast the fly above the spot where the big fish had fed, placing the leader carefully in an upstream curve. Slowly the fly drifted over the spot marked X. Nothing happened.

Experimentally I offered the fly to a smaller fish some twenty feet to one side, and it was taken solidly on the first drift. With a minimum of fuss I brought in the little fish and released him. Then I stood quietly and waited, meanwhile making mental note of the other flies that were drifting.

Before long the big boy rose and fed again. This time I showed him a Light Cahill. He refused that one also; so I picked up another small trout with it, released him, and changed flies again. Once more the big trout rose and took a drifting fly, and once more he refused the artificial. In the course of an hour I had offered the big fellow seven different patterns, and he wanted none of them. Still he kept on feeding.

By this time it was getting dusk and I was running out of ideas. Seven smaller trout had taken my flies without hesitation, but the big trout insisted on naturals. A search of my fly box turned up a spentwing Coachman, freshly tied and unused. It resembled nothing on which the large fish was feeding, but I knew it to be a good fish-getter. As a last desperate measure I tied it on, straining my eyes in the gathering dusk. Then I drifted it down over his feeding station. On the first drift, up came the big nose, and the spentwing Coachman disappeared from the surface. My heart turned completely over as I raised the rod tip and pulled home the barb.

For several seconds the fish didn't move; he simply sat there and thought it over. I applied more rod pressure, and away he went, upstream. When he reached shallower water, he turned and headed downstream. I took in line until he had passed me; then the line melted once more from the reel drum. I knew I couldn't turn him with such light tackle; so I backed into shallow water and waded down the bar toward him. At last he stopped and turned of his own accord.

For ten minutes the big trout swam about the pool. I don't suppose I could be credited with playing him. Such a thing as controlling his movements was out of the question. All I could do was to hang on, keep tight line, and hope for the best. The best, however, was not fated to happen. As he passed me on his third or fourth trip upstream my line went slack. There was no sudden strain, no jar against the leader; the line was tight one moment, the next it hung slack from my rod tip.

With heavy heart I reeled in and inspected the hook. It was in good shape, sharp and factory-new, but it had pulled free, and that was that. Then I looked at the fly. To be sure, the fish had not been landed—it is not easy to land fish of that magnitude on a dry fly tied on a tiny hook. Just the same, the spentwing Coachman had delivered the goods again. It had hooked a large fish where seven carefully tied exact imitations had failed. That, I find, is quite typical of the Coachman series.

The Coachman is not a new pattern by any means. Its origin goes back to an earlier century—for that matter, back some 2,000 years to the original trout fly, the Macedonian, which had the same basic color pattern minus the white wing. In the early eighteen hundreds, the royal family of Great Britain had a coachman named Tom Bosworth. Tom was a fisherman and, from what we can learn, tied his own flies.

Bosworth had found that the Brown Hackle, or Red Hackle, as it was then called, was an excellent trout fly. Perhaps with the idea of giving this fly a bit more flash to attract the attention of the trout and to enable him to see the fly more plainly when fishing it in clear water, or to turn out a fly that was his own pattern, Bosworth added a pair of white wings to it and gave it a new name. He called it the Coachman.

The original dressing of the fly was as follows: body, bronze peacock herl; legs, a red hen's hackle; wings, part of almost any white wing pinion. The original pattern had no tail.

Fly tyers since the days of Izaak Walton have evidently not been content to leave established standard patterns unaltered and in their original form. Thus it was not long until Tom Bosworth's Coachman, a Brown Hackle with white wings, was given what the Scotch tyers call blae wings instead of white wings. These wings were made from clippings from wing pinions of the starling. Thus altered, the fly was called the Leadwing Coachman. Still the dressing had no tail.

The next step in the process of adulteration or, if you like, development was the Royal Coachman. Harold Smedley in his book *Fly Patterns and their Origins* gives the history of this fly as follows:

In 1878 John Haily had a shop at 320 Henry Street, New York City, where he tied trout and salmon flies, gave instructions in fly tying and sold fly-tying materials. To suit the whims of an unidentified customer, he tied some Coachmen with a red silk band in the body and with a few stylets of barred wood-duck feather as a tail. He thought this creation to be rather handsome; so he sent some samples of it to Charles Orvis of Manchester, Vermont. Orvis, his family and some friends looked over this new Coachman and christened it the Royal Coachman.

When Theodore Gordon, under the remote but constant guidance of Halford and Skues in England, began his famous research with floating or dry flies on the waters of the Neversink and the Beaverkill of New York State, it was only natural that he should tie dry versions of the standard wet-fly patterns, both English and American. This included the Coachman and the Royal Coachman. I can't say with certainty that he included the Leadwing Coachman in his dry patterns, but the probabilities are that he did.

Gordon, as you no doubt know, depended in part for his livelihood upon the sale of trout flies to the old-time Catskill fly fishermen. Two of his regular customers were Guy R. Jenkins and the late Leslie S. Petrie, both of New York City. On one fishing trip Guy Jenkins saw Gordon use some Royal Coachmen that were tied with what we now know as "fan wings." These were the tips of small white feathers from the breast of a male wood duck. Jenkins took a fancy to this fly, and until Gordon died he ordered a supply of them annually. Petrie went him one better. He had Gordon tie his fan wings with a yellow silk band in the body instead of the then conventional red band, and this alteration was called the Petrie fanwing Royal Coachman, or, more briefly, the Petrie Royal.

For some years I had in my collection a size 14 fanwing Royal that was tied by Gordon in 1907. This fly was given to me by Leslie Petrie and the date fixed by him from his Gordon correspondence. This fly is now in the Gordon Collection of the Anglers' Club of New York.

There have been many variations of the Coachman since the days of Tom Bosworth. Consider, for instance, the Royal Coachman, the Leadwing Coachman, the California Coachman, the bivisible Coachman, the Cahill Coachman, the Crazy Coachman, the spentwing Coachman, the more recent Teal, and goodness knows what other deviations. Regardless of variation in design, the fact remains that they all catch fish. There seems to be something about the basic combination of bronze peacock herl and brown hackle that has strong and proven trout appeal. Not only that; all game fish, without any exception that I know of, will go for the Coachman variations in a large way, from the lordly Atlantic salmon of the northern Atlantic Coast to the flashy bonefish of the Florida Keys.

The Coachman and its relatives seem to lend themselves better to the complexities of brown-trout fishing than does any other pattern. In the matter of selectivity and all round perversity the brown trout of our Eastern waters just about tops the list. To be sure, Atlantic salmon can be superselective now and then. So can squaretail or rainbow or black bass. But none of them, at least in my experience, can compare with the brown trout of our central Pennsylvania streams and those of the Catskills and the Adirondacks of New York State. When these fussy feeders settle down to a meal of drifting insects, they can be about as contrary as any fish I know.

Selectivity in feeding is a peculiar characteristic when you stop to consider it closely. A brown trout in a mountain stream, when he is not occupied with a drifting hatch, seems to relish any of the standard patterns, such as a Quill Gordon, a Hendrickson or one of the varous Cahills. If he is in the mood to feed, he will take just about any standard pattern that you care to drift over him. Yet once let him start to feed to an established hatch of insects, and flies that he would have relished half an hour previously will be completely ignored.

One afternoon on the East Branch of the Delaware River near Arena, New York, I found a school of brown trout rising actively in a smooth run flowing along by a rocky wall that supported the railroad bed above it. From my position in the shallower water I could see no flies on the surface. The water was too deep for me to wade out into the current to see what was drifting. Nothing to be done but stand there and attempt to identify the hatch through the laborious process of trial and error.

Not being able to see insects on the surface, I concluded that the fish were feeding to a developing hatch or one that was drifting spent. I tried nymphs and wet flies of all sizes, colors and shapes. Nothing doing, but the trout kept on feeding. At last, more in desperation than anything else, I tied on a fanwing Royal Coachman, size 12. When this came drifting down with the current, it looked as big as a seagull. To my great surprise, a fair trout took it solidly on the first drift. An autopsy of this fish disclosed that the trout were taking some tiny wormlike larvae, something I had not seen before and, incidentally, have not seen since. Having nothing like it, I sat down on the bank to smoke and think it over, meanwhile rummaging about among the flies in my fly boxes.

Close inspection of the larva showed that it had a well-defined head and thorax and a segmented body, similar to that of a quill-type fly. As a makeshift measure I trimmed the wings, hackle and tail from a wet Gray Quill, size 16, and with this affair, which looked almost like a bare hook, I actually did manage to take a few of those trout before the rise came to an end. Had it not been for the timely aid of that fanwing Royal, I would still be wondering what those trout were taking.

As I say, when brown trout are hungry and ready to feed, almost any well-dressed standard pattern will take them, always provided they have not settled down to steady feeding to an existing hatch. When the stream is quiet and the fish are not moving, however, a man must use care in his selection of flies if he would take fish. There are several flies we call fish finders that seem to have the capacity at least to make the trout show themselves, notably the gray and brown gold-bodied variants, the spiders, etc. Probably as good as any other for this purpose is either the fanwing Royal Coachman or the bivisible Royal Coachman. These will not only raise fish; they will usually hook them as well, as they are smaller than the other fish finders and easily taken.

One trout season a local fishing club was kind enough to extend to me the privilege of fishing its waters. Naturally, I killed no trout from that stream, but it gave me the opportunity to list the fly hatches and to fish in undisturbed water where I could finish some experiments then in progress. One day on the stream I met one of the club members, who complained that the trout were particularly uncooperative. He had fished over a mile of water with his favorite pattern of Cahill and had turned up only three small trout, all of them squaretails. No brown trout had so much as looked at his fly.

This man is a good fisherman and usually brings in his share. After he had left me I decided to try something that had been in the back of my mind for some time. I had always felt that the Coachman was a grand fly to use when the going was tough, and this seemed like a good time to make sure. So I walked down to the place near the clubhouse where he had started fishing and began to fish up through the same water. The fly I had chosen was a size 12 bivisible Royal Coachman.

I took my time and fished carefully, exploring every pocket and hiding place. When I arrived at the place of our previous meeting, I had hooked and released forty-eight brown trout. As there is not enough difference in our fishing techniques to account for this variance in results, I am convinced that if he had changed to one of the Coachman series he no doubt would have done as well as I.

Have you ever noticed that some flies seem to have greater appeal to large fish than do other flies? There are some excellent standard patterns that on some days will take small and medium-sized trout to beat the band, but they simply do not produce large fish. Conversely, other flies appeal to large fish, but they do not produce many smaller trout. The spiders and variants are typically in this group. By and large, however, the Coachman series seems to appeal to all sizes.

Some years ago the Pennsylvania Fish Commission instituted a sport-fishing playground known as the Fishermen's Paradise. Near the city of Bellefonte, a mile of Spring Creek has been set aside for this project. The area has been fenced in, the grounds have been landscaped, and the stream is kept copiously stocked with large trout of all three varieties. A handsome clubhouse has been built, and over the fireplace in the main lounge hangs the mount of a brown trout which is almost 30 inches long and which weighed, while still alive, slightly more than 9 pounds. The lure? You guessed it—a No. 10 Royal Coachman wet fly.

This is not an isolated instance. A friend of mine has a summer camp on the bank of one of our large trout streams. On a June day in 1949 he chanced to stroll down to the edge of the high bank, and there, near the far shore, he saw a man fighting what evidently was a large fish. The battle had arrived at a stalemate of sorts; evidently the trout was sulking near the bottom of the pool while the angler stood knee-deep, with fly rod erect, applying constant pressure on the fish.

My friend watched for a while and then called to the fisherman, "How big is that fish?"

"Don't know. Ain't seen him yet," was the reply.

There being little action, my friend went in to lunch and then drove to the store for supplies. Some two hours later he went back to the bank of the stream. There, on the far side, stood the same fisherman, rod erect, fighting a large fish. My friend called to him, "I see you hooked another big one."

Without looking up the man replied, "Nope. Same one."

After a battle that lasted somewhat more than three hours the fish was landed. It was a big brown trout weighing a shade over 7 pounds. Again the lure was a No. 10 Royal Coachman wet fly.

In June, 1950, another friend of mine who was fishing in the same general area hooked and landed in one afternoon two brown trout that weighed 4 pounds and 6½ pounds respectively. Again the lure that did the execution was a size 10 Royal Coachman wet fly. No doubt about it, the Royal Coachman does appeal to large trout.

Back in the early days of American trout fishing, before the brown trout was an established citizen of our waters, fancy flies were very much the order of the day. Brook trout (*Salvelinus fontinalis*) are not insistent upon exact imitations of the natural insects. Flies with color and flash appeal to them; such things as the Professor, Parmachenee Belle, Wickham's Fancy, Montreal and Silver Doctor are taken readily. Quite naturally the Coachman series—as many of them as then existed—fitted into this list very nicely.

With the increased interest that developed over the years in brown-trout fishing, particularly after the introduction of the dry fly, the use of fancy patterns gradually fell into the discard. Replacing them were the typically American patterns such as the Quill Gordon, the Hendrickson or the Cahill series. All of these are of the exact-imitation classification. In other words, all of them imitate or suggest certain types of insect hatches. Surprisingly, however, the Coachman series has held its own with these comparative newcomers. Obviously a Royal Coachman looks like nothing else on earth save another Royal Coachman, yet it compares favorably as a fish-getter with any of the exact imitations.

The late Lee Allen of Philadelphia had an interesting theory regarding trout flies. He maintained that trout flies, even tied with the finest craftsmanship, are at best merely crude suggestions of the natural insects and that there is no such thing as an exact imitation. Place side by side a natural insect and its artificial counterpart (as it is conventionally tied today) and compare them. The resemblance is exceedingly slight. Thus he contended that size is the important factor, other things such as color and shape being relatively secondary. Any proven standard pattern, whose color is not too radical, would, according to Allen, take fish just as well as the exact imitation of a drifting hatch so long as the size of that fly was the same as the size of the hatch.

I knew Lee Allen quite well. He was a meticulous fisherman, a perfectionist. Moreover, he had the courage of his convictions. The fly that he chose to prove his contention was the Leadwing Coachman. It is classed as a fancy, but he knew it to be a dependable fish-getter; so he selected it in preference to any of the established exact imitations, as these, in view of the seasonal color cycle in hatches, are apt to clash too much with various color phases of the naturals at one time or another. The Leadwing Coachman is more or less neutral and, moreover, dependable; so that was his choice. In the fly boxes that he carried with him he had only wet and dry Leadwing Coachmen in sizes that ranged from No. 2 to No. 20. Lee may or may not have been completely right in his size theory. Again, it may have been that he was a finished angler. The fact remains that he always managed to bring in his share of trout.

One day in Paradise Creek in Pennsylvania's Pocono Mountains I watched Lee Allen make an interesting experiment. There was no hatch drifting at the time, the sun was bright, the water was clear and the stream was void of activity. Lee had located a particularly fine trout the evening before; so, knowing the home of his fish, he set out to show me that it is possible to stir up activity if you have the skill and the patience. He took his position in the stream downstream and somewhat to one side of the rock where this fish lived. Then he began to cast.

Time after time his No. 12 Leadwing Coachman drifted down the natural thread of the current. On the two hundred and seventy-sixth cast the big trout rose and took the fly solidly. Maybe a hatch could be created just as well with some other pattern. I wouldn't know, as I certainly haven't the patience for the tiresome business of creating hatches. The fact remains that the Leadwing Coachman, in a size that might be considered average, certainly turned the trick.

I have put Allen's theory to good use many times when I was having trouble in trying to find a fly that would match the drifting hatch. It doesn't seem to make much difference what Coachman is used, either, just so long as the size is right. For instance, consider this one that my son Dick came up with not long ago.

Every fisherman has been confronted at one time or another with a school of trout that are feeding on drifting midges, tiny little black flies, usually drifting spent. Dick found such a school and, through the devious means of hooking a luckless chub that was rising in company with the trout, he learned what was drifting by performing a quick post mortem. Not having any No. 20 midges, he put on, of all things, a No. 20 Royal Coachman. Goodness only knows where he got the thing or who would have the patience to tie it in the first place, but he found it in his fly box; so he tied it on. For the next hour or so he worked his way up through that feeding run, hooking midging trout. To be sure, he lost most of them on that tiny hook, but he was able to make them take the fly. That is not easy with midging fish.

For a long time I have felt that the trout do not regard any of the Coachman series as a fly. Why they take one of them I'll never know, but they do, and I'm sure they recognize the fraud before they take it, as the manner of their rising is not the same as when they take a natural. Hundreds of times I have watched feeding fish drift up and take naturals from the surface without making a splash or causing any disturbance. Then a Coachman—plain, leadwing, spentwing or fanwing Royal—comes drifting along. Invariably the rise is what we call a smash rise, with a splash and a flurry of spray.

Every fisherman, I suppose, carries many more flies than he can possibly use. I know I do. Moreover, I carry patterns that I rarely, if ever, have occasion to use. About all they do is take up useful room in my fly boxes. However, I'm learning. More and more each year the seldom-used patterns are being relegated to the stock box in the car, thereby making room for more Coachmen.

I'm more and more inclined to agree with Lee Allen. If I have a Coachman in almost any of the patterns in the correct size, I do just about as well as the next fellow who sticks to exact imitations. To be sure, the idea is not completely fool-proof, and Coachmen don't always solve the problem. But then, what fishing idea does work out one hundred per cent? I think I'll stay with them, at least until better patterns come along.

Midwinter Night's Dream

HOWARD T. WALDEN 2d

How a green-hackled "joke" fly, created during the doldrums of winter,
turned out to be the real thing, after all. (February 1953)

Along about Thanksgiving I said to Tom Garrison: "Why not do something constructive this winter? You know how to tie flies, but you never start tying 'em until two weeks before opening day. Now, with four months ahead in which you'll do nothing but dream about the Big Stony—"

"I'm planning to hibernate this winter," Tom interrupted, "like a bear. I told the telephone girl to ring my number early in the morning of April first."

"Okay, I'll hibernate with you. But we'll have your vise and some mandarin necks, peacock herl—all that stuff, and a couple of tall glasses. And come April we'll be set with forty dozen Leadwing Coachmen, Quill Gordons, Hare's Ears. . . ."

That was how it started. We planned to amass a sufficient backlog of the dull, orthodox patterns that kill the Big Stony browns to keep us in business a whole season. While the snow rustles against the window-pane April, May and June are far off and fabulous, and fishing seems as easy and unworried as things remote in the future always appear. I would put another log on the fire and watch another quill body sprout wings in the little vise. Tom would apply the last dab of lacquer to seal off the final turn of thread around the hackles of a Wickham's Fancy, loosen the vise jaws, drop the fly on the green-felt table top to see how nicely it landed, relax in his chair, take a draw on his pipe and say, "So." The single syllable was eloquent with accomplishment. Another fly tied, another trout as good as caught, another step toward the sum of our preparedness for April.

It was nice and comfortable for a while. Because I don't tie flies very well my function was to keep the fire from getting low and to provide a certain moral support for Tom's industry.

But one evening, after a couple of weeks of building a small stockpile of Cahills, Hendricksons and others of that drab, murderous ilk, Tom was suddenly inspired. "Look," he enthused. "Let's try something different. A red-squirrel body, nylon-quilled, a mallard tail, indigo hackles and wood-duck wings, eh? Do you want it long-shanked or short shanked—No. 10, 12 or 14?"

Finally it came to full flower, looking like no trout fly we had ever seen, and again Tom said "So." We gazed at his conceit under the magnifying glass, floated it in a transparent dish and looked up at it from beneath to get a trout's-eye view, and told ourselves in all seriousness that it was good for a 20-incher. We thought of the wood-thrush-haunted dusks along the Big Stony and how the Pasture Pool would look, black below its murmuring riffle. A lunker just had to be there, all primed to grab this fantastic hybrid.

"I'd rather catch a fish on that baby than six on a Cahill," Tom said. "Let's try something else, a bit different. I'm fed up with the theory that a fly has to be dull to be smart. Imagine such beautiful things as the Parma Belle and Silver Doctor being out of fashion, mere museum pieces."

So we decided to spark a renaissance in fly-fishing, bringing color—judiciously, of course—into our flies.

We started judiciously enough, but one fall from grace leads to another, as the moralists say; and a couple of hackle feathers, dyed a pale indigo, led to whole cockerel necks dyed royal purple, emerald green, cerulean blue. Nature ran out of colors early in our campaign, and those we improvised with dyes would have set any barnyard flock to screaming. We made an orange-and-black, flamboyant fanwing on a bass hook and called it Old Nassau. When the dyes ran out, we pushed our experiments into the field of design, ultimately achieving a double fly—a four-winged, two tailed job seemingly fixed in a mating act—and called it Wickham's Ecstasy.

Tom took a couple of hundred such steps toward April, announcing each with a "So" as he let the fly drop on the green felt. It was like checking off on some tabulating machine the step-by-step passage of winter. And we believed in them all while the snow eddied against the window. All fishing is so easy in that off-season interlude. Winter is the angler's time to dream, and in his dreams his flies are right and his casts true. There are no hang-ups or snags in this winter fishing, no aching legs and wrists, no waders full of cold water. There are only trout.

But spring came, as it always does, like an alarm clock on Monday morning. With her spurious reputation as the time of poets and young love, spring is the realist among seasons. There was a day when my winterlong faith began to lose its solid core. Suddenly, one noontime, as March was running the last of winter down the gutters, a tackle-store window brought me back to fishing. Here, in these bright new gadgets, was the real thing again—fishing as it is, full of all its hope and striving, promise and pain.

I didn't need any flies, of course, after our winter's industry. But once inside, I took a look at 'em, anyway. Here they were again, like moths out of their winter cocoons. I pored over the neatly labeled trays, looking for something new. Had the fly tyers, for once in their lives, used their imaginations, as Tom and I had used ours? The labels didn't indicate it. Here were the ancient standbys, as I had seen them every spring for more years than I like to count: the March Browns, Cowdungs, Royals, the he and she Beaverkills, the Whirling Duns and Ginger Quills. The old recital of names. Beautiful names, yes. But what about that green-and-gold thing that Tom and I had made the night of the blizzard, the one we called Brodhead's Incomprehensible? Why wasn't something like that here—at 50 cents apiece, $6 a dozen? Could it be that no demand for it existed because it wasn't likely to take a fish? And all that stuff from the magenta-dyed neck—the magenta-hackled, silver-bodied spiders? It was hard to remember how good they all had looked when it was 10 degrees outside and a great feat of natural chemistry had yet to melt a foot of snow and bring the buds on the forsythia and the geese on the south wind before our fancy flies could feel the bounce of a riffle in a real April stream.

From their show cases the killers spoke to me again of the gross satisfactions of a weighty creel. "If you want to get trout," they said in their special language, "here we are, and you'd better respect the wisdom of the years." Come to think of it, maybe Tom and I should have tied more of the orthodox flies. Our theory about the fancy stuff was pretty, yet we shouldn't slight those members of the old guard that have a way of bringing home the bacon.

I didn't revert whole hog to the extreme right, of course. The winter fancy died harder than that.

Opening day came in warm and dry-flyish, the water low for April. Just to be stubborn, I would start with one of our fancy Dans. A sparse hatch of a yellowish fly was astir as we approached the stream. "See that?" Tom pointed out. "A Light Cahill is my baby to start this season off."

An old meat-in-the-pot fly, the Cahill, at whose eminence in history Tom had sneered last winter, if I remembered right. I reminded him of that and added that I'd back the lavender and tea-rose job we named Campbell's Lunacy.

"Oh, *that*," he said. "Well, I kind of think the Cahill—for the first fish, you know. After that maybe I'll give some of our beauties a play."

I called him a sniveling coward, but he pretended not to hear.

An hour with the Campbell's Lunacy was pleasant enough. Nothing happened, but it was nice just to cast again and to feel the press of the stream after the long months away. And of course my gamble with the C. L. proved me a man of character, a sportsman able to resist the easy, tempting thing. But, after all, I did come up here for trout. I sat down on a streamside rock, took out my fly box and looked inside. A lot of good old stuff there from last year. Four or five Light Cahills, for instance.

Behind me I heard a voice above the sound of the water. "Any luck?" It was one of the younger members of the March Browns, passing on his way upstream.

"Nothing—yet," I said, with the inference "but give me time."

"No? What fly you using?"

"It's a little invention," I replied feebly. "It hasn't any name, I guess." Of course, I should have confronted this upstart like a man, asserting, "I am fishing the Campbell's Lunacy, sir, whose exquisite genius I have kept out of the manuals for beginners. It tempts no fish under three pounds." But I didn't.

"Got any Light Cahills?" the youth asked.

"Yes. I was about to change to one."

"You better," he said. "They're hitting 'em." He had in his tone the smug authority that every man somehow achieves when he has trout in his creel.

"You do any business?" I asked.

He lifted his creel lid and drew out a 13-inch brown and a 10-inch native. "Both on the Light Cahill," he reported, confirming his unimpeachable wisdom.

That ended my go at the Campbell's Lunacy. Indeed, it almost ended my whole winter's dream, the sum total of our hours of industry before the fire.

But not quite. There was a time, before the trout season waned to its late-summer slack, when one of our private brands did have its moment. With a backlog of four trout in my creel—victims, of course, of one of the meat flies— I could afford to speculate that evening. It was the rare sort of moment that comes when the weight of my creel allows me to gamble. Now, when all my conservative instincts told me a Pale Evening Dun would draw a good fish from the darkening pool upstream, was the time to get out a certain pink-bodied, emerald-hackled, spentwing beauty from last winter's harvest. "It's some kind of a dun," Tom had announced dreamily over his glass. "Let's call it the What-Have-We-Dun."

It had looked trouty then; it could be trouty now. There is a brief period of every year, usually a few days in June, when the Big Stony's browns exhibit a sort of holiday spirt, an irresponsible abandon in their choice of food. Here was a soft June dusk, with the streamside woods wet and clean and steaming after a shower, the wood thrushes singing in the washed trees. A good trout rolled up lazily thirty feet away, exposing his spotted flanks as he went down. If there was ever a time to try the bright coinage of our winter, it was now. Let the pork-and-beans flies stay in the box. This trout was playful rather than hungry, a little drunk with the fat and easy living of June. The What-Have-We-Dun could be a nice liqueur after a full meal.

Play up to his mood, I told myself. Don't make him work by casting below him, where he'll have to turn and rush for the fly as it floats down-current. Put it above the point of his rise, so that he can take it lazily as it comes opposite.

A few minutes later the miracle had been wrought—a pound-and-a-half brown had actually taken that dream bug, that caprice in feathers, that absurd fantasy of a winter's night. In five minutes I was bringing him in, a tired fish now, fair-hooked by the What-Have-We-Dun. I eased him over the net, lifted him clear, took him ashore and administered the coup de grace. Laid out on a flat rock, with the tape on him, he was 15¼ inches long. I stowed him in my creel. Maybe this was the way, after all—the bizarre thing that no one ever uses. A fly I had ceased to regard as legitimate had killed the best fish of the day.

It would be nice to surprise Tom when he stopped on his way upstream and asked, "What'd you take him on?" A hundred times I had met that inquiry with one or another of the old expected names: "On a Leadwing Coachman" or another of the elect. It was never news, never a surprise. But now at last it would be.

In a few minutes Tom came up the path, accompanied by an old-time March Brown member who used to fish the Big Stony before we had a club there. The old boy and I greeted each other. Then Tom said, "Well?"

For answer I opened the creel. They looked inside, where the big one lay on top, and both said at once, "What on?"

I gave them the name, held up the What-Have-We-Dun, still on the tippet, and watched the swift, incredulous surprise jump into Tom's face.

The old fellow said, "Let's see that fly." He took it in his fingers for a close scrutiny, turned it around, held it up to the waning light. "Yep," he said, as if to himself, "That's what it is." Then, to me: "What was that name you called it?"

"The What-Have-We-Dun. It's a crazy thing Tom and I dreamed up last winter, and we gave it a crazy name, just for the hell of it."

"I'll say you did," he said. "Craziest name I ever heard for the old June Witch."

Tom and I looked at him, then at each other. "You mean—" I said, "you mean it's a real fly?"

"You bet it is—or it was. I haven't seen one of them on the Big Stony in a long while. But years ago we used to see 'em, only a small hatch or two each year, and always about this time of June. Then for some reason they disappeared.

But when they came on, in the old days, they were always the hottest thing you could use. I've tied dozens of 'em, about like yours. Your hackles are a little too bright a green."

That's how to take the edge off a miracle, I was thinking. In all that fabulous production of flies, Tom and I were bound to imitate nature, without knowing it, at least once. The What-Have-We-Dun was no longer a dream bug. It had lost caste, perhaps on that account, but it had gained on another. A 15-inch brown is no slouch of a fish, even in the Big Stony.

Feather Merchant

A. J. McCLANE

What's the recipe for great dry flies? According to the late Harry Darbee, it started out, "Take one rooster, add a few hens . . ." (July 1955)

Although a President may change the date of Thanksgiving with no stress, Harry Darbee would fall into infamy if he changed the hackle color of a customer's Royal Coachman. To a man who must keep an inventory of 200,000 fly hooks, who has made flies for twenty-four hours without stopping to eat, who has tied eight dozen flies a day for thirty days straight, who once filled a single order for 800 dozen wet flies, and now finds he needs a few thousand dozen in stock to get caught up, the world is a whirling hive of synthetic insects. Men whose decisions divert golden streams of dollars one way or the other wait at his side like members of the South African Diamond Syndicate while he creates with inexplicable alchemy those gems of tinsel and feather that look exactly like the hundreds of thousands he has made before. With a quiet, measured speech and spongelike mind, Darbee sits squarely among the best in his trade, behind walls that have been frescoed in tobacco smoke and spatterings of old varnish; walls that echo to the legends of Eli Garrett, Pop Robbins, John Taintor Foote, Ted Townsend, and the fabulous Bill Johnson.

Darbee lives in the Dutch, Rip Van Winkle, rocky, short-legged cow country of the Catskills. "It's all sidehill," he says. "Even the hay riggings have two short wheels." At night you see the deer go off through the trees, then stand looking back at your headlights, and a grotesque parade of hotels marches over the ridges, so that tourists can find any atmosphere from South Sea Islands complete with papier-mâché palms and rubber coconuts, to Swiss chalets, dude ranches, and a native form of architecture best described as Early Nothing. The mountains are old in all senses and dimensions, for just a few miles beyond the Borscht Circuit, away from pounding truck arteries, the rivers are so natural that they can be traced like veins in the neck of a Catskill farmer.

The angler gets a wonderful feeling of continuity in finding that the Willowemoc flows to the Beaverkill, the Beaverkill to the East Branch, and the East to the West Branch where both pour into the Big Delaware. Men who derive their nourishment from a weekend contact with these rivers usually stop at the eight-room, two-story farm-style house with a high-angled green shingle roof, which stands nervously at the roadside where the concrete drops rapidly into the flatness of the Willowemoc valley.

"I don't mind the traffic out there," Darbee said, waving at the road; "it's the traffic in here that's killing me. I didn't get to bed until three o'clock this morning. At six o'clock two guys were pounding on the door, wanting me to tie some flies for them. I guess I can hold out until the trout season is over, though. Elsie tied until three this morning. She's out back now putting a new spring leaf in the car," he added proudly, "but tonight this place will look like Grand Central Station."

The attitude of the purist toward his fly dresser is one of remarkable devotion. When the home of Reub Cross burned down in Lewbeach back in 1941, his frenzied followers took up a collection to put him back in business, for the balding, corrosive, caustic-tongued wit of the Beaverkill tied trout flies like no other man. And there were those who couldn't fish without flies made the Cross way. But a professional fly tyer is also able to prescribe accurate remedies for local fishing conditions, tackle, the mood of the trout, the state of the nation, and will dispense blood-circulating medicines to clients who just crawled out of the river.

Darbee has not only survived twenty years in the feathered jungle, but has spent much of that time ferociously biting the hands of the Audubon Society. "Damn bird watchers are ruining our business. Last year they pushed through section 1518 of the 1930 Tariff Act, which is a general prohibition against the importation of feathers and skins, whether they're wild or domestic. That means that only 5,000 skins of gray jungle fowl, and not more than 1,000 skins of mandarin duck, can be shipped in during the year. Then we have to split up about 45,000 Oriental pheasant skins with the millinery trade. As the law stacks up now, teal, kingfisher, partridge, woodcock, starling, snipe, grouse, coot, and bronze mallard are gone.

"The bird watchers bagged Reub Cross back in the thirties," he continued, "but he got them all fouled up. Actually, they had nothing on him. The crazy horse-feathers law demanded a certified public accountant to itemize every feather you had, and all Reub had was some feathers that I had sold him. He wasn't even selling flies then. But the warden and the game inspector who made the arrest didn't know which feathers were on the banned list. So the whole business was dropped and the law was amended.

"Now they're riding herd on us again, and we have to keep a record of all purchases and be open to inspection at all times. Of course we're licensed by the state, but the Audubon creeps have us up a tree. I used to import thousands of necks from Japan—I'd buy them in bales. Most necks are no good; so it would take a lot of them to get the few quality skins I needed. I still get some necks from the big feather houses in New York City who supply the millinery trade, but my best skins are the ones I raise myself."

Darbee is most proud of his near-pure strain of blue dun roosters. The blue dun is a dingy, grayish-blue chicken that runs from light to very dark, and its neck provides hackles for such popular patterns as the Hendrickson, Quill Gordon, Blue Quill, Blue Dun Variant, Blue Caddis, and the traditional Blue Dun fly. Although the blue dun rooster wouldn't win a beauty prize in the barnyard, his hackles are the most sought-after feather in the fly-tying world, because no blue race of chicken runs true to color. The blue dun is a Mendelian freak, unless you want to spend twenty years in crossbreeding, which is what Darbee did.

"My buff rooster is just as likely to have blue chickens as a blue dun cock. But I've worked my present three hundred birds to a point where I'm reasonably sure of getting blue duns. I started my stock out of blue Andalusians. Always in a large hatch of Andalusians you'll find a few sports," Darbee observed, "and these might turn out to be natural blue duns, but you don't know until you raise them. Some Andalusian sports throw back to whites or blacks when they mature. It can be very disappointing.

"If you do get a few natural blue duns, however, then you have stock to work with. You can't breed them to a dominant strain like the White Leghorn unless you're going to use a black dominant, too. I found you can throw generic laws out the window," he continued, "because we have very critical problems in fly tying. I've worked my blue dun strain up with recessives. A recessive white and a recessive black. I use Buff Leghorn for blood, and Buff Cochin Bantam for early maturity and narrow, stiff hackle. I tried pure Buffs for a number of years, but they made the hackle quills stiff. We have to have flexible quills for tying, you know."

The Darbee chicken houses range from old shipping crates to orthodox coops that are scattered down the hillside in back of his house. Unlike production-minded egg farmers, who keep thousands of birds, Darbee maintains two to three hundred choice roosters, many of which have to be kept in solitary confinement.

"I can't get the gamecock blood out of some of them. They have to be culled, because they cut each other to shreds. My natural duns aren't really cooped, you'll notice; they just stay behind wire, even when it gets down to twenty below zero. That makes a quality feather." Although the present market price on top-grade blue dun necks is fifteen dollars, Darbee doesn't figure that this is a very high tab from a cost standpoint. "My ratio of good dun necks now is about one in five. The rest will be patterned or rusted. It used to be one in ten. Cripes, I was up to my button in fried chicken then.

"All my naturals are sold a year in advance," he continued. "I've got orders now for twenty that I haven't even raised yet. I don't kill all my birds. They average three or four crops of hackle a year; so I pluck them whenever I need material. I had one bird who gave a crop every six weeks. Sure miss him. They say the Old English Blue Gamecock runs true to color. Maybe it does, but those I've seen had very poor hackle. Sooner or later they must throw back to some other color, because all blue races run out. Then the hens are more often blue than the roosters.

"I have people writing to me all the time about my birds—in fact, I've sold some chicks because I want to perpetuate the race," he added. "And if you think fly tying is competitive business, I'm raising blue duns for half a dozen fly tyers right now. We don't compete, because first of all there's too much work and secondly, we all have different styles in our tying.

"It's a funny thing, though, if we had to have as much black hackle as blue dun hackle, we'd all be out of business. Good black hackle is extremely rare. The Black Minorca strain provides most of what we use, but it isn't stiff enough. The same goes for dark brown. The darker it gets, the poorer the quality. A real chocolate color that dresses so well on a Royal Coachman generally has hooked fibers. Wish I knew why. Furnace and badger are fairly easy to come by; but when you get right down to it, we can never get enough top-grade hackle of any color."

Fly tying as a business runs the gamut from part-time professionals who wrap feathers in the back room of a grocery store or gas station to the half-million-dollar enterprises run by venerable firms like Hardy Brothers in Alnwick, England, and the Weber Lifelike Fly Company of Stevens Point, Wisconsin. The big plants are conducted on a piecework basis, the Europeans demanding long periods of apprenticeship in single steps of tying, such as forming a wing or wrapping a tinsel body, whereas the American system prefers female tyers who can make complete flies.

"One chap up in northern New York made a time study on each operation in tying," Darbee said, "and then built a rotary table which a dozen women sat around, each one doing a separate stage of the same fly that took the same length of time. The idea was that for each revolution of the table one fly would be finished, but it didn't work out," he concluded.

The demand for artificial flies has always far exceeded the supply. Even with an estimated 250,000 amateurs making their own, a small corps of talented individuals scattered throughout the land work around the clock to keep critical anglers supplied. Professional fly tyers won't talk about their incomes, but presumably the best of them make $4,500 to $5,000 a year.

In spite of the fact that Darbee is a regional specialist, his orders come from all over the world, the bulk of his foreign trade centering in South America and Ireland. On the prevailing market he tabs $5.40 a dozen for dry flies, and $9.00 a dozen for salmon dry flies. Salmon fishermen like American Airlines prexy C. R. Smith and John J. McCloy cause Harry to split his work with Elsie. "She doesn't like to dress salmon patterns. Too much work in sorting materials. That's where the real work is," he continued. "When we're turning out flies as small as No. 22 up to No. % Long Dees, we have to spend a whole day just laying the materials out, grading the hackle sizes, matching wings, and so on. You have to be systematic. If I stopped to pick out new materials after each fly, I wouldn't be able to do more than two or three dozen a day."

Odd orders bother Darbee during his busy winter and spring seasons. "There's always some guy who wants one of each of thirty or forty different patterns, and somebody who wants all his flies dressed with four wings so they won't land upside down. I like to do the work, but it throws me way behind. Year in and year out, we tie more No. 12 Light Cahill than any other fly. Good patterns aren't an accident," he cautioned, "and I think that's where amateur tyers go haywire. They work at freaks, you know, things they dream up instead of the standard patterns.

"Basically, all an amateur needs is practice, a good thread, and good wax. I use 6-0 Holland thread and a homemade wax which I make from beeswax, rosin, and paraffin in mixture; then I add a little castor oil to keep it from drying out. Putting the materials together is easy. Really easy."

Born in 1906 in Roscoe, New York, young Darbee grew up in what was then America's most fertile trout country. While still very young he made an attempt to go to Alaska, but went broke in Wisconsin and gradually worked his way back to the Catskills where he resumed fox trapping, a profession that Darbee pursued right up until the depression. "I could get six foxes in one night," he said, "but that wouldn't be unusual those days. In fact, it was easier to get the foxes than the bait. I used house cats. Small, well-aged pieces," he said carefully. "When money got really tight, I began commercial fly tying because fishing seemed to be the only business that wasn't too affected by the depression."

Anybody can buy the few tools and materials needed in the fly-tying trade, but it takes great personal skill to become popular enough to conduct a business. Darbee advertised in all the outdoor magazines during his first professional year to build up a clientele, and after a brief partnership with Walt Dette he met and married Elsie, who not only learned the trade in thirty days but is now skilled enough to whip out a wet fly in two and a half minutes flat. Regular customers agree that Elsie is the spark plug in the Darbee combo, as Harry is inclined to wander off to the Big Delaware instead of sitting at his bench. "I painted one side of the house once," he added reflectively, "but there's no sense in finishing now because they're going to widen the highway out front."

To help others to take over wherever he may be compelled to leave off, Darbee has taught his art to many youngsters in the Catskill area, and to further assist unborn generations of fly makers he has collected thousands of original patterns dating from Theodore Gordon to contemporary experts and filed them for future reference. In an art form that demands strict adherence to the rules, one would expect all flies of one pattern to be exactly alike. But even with the same ingredients no two fly dressers achieve precisely the same result.

"You can't really dress a pattern correctly from a book description. You've got to have the fly in your hand. Give one printed description to twenty different tyers, and you have roughly the same fly, but twenty distinct styles. It's like playing the piano. Walt Dette is more precise about selecting his hackle for length than I am," Darbee continued, "because I can spot his flies right away. Reub Cross cocks the tails on his flies and he uses a shorter body. Mike Lorenz brings the bodies of all his flies down around the bend of the hook. Del Appley over on the East Branch makes a larger, rougher-looking fly, whereas Herman Christian on the Neversink ties so sparse that his flies are for experts only.

"I guess most of us aim at sparseness these days. I tie what looks like a bulkier body than most. But actually I pick the material out a little. When we first started in the business, I used No. 11, No. 13, and No. 15 hooks instead of the regular 10, 12, and 14. People knew there was something different about my flies, but they couldn't quite figure it out. It was a good gimmick," he added.

Darbee's friend, ex-game protector Roy Steenrod, stands as a link between past and present in being one of the few men alive today who knew and fished with Theodore Gordon. Steenrod, creator of the famous Hendrickson trout fly, used to visit Gordon in his Neversink retreat before he died in 1915. Eroded by the culture of the Gay Nineties, and with a tendency toward hermitage, Gordon had the foresight to develop American dry-fly fishing, and thus is remembered in a class with such other permanent benefactors of the human race as the inventors of the cotton gin, the light bulb, and the wireless.

"I wish I had known Gordon," Darbee said. "He actually changed the anatomy of the fly. He set his wings with butts toward the rear and placed his hackles at right angles to the hook. He was smart enough to use nonabsorbent materials, which made a big difference. English dry flies at that time were nothing more than modified wets. They still tied their wing butts toward the eye of the hook. I have thirty or forty of Gordon's original Quill Gordon flies. That man had a beautiful style. He tied on slightly long shank hooks, which gave his flies a real mayfly appearance."

Darbee feels that it is bad for a man to love one country too much, and when the wind sweeps a gale down the dark valley in the winter he gets up from his bench once in a while and thinks maybe he will leave, or maybe he will go trap a fox, or look for the blind deer that almost knocked George Stewart into the Beaverkill. "Somebody should kill that deer. The poor beast is half crazy. The boys find him floundering in the river every so often. His eyes are as white as marbles. By rights, though, I guess I'll have to wait until the season opens, won't I?"

Count-Down for Trout

EDMUND WARE SMITH

During an endless winter and snowy spring, they dreamed about their first-of-the-season trip into Maine's wilderness trout country. How could any outing live up to such expectations? (April 1959)

As a sprightly epic of spring fever—its contagion, witchery, horsepower and highjinks—I offer herewith the case history of Jake's Rangers of Damariscotta, Maine, and the handful of magic pine shavings that lured us, one and all, through the core of New England's last wilderness in quest of trout. The enchanted expedition took place during an unforgettable week in May last year. But before it ever got off the launching pad, many strange things came to pass.

I must explain that Jake's Rangers is a group of seven normally sane business and professional men. Our roster includes Damariscotta's postmaster, its veterinary surgeon, a leading physician, a grocer, an artist and an insurance man. A nonmilitary and nonbelligerent organization, we are called Rangers only because we range far and wide throughout our home state in search of trout and the blue horizon.

Dedicated to the outdoors, open water and fishing, I suspect we resemble sportsmen's groups in small towns all across our land. We have no bylaws, no regular meetings, no dues and no headquarters, unless you count Perley Waltz's drugstore on Main Street or the post office next door. Our claim to distinction is our leader, the man for whom the Rangers was named: Maurice "Jake" Day, artist, naturalist, longtime explorer of Maine's wilderness region—and shrewd alchemist of the Rites of Spring.

Last year it seemed to us that spring was deliberately avoiding Maine. Just when you were about to inventory your trout flies or paint your canoe, another blizzard wrecked your dream. Six or seven of them pasted us in March. The most detested object in town was the snow shovel. Jokes about the weather wore out and fell flat, and by late March the morale of Jake's Rangers hit an alltime low.

But, unbeknown to the rest of us, Jake himself had taken on the task of reviving our hope of spring and sun-warmed brook banks. Secretly and single-handedly he had been at work on this problem through many consecutive snow-storms.

The first inkling I had that Jake was making medicine came one dismal, ice-gray morning when I walked into Perley Waltz's drugstore for coffee. Three of the Rangers were already entrenched at the marble counter: Dr. Sam Belknap; Eddie Pierce, whose Yellow Front Grocery is a Damariscotta landmark; and Jack Glidden, our insurance man. They were talking with an animation long subdued. Dr. Sam and Eddie wore wide smiles, and Jack Glidden was laughing right out loud—a sound I hadn't heard since the winter solstice.

"What right have you guys got to be happy?" I asked. "Don't you know it's snowing again?"

They exchanged secretive glances, and immediately clammed up. After a moment Dr. Sam said, "Stop at Jake's on your way home."

"What gives?"

"Obey orders, and you'll find out," said Jack.

I left them and went into the post office, next door. Dr. McClure Day, our veterinary surgeon and Jake's son, was in the act of plucking the mail from his box. He held up a fishing tackle catalogue he'd just received, waved it like a banner, and said, "Hurray!"

"Hurray for what?" I asked. "Who do you think is going fishing?"

"You are," said Mac mysteriously, and went out into the snow.

I stepped up to the mail window. Behind it was the round, merry face of Bentley Glidden. Bentley, Jack's younger brother, is Damariscotta's postmaster. He seemed to be shining like a portly, human sun as he slid my mail under the wicket. My mail consisted solely of a seed catalogue.

"That's a personal affront," I said. "I refuse to accept it."

"It's for your wife, not you," said Bent gayly. "And there's two cents postage due. Drop in at Jake's on your way home."

Jake Day's house, up near the Baptist Church, is one of those solid, foursquare white colonials. Mellow with age, it was built by Jake's great-grandfather, and the door has seldom been locked in 161 years. I let myself in, scowled at the snowshoes stacked in the front entry, and went up the stairway to Jake's studio. It isn't the kind of artist's studio you read about. No skylights, plate glass or folderol. It's just a big, cluttered, upstairs corner room.

Nor does Jake himself resemble the standard concept of an artist. He doesn't wear sandals; he wears moccasins. His smock is an old flannel shirt, and instead of a beret his head is adorned with a vagabond felt hat abused by countless rains and suns, its band a beat-up leather strap.

At 67, Jake is lean, wiry and feather-light on his feet. On mountain fishing trips he can walk the ankles off his Rangers, all of whom—except me—are his juniors by about thirty years. This gifted man has the spirit of youth and a genius for embellishing life. Perhaps they are the same. He met me at the door of his studio, a corncob pipe between his teeth.

"There was an emergency meeting of the Rangers last night," he said, removing the corncob. "We tried to reach you."

"I was in Portland," I said morosely. "What happened? Making plans for a snow festival?"

By way of answer, Jake stepped aside from his doorway and—with a magician's gesture—waved me into the room. Suddenly I found myself, to all intents and purposes, in the wilds of Maine's immense Baxter State Park in the green benediction of spring. The impact and the scene itself, in contrast with the bleak reality of the March day, are almost indescribable.

Flanking me on each side of the room were twenty or more of Jake's wonderfully realistic watercolors of the unpeopled Katahdin wilderness we loved and knew so well. Some were from his old portfolios and sketchbooks. Others he had painted for the occasion. They haunted me with ghosts of old campfires and inspired the promise of new ones. I saw Russell Pond under a blue sky, a pair of wood ducks near shore. I saw South Branch Pond, its fringe of birches misted with green. There was a lone canoeman on Wassataquoik Lake, and I saw Traveler Mountain and an old black bear and her cub on Pinnacle Ridge. Trout were rising in Six Ponds, and a kingfisher rode on a cedar frond; there was a tiny, flickering campfire with its smoke skeining through the spruces. You could smell it! The total effect was uncanny—as if Jake somehow had been working hand in glove with spring.

"Jake," I said, "you've broken up a hard winter with a paintbrush. I shall go home and burn my snow shovel."

"Wait!"

Jake stepped to an easel that stood between the two aisles of paintings. The easel was veiled with the cover of an old sleeping bag. Sweeping this shield to one side, Jake disclosed the Katahdin and Traveler Mountain quadrangles of the U.S. Geological Survey. He had mounted the maps on cardboard, and in red pencil scored the 17-mile foot trail that traverses the wildest part of Baxter State Park, from Roaring Brook Campground at the southern border to South Branch Ponds Campground near the northern extremity. About midway of this trail, in the heart of the park, and accessible only on foot, is Russell Pond Campground. This mountain solitude, in Jake's lettering, was tagged: "Base Camp, Jake's Rangers, Spring 1958."

"Does this mean we're going to fish those hidden ponds this year—at long last?"

"It does. Takeoff day is May eighteenth."

"How are we going to sustain life till then?"

From his shirt pocket Jake ceremoniously removed a small cardboard box. He rubbed the box lovingly, which somehow made it resemble Aladdin's lamp. "I have here," he said, "lifegiving medicine—the smelling salts of the wilderness."

He opened the box and held it under my nose and the scent of clean, sun-dried pine pervaded me. Resinous, pungent, supreme! It seemed to put a kind of hex on me. I thought I heard the song of a white-throated sparrow proclaiming life from a spruce top, a loon calling from a sequestered deadwater. Wind seemed to whisper in young leaves, and the full trance and heartache of spring were upon me.

"Jake!" I said. "This is alchemy!"

"No," he said, tapping his magic box, "it's just a handful of pine shavings. I whittled them from that old stump above Trout Brook Crossing in the park last fall. I've been sniffing them for weeks. I call them Old Doctor Jake's Golden Spring Medical Discovery."

What with his wilderness watercolors, his maps and his siren pine shavings, Jake had deliberately created the worst case of spring fever since the Song of Solomon. The Rangers—including Jake himself—were smitten to the point of frenzy. And in April, when wild geese, green grass and lilac buds began to show, we could talk, think or dream of nothing but May 18 and our expedition.

The rigors of the trail to Russell Pond were forgotten, though the inner core of the park is a hundred square miles of jumbled peaks, ravines, glacial boulders, forests, ruffian watercourses and isolated ponds, many of them rarely fished, a few never.

Only two of the Rangers had experienced this rugged terrain in spring, but in our zeal we forgot the facts of life on a hard trail and all fell into the Old Map Trap, or the Pitfall of the Contours. The trail looked easy—on paper. We simply leveled off the mountains. The congested contour lines were nice, artistic arrangements of brown curves. The streams we would have to cross were innocuous ribbons of blue. Trout seemed to be breaking up through the surface of the paper. We had breathed the giddy incense of Old Doctor Jake's Golden Spring Medical Discovery and were infected with invincibility.

On the back of his pack, as a challenge to the Russell Pond Trail, Bentley Glidden stenciled "U.S. Domestic Air Mail." Jack Glidden, during his day's travels as an insurance man, stopped at any convenient field or bit of open water and practiced fly casting. Jake and his son, Dr. McClure Day, our veterinarian, drew up the trip's supply list and submitted it one evening to the full roster of Rangers at Dr. Sam Belknap's house. This meeting was called a "survival seminar." The supply list was as lovely as a sonnet. Not a single item had been forgotten—except dry matches and salt. For this crucial oversight, we reduced Jake in rank. But we acclaimed him full colonel the next morning shortly after Bentley handed him a letter from Mr. Helon Taylor, who is supervisor of Baxter State Park and a longtime friend of Jake's.

Unbeknown to the rest of us, Jake had written Mr. Taylor of our expedition. And Mr. Taylor was greatly interested. He was eager for a report on the park's remote trout fishing. There had never been one; so our survey would be the first.

All this was climaxed by a second letter. Addressed to Jake and me, this letter simply wished us godspeed, good fishing and fine weather. It was signed by no other than the Honorable Percival P. Baxter, Mr. Maine himself—the man who, singlehanded, bought and gave Baxter State Park's two hundred thousand acres and fifty mountain peaks to us and all men, "to be forever held . . . forever left in its natural, wild state."

In their homes at night, some of the more earnest Rangers had taken to sleeping in their sleeping bags for practice. This form of training was finally outlawed by their wives as being irrelevant, uncomfortable and unfriendly.

On May 8, Jack Glidden started the count-down to our takeoff day by yelling "Ten!" at the top of his lungs on Main Street. He startled the seagulls from their perch on the ridgepole of the Gay Block. Rangers within hearing took up the cry, as did many sympathetic bystanders. Thereafter, any morning at coffee time you could hear the current count-down resounding anywhere from a point near the town library clear down to the Newcastle Bridge. "Nine!" . . . "Eight!" . . . "Seven!"

Suspense mounted daily. Sleep, fitful at best, was disturbed by dreams of fishing the mysterious waters of our destination. Daydreams gave our eyes a glazed look. On the morning of the six-count, Eddie Pierce, while chalking the day's offerings on the big front windows of his grocery store, marked up this eyecatching Special Sale item: TROUT, 59¢ a Peck. Eager purchasers filed into Eddie's store and filed out again in disappointment when Eddie, reorienting himself, explained that he had meant "potatoes."

Even Jake himself, severely stricken by his own alchemy, went into Don & Bob's Barber Shop on the afternoon of the four-count and emerged, half an hour later, with a crew cut.

That same afternoon, Dr. Sam's charming wife, Lucy, sailed into Perley

Waltz's drugstore for films, complaining that Sam had packed every roll in the house for the Rangers' trip.

"Why don't you unpack them?" asked Perley.

"I can't. Sam's mowing the lawn."

"What's that got to do with it?"

"The pack is on his *back*!"

It was a fact. Dr. Sam, carrying his full pack—and with a pedometer affixed to his belt—was mowing his spacious lawn as a kind of dry run for the Russell Pond Trail.

Count-down "One!" Late Saturday afternoon all seven Rangers gathered in the alley back of Eddie Pierce's store for the ceremony of loading the packed supplies into my station wagon. It's entirely possible that some of us managed to sleep soundly that night, but I doubt it.

Next morning, in deceptively beautiful weather, we were on our way, rolling up the seacoast from Damariscotta, then swinging northwestward, inland, to Maine's mountain region. That afternoon, with two hundred miles behind us, we entered Baxter State Park and halted for the night at the bunkhouse at Roaring Brook Campground. We stood in the shadow of that great, gaunt mountain, Katahdin—majestic, lonely, its ravines and higher elevations wearing the white scars of snow. In the camp clearing a sign said: RUSSELL POND CAMPGROUND 7 MILES.

"That means us," said Jake. He pointed to the wilderness stretching to the north, then to the log bridge that spanned Roaring Brook. "The trail," he said, "starts right there at the bridge."

There it was—the trail! We were looking at it. Anticipation was over. Realization was at hand. But reality is the truer word. On the bunkhouse roof that night came the deafening drumfire of rain—an all-night, four-alarm downpour.

In the morning Roaring Brook was in flood and our bridge had vanished. The first baptism in ice water occurred right there and then. Soaked to the waist, chilled to the marrow, but with spirits never so high, we were feeling with the soles of our feet the trail we had been dreaming about for six weeks.

Some trail! In less than a mile snowdrifts loomed. Blowdowns barred the way. Laughter and bright banter tapered away to silence. You heard only the tinkle of the tin cup suspended from Jack Glidden's belt; the scuff of boots on rock; a groan as someone made a misstep or sank to his hips in a ridge of snow; the pounding of your own heart. Shoulders lunged into packstraps on a steep ascent. Sweat trickled. Breath steamed. The pace slowed and steadied for the long pull. This was the shakedown of Jake's Rangers on the Russell Pond Trail. Not a Ranger will ever forget that 7-mile trek.

In August it's an easy two hours or so. In an ordinary spring you'd make it in three. But in the spring of '58, with 3-foot drifts, blowdowns, bridges washed away and rivers in flood, it was 7½ hours of heartbreak and hazard. Eddie Pierce went in all over while fording the iced rapids of the South Branch of Wassataquoik Stream. On the Main Wassataquoik crossing we thought Bentley was a goner when he stumbled, plunged through the last ten yards of white water but finally made land, with helping hands yanking him ashore. Each crossing was a point of no return. You wouldn't dare cross back again. You couldn't. So you went on.

If the trek is unforgettable for its bone-wearying, all-out effort, it is even more so for the sweet last turn in the trail and the triumphant, heart-lifting moment of stepping into the clearing at the Russell Pond Campground. There were the log lean-tos; the log cabin bunkhouse; the encircling mountains; the blue, sunlit expanse of Russell Pond—and trout breaking the surface! And, above all, the solitude.

"I'm dreaming," said Jack Glidden, dropping his pack. "Don't wake me."

Myrle Scott, the big, able, redheaded park ranger, came from his cabin to greet us. Myrle was pinch-hitting for Russell Pond's regular ranger, Ralph Dolley, who had been delayed. He said, "I declare, I'm gladder to see you boys than you are to see me and Russell Pond."

"We have just heard the misstatement of the year," said Mac Day.

It was Bentley Glidden who summed up the trail's anguish and the sense of achievement that now pervaded us. Bent had his boots and socks off and was gazing in open wonder at his bare feet. He wiggled his chubby toes. Admiration mounted in his eyes as he reckoned up what they had just been through. In an awed voice he said, "They ought to be buried in Westminster Abbey."

In the isolated ponds of Baxter Park, the best time for trout, if not for men, is mid-May. In all ponds the limit is five fish a day. The trout are exclusively *Salvelinus fontinalis*, variously called brook trout, speckled trout, natives or square-tails. These inner waters have never been stocked. Neither the trout you catch nor their ancestors ever saw a hatchery or a rearing pool. Their color is sunset-brilliant, their flesh pink and firm, their flavor matchless.

The fishing began that afternoon right at Russell Pond after a rum ration and an hour's rest for all hands. We fished from canoes, which you can rent at Russell. No one carried those canoes over the trail. They were flown in by a bush pilot, Elmer Wilson, on the pontoons of his Jet Cub plane.

Eddie Pierce scored first with the beautifully colored 14-incher. In that first hour's fishing the Rangers caught and released thirty-two trout. We kept a dozen more, ranging in size from 8 inches up to Eddie's 14-incher. They came to standard flies and to gold-bodied spinning lures, and they were strong and belligerent.

A large moose wandered out of the forest and stepped into the pond to view proceedings. He seemed to take a special liking for Mac Day, and waded in a leisurely manner toward Mac's canoe.

"My office is closed, fella," said the veterinarian. "But I'll take your photograph." He did. So did Eddie, Jake and Dr. Sam.

At sunset we gathered in the bunkhouse and started a fire in the stove. When the cabin warmed up, the little spiders that had wintered there came creeping from their cracks in the wall logs to see what was cooking. The answer was native trout.

We were in our sleeping bags at dark, too tired for chatter or wisecracks. You could hear bone-limbering sighs of comfort and the tap and hiss as someone's wet socks dripped onto the hot stove. A whippoorwill tuned up, and 'way back in the forest an owl hooted. That was all—except for the distant roar of rapids reechoing from the walled valley of Wassataquoik Stream. It couldn't touch us now!

There are miles of Wassataquoik Stream that are seldom, if ever, fished. They are too far, too hard to reach from either approach, upstream or down. We had "map-fished" these enticing reaches back home but now unanimously abandoned the idea. The ponds were our real objective. Besides, we were on the outs with the Wassataquoik after what it had almost done to Bentley.

Within a day's round trip of the Russell Pond base camp, you can fish approximately fifteen ponds—not all of them in a single day, by any means. Wassataquoik, Draper, Six Ponds (there are six of them), Deep, Long, Pogy, Weed, Bell, Russell itself and a couple that are unnamed. We fished all but two or three. Mac Day and the Glidden boys caught fifty-odd trout in Bell Pond. They were the first to fish it within the memory of man. The trout ran uniform in size— 8 to 10 inches.

The fastest fishing was at Deep Pond and Six Ponds, where four of us landed and released over 150 fish. The largest was Jack Glidden's 15-incher. Back at camp that evening, Dr. Sam Belknap treated Jack and Bent Glidden for an ailment that he, or any of us, had never seen before. To wit, multiple tiny lacerations on the patients' forefingers caused by the teeth of countless trout as the anglers released them to the waters of the ponds.

But no report—this first one or any that may follow on the park's wilderness fishing—can pin itself to trout alone. Climb to the Lookout, a high crag two miles from Russell Pond, and you know why. The view from the Lookout, as described by an unidentified observer, produces sensations like this:

"From here you sense the full power and grandeur of the wilderness into which you have penetrated. You feel that right here is the place man has gone too far away from in his search for something he has never clearly defined. You feel that whatever you have longed for is here, around you, a full 360 degrees of mountains, streams, lakes and ponds, named, unnamed, solitary."

As you stand on the Lookout you can see, near at hand, the spindles of the young spruces, silent and steady in the still air, aspiring to the sun and aloof to the presence of man. Then, lifting your eyes to the northward distance, you see the rolling peaks of the Traveler range and the valley where the Pogy Notch Trail leads to South Branch Pond Campground. That was our trail out, and it was time to go. With hardened muscles and lightened packs, it was a lark compared to the Russell Pond Trail.

We had arranged to have our cars driven from Roaring Brook around the park's peripheral road to meet us at South Branch Ponds. This campground, with its two clear-water ponds lying blue between the steep crags and faces of Traveler and South Branch Mountains, is one of the most beautiful on our continent. Here Jake's Rangers spent the last night of the expedition. And it was here we realized that something had happened to us, over and above our adventure. Our spring fever had been cured! But you don't actually cure it, like a disease. Recovery is a little like falling out of love. Suddenly it is there no more, and you can hardly remember its yearning and heartache.

But there was one among us who didn't treat it so lightly. On the start home, just after we left South Branch Pond, a white-throated sparrow sang. It sang as I'd imagined it in Jake's studio that bleak March day so long ago. It may be that Jake heard the white-throat too. Because down near Trout Brook Crossing, just before you get to the main park road, Jake stopped his car, got out, and approached an old pine stump, drawing his sheath knife as he went. He came back presently with a handful of rich, yellow, resinous shavings tied in his handkerchief. "We'll be needing these next spring!" he said. "Now—home we go."

The Best Fishing in America

TED TRUEBLOOD

High on high mountain lakes, Ted claimed you'll take both the most, and the biggest, fish here if you know how. (June 1959)

I am convinced that the best trout fishing in the United States is in the mountain lakes of the West. It is the best from any standpoint—from numbers of fish, if you want to catch a lot; from the size of the fish, if you want to catch big ones; from the ease with which you can catch them in some lakes, and from the difficulty of fooling the smart lunkers in other lakes if you prefer angling with a challenge.

One evening last summer a friend and I were sitting in my canoe on a difficult lake. It had plenty of fish, including both browns and rainbows up to better than 10 pounds, but they had been hard to catch. We'd been fishing all day, and I think one hungry mink could easily have eaten every trout we caught. We hadn't kept any. When you see cruising fish that would go all the way from 2 pounds up to 4 or 5, you just don't keep 8-inchers. And we hadn't caught a single trout that would shade a pound.

Now we were beat. We sat there over the edge of a moss bed, our leaders trailing in the water, and looked dumbly at the scattered rises that broke the glassy surface. The colors of sunset were on it. The white-trunked aspens on the western slopes stood out in bold relief, etched against dark fir and lodgepole by the lowering sun. The sagebrush across the lake was soft blue-gray. Its rich aroma mingled with the spicy odors of the conifers.

Just being in a place so perfect should have been enough to gladden the heart of any angler, but our hearts definitely were not glad. Eleven hours of frustration does not lead to gladness. We were, however, perfectly primed for one of those wild, wonderful hours that none but the fisher who has first drunk the bitter dregs can fully appreciate. We were ready, and it came.

First, we saw a few fluttering insects in the air. Their numbers increased rapidly. Then we saw that they were rising from the lake everywhere around the canoe. They were Mayflies, and they came up through the clear water above the moss to shed their nymphal husks, dry their wings and weave off in dancing flight.

Shortly a trout rose. Then another. Then a dozen. Meanwhile the hatch thickened. Fatigue was forgotten as we sent our lines hissing out, but almost before we could cast the air was full of insects and the water was boiling with trout.

It took us twenty frantic minutes to discover that the fish were not yet taking the adult insects. They were bulging to the nymphs, either on or just below the surface, and we eventually tied on the proper nymphs with trembling fingers and laid them out. It was better than anything we had hoped for!

We'd cast to a rise—any rise of the hundreds now within reach—let the nymph sink for an instant, then start drawing it in with little pulls. Every trout struck going away. I can't remember any other time when they struck so willingly—or so hard. I left two nymphs in fish before I could bring myself to keep the rod tip high and hold the line loosely between my fingers. It wasn't necessary to set the hook; the hook was set and the trout was yards away before we could possibly react.

We kept two fat 1½-pound rainbows to eat. Then we just fished. We played them and turned them loose. We played them and lost them. Some came un-hooked; others broke our leaders. This doesn't mean, however, that we tied into any really big fish.

I wish some of the cynics who've told me that trout in lakes don't fight like those in streams could have been there that evening. How often do you hook a stream trout that comes out of the water with its tail buzzing—actually making an audible buzz? These fat rainbows did, many of them. Trout of a pound or two would shoot a yard straight into the air, tails buzzing like skipjacks, turn over and go back down headfirst. I saw a trout that couldn't possibly have weighed more than 2 pounds—saw him well when he jumped close to the canoe—take out all my companion's fly line and thirty yards of backing and break the 2X leader. It takes a good fish to do that.

When the light began to fail, our nymphs would no longer work. The sun was down and the bats were darting among the myriad insects, snapping their little teeth and squeaking in gustatory delight. The long mountain twilight was still with us, however, and the trout still fed. We switched to dry flies and the fun went on.

At last the time came when I knew that I should tie on a fresh fly but was afraid to try it in the poor light. The Mayflies were growing scarce. There were not so many rises. We made a few more casts with our worn-out, sinking dry flies and managed to hook a lone late-lingering rainbow as darkness settled, with finality, upon the lake.

This was a tough lake. We were rewarded because we happened to be in the right spot at the right time. I have also, on occasion, been rewarded on it by hooking a really big fish. Generally, however, I've put in a lot of hours there for each good trout I've taken. That kind of lake is humbling, but I enjoy it the best of all. For others, whose angling might not necessarily be the same as mine, there are other lakes.

Suppose, for example, that just for once you'd like to catch trout until you were tired of catching them—hundreds of trout. There are many lakes where you can do it. I fished one of them last summer. As I walked down the grassy mountain to this lake I saw they were rising. Did you ever see a million trout rising? Well, a million trout were dimpling the surface of that lake, and I defy anyone who doubts me to go there and prove me wrong.

I made a cast near the inlet, hooked an 8-inch brook trout, led him in and turned him loose. I made another cast and caught another 8-inch brook trout. Another cast, another trout. Ten casts, ten trout, each 8 inches long. I tied on two flies and caught two brook trout, each 8 inches long.

I decided to see how many casts I could make before I failed to catch a trout; so I smashed down the barbs and continued catching them. Sometimes one got off, but it didn't matter—another struck before I could retrieve the fly for a new cast.

There seemed to be a concentration around the inlet; so I started fishing and walking away along the shore. I still caught an 8-inch brook trout—and sometimes two—on every cast. It began to get monotonous. I decided there was a concentration all over the lake. I finally quit. I hadn't succeeded in fishing out a single cast without catching a trout, but I gently turned the last one loose, hooked my fly in the keeper and hiked on to another lake where the fish were bigger and harder to catch.

That first lake was, of course, badly overstocked. There were too many trout for the available food. I actually should have kept all I caught, but after you get into the habit of turning trout loose it is hard to make a hog of yourself, even when you should. Generally speaking, lakes with a superabundance of small fish don't have any big ones. The fish population has to be in keeping with the food supply to provide the best fishing. When you do find such a lake, however—and there are thousands of them—you can expect to have fabulous sport.

There are several reasons why mountain lakes provide the best fishing. For one thing, there is now a good road along virtually every major trout stream in the West, so the streams are fished many times harder. Most lakes are in the high mountains where the roads don't go, and a 4- or 5-mile hike is too much for many anglers.

I should point out, however, that some of the very best lakes can be reached by automobile. Year after year they continue to produce good fishing, long after the nearby streams have gone from superlative to fair to darned tough. There are reasons for this. A good lake, particularly one in a limestone or a basaltic formation, with large areas of shallow water, is far more productive than any stream of equal surface area. The *Chara*, commonly called moss, teem with fresh-water shrimp and the larvae of aquatic insects. Minute water fleas and copepods thrive by the billion. All these little creatures are the finest possible food for trout. Consequently the fish grow fast, and if the spawning areas are limited so they can't overpopulate the lake, or if the fishing pressure is heavy enough to remove the surplus, the sport is superb.

There is still a third reason. Once a trout reaches the age of discretion—say a pound or so in weight—it is usually harder to catch than one of similar size in a stream. Mountain lakes are always crystal-clear; there never are periods of muddy water when the fish are vulnerable to bait. Since food is always abundant in the better lakes—the only exception being those that are overstocked—the trout are never particularly hungry. They feed every day, but if a tidbit looks suspicious they can afford to pass it by in the sure knowledge that something else will be available in a few minutes.

Furthermore, by the nature of their environment, the feeding of trout in lakes is more deliberate. When a trout lying behind a rock in a stream sees a fly—real or artificial—floating by, he knows that he must grab it instantly or it will be gone forever. Trout in lakes have plenty of time, and as a result they are harder to fool.

One of the most amusing trout fishing experiences I ever had was with a lake rainbow of 2½ pounds. I was fishing a dry fly that I tie to imitate the blue damselfly. Trout seem to love these little cousins of the dragonflies, and feed on them enthusiastically whenever they are available. I saw this particular fish cruising in shallow water and, luckily, made a perfect cast. The fly lit right in his course, about ten feet ahead, and the last two or three strands of the leader sank quickly. He came leisurely on until he saw the fradulent blue damsel, then darted ahead.

My muscles tightened to strike, but when he was a foot from the fly he stopped. He hung in the water a moment, then turned away. I let the fly remain motionless. He swam a yard or so, then drifted back. Again he started away. Obviously he realized that something was wrong, although he wasn't sure what.

For the second time he turned and started back toward the floating fly, moving very slowly. Suddenly he shot ahead. He struck with a splash like that of a 5-pound bass hitting a top-water plug and raced toward deep water so fast that the leader fairly sizzled. It was hardly necessary to set the hook.

There are thousands of trout lakes in the West. Nobody knows exactly how many, but California alone boasts about 5,000. Montana has around 1,500; Idaho, 2,000; Wyoming, 1,600; Colorado, 2,000; Washington, 5,500; Utah, 2,000; and Oregon, 1,200. Only a small number are posted because most of them are on national forest land, the property of the United States.

Attempting to list them all, much less give directions for reaching them, would be like trying to list all the brooks in New England. Some of the states have prepared booklets, complete with maps, on their mountain lakes, and you can obtain them by writing to the state game commission.

When you have chosen an area within a state that you intend to fish, stop at the nearest ranger station and ask to look at a Forest Service map. It will show lakes, streams, peaks and trails. The ranger can give you a list of packers and outfitters serving his district. One of them will take you to any lake that can't be reached by car—unless you prefer to put a pack on your back and hike. Thousands of anglers provide their own transportation in this way each summer.

You can arrange to have a packer take you and your camp outfit to a lake, leave you, and come back at a prearranged date. Often there will be several lakes—sometimes stocked with different kinds of trout—within easy hiking distance of each other. Or if you prefer, you can have the packer stay with you to serve as guide and keep horses available for exploring.

Most trout lakes, though not all, are in high country. Because of the elevation, the rough country, the small size of many of the best, and the fact that most western bush pilots land on wheels rather than on floats, flying to your fishing is hardly practical. Hiking, riding, or, where you can, driving are the three standard means of transportation. Local inquiry is always advisable, no matter which you choose.

Once you get there, you'll have to stop and gasp at the scenery. It probably will be magnificent. I think this high mountain country is the most beautiful in America. As soon as you've taken a quick look and set up camp, however, you can start fishing. Then, if you're a stream fisherman—as most trout men are— you'll have problems.

There are several important differences between stream and lake fishing. Pausing to consider them will shorten the time between bites.

First, trout in a stream find suitable spots and stay put, letting the moving water bring their food to them. The water in a lake doesn't move; so the trout must. Feeding trout cruise continually, and it usually is better to find a good spot and stay there. Let the trout come to you.

There are exceptions to this rule, just as there are to every other rule in angling, but the basic point is a good one to remember. Many times, after once locating the general area in which the trout were feeding, I have fished half a day without moving more than a few yards.

Second, most of us have learned to look for deep water on a stream. A big pool is often the home of a big trout. The deep water in a lake, however, is comparatively sterile. The shallows produce most of the food, and hungry trout turn to them in search of it. It is true that big trout, especially browns, often lie in deep water during the day, but the feeding fish—the ones you have a chance to catch—cruise the flats and the moss beds.

For this reason, a boat is seldom necessary in fishing mountain lakes. There are exceptions, such as wide, shallow bays and rocky bars out from shore, but more often you'll catch most of your trout within an easy cast from the bank. A great many lakes lie in open alpine country, and you can fish them more effectively by walking the shore than from a boat or a raft.

A third point to remember stems, like the first, from the difference between the water in lake and stream. The water in mountain lakes is nearly always crystal-clear. It is motionless, of course, and the surface is frequently glassy. There are no swirling currents to hide the angler or his rod or line. A breeze that ruffles the lake serves this purpose, of course, but sometimes there is no breeze.

In that case, extra caution is always necessary to keep from alarming the trout. A lure—even a fly—that strikes the water too close to a fish will scare him. I habitually cast farther on lakes than on streams, and I try to cast far enough ahead of cruising trout so as not to alarm them, but still close enough so they won't change their course before they see my fly. This cast can be tricky, but it's fun. It pays to stay low and to keep rod and line as low as possible, because the higher a movement, the farther a fish can see it.

All sorts of methods are used to catch trout in the high lakes, depending on the skill and the preference of the anglers. Trolling, bait fishing, spinning and fly fishing are all effective.

If you're a beginner you can troll. Follow the dropoff from shallow water to the deep, trailing a small wobbling plug or spoon or a multibladed spinner. You'll catch fish.

Casting small spoons with bait-casting or spinning tackle is also effective and has the advantage of not requiring a boat. You can fish from shore. All-copper, all-nickel, all-brass, red-and-white with nickel and black-and-white with nickel are good colors. Weighted spinners and small plugs are sometimes more effective. When a steady retrieve fails to produce strikes, try letting your lure sink longer and then reel it in with pulls and pauses, or make it flutter by jiggling the rod tip.

Live minnows are not permitted in some states because many fine lakes have been ruined through the introduction of trash fish by careless minnow fishermen. Salmon eggs, likewise, are illegal in some states—and should be in all—because they are particularly well adapted to an abuse that can result in the virtual extermination of the trout in any body of water.

Actually, a plain old worm probably is the best trout bait of all, and it can be used anywhere except in the few lakes that are restricted to fly fishing. It seems odd, but trout that never saw a worm before will take one readily. There are no earthworms in the high country where most lakes are found, but the fish are always glad to see one.

Most anglers cast a worm, using the lightest possible sinker, or none at all, and allow it to sink. Then they simply let it lie until a trout comes along and picks it up. Eventually one will. If you're restless, you can walk the shore, casting and retrieving your worm, and occasionally letting it lie on the bottom awhile.

Grasshoppers, in season, are another good bait. You can fish them on the surface, preferably along the shore where they're tumbling in and the trout are hunting them, or you can sink them like a worm. They'll take fish either way, but the former method is more fun.

If you can handle a fly rod, however, you'll take both more and bigger fish from the mountain lakes on a fly than in any other way. Your flies imitate the aquatic insects and other minute creatures on which the fish feed every day. The old residents eventually get wise to glittering, flashing lures, but they never get wise to flies.

I've caught more trout by far on wet flies and nymphs than on dry flies, but occasionally the latter are better. Conventional patterns, the kind you use any-where, will work. A long tapered leader, as light as the size of the fish and the natural hazards—moss, snags and weeds—permit, is always a help. Don't hesitate to use a leader twelve or fourteen feet long, and if you can get by with two feet of 2- or 3-pound-test nylon for a tippet you'll get more strikes.

You definitely need two lines, a floater and a sinker. The floater is, of course, for dry flies and for fishing a wet fly or a nymph near the surface. But when the trout are feeding from six to fifteen feet down, as they often do, you'll starve to death unless you have a line that sinks.

I often fish a lake unique in the respect that it is seldom clear. It is shallow and so fertile that it blooms most of the summer. The first time I tried it, rising trout—at least I thought they were rising—nearly drove me frantic. They were big, and boiling everywhere. I tried all my dry flies and all sorts of wet flies, nymphs and streamers near the surface. However, I didn't get a single strike.

Eventually, after I started fishing deeper and deeper, I finally began to connect. The trout were feeding just above the moss, which was about eight feet beneath the surface in the spot where I first got into them. They always seem to feed there in this particular lake, and though they boil frequently, I have yet to hear of anyone's taking even one of them on a dry fly.

At any rate, one morning after I had learned to fish a wet fly very deep with a pull-pause retrieve, I caught five native cutthroats. They all looked as though they had come out of the same mold, and the one I kept to eat weighed exactly 5 pounds. I hooked two bigger fish that broke off!

I don't know a river in the West that can provide such sport. But there are plenty of lakes that will. Any way you look at it, this is the best fishing in America.

I'll Fish Again Yesterday

COREY FORD

The secret of going back to the trout streams of yesteryear and finding them as good as ever is really very simple when you learn it.
(September 1959)

I could close my eyes and see it all again. The stream made a bend to the right, I remembered, and there was a long slick pool, and below it was a boulder shaped like a coffeepot. No—come to think of it, the boulder must have been at the head of the pool, because the stream parted around it and the main channel ran dark and deep along the far bank, and that was where Old Faithful had risen to my fly.

I called him Old Faithful because he had been rising regularly, every hour on the hour, and I had been trying for him for three days. I'd offered him every pattern in my book, and a few others I made up on the spot. I had worked him in the early morning with a Black Gnat, and in the evening with a White Miller, and once when it was almost dark he had turned under a spentwing Cahill, but I retrieved the fly too soon. And then on the morning of the fourth day I had tied on a No. 16 Quill Gordon, which is my favorite fly, and made a long cast, so that the fly lit on the grass above the bank and fell lightly onto the slick, and he sucked it in.

He had come clear out of water as I lifted the rod, and my mind snapped a mental picture of him hanging there in space, the fly embedded in his lower jaw and the leader slanting down to the stream. Everything was immobilized at the instant my mind clicked the shutter: the great trout suddenly rigid at the height of his leap, a few shining drops of water still suspended in the air; a blue heron halted in midflight with its disjointed wings bent backward like a Siamese dancer's arms; a marmot frozen on the bank in an attitude of permanent horror. That was the picture I had carried in my mind for—how long was it?—twenty years.

So now, twenty years later, I was going back to fish the stream again. I had never told anyone where it was, of course. A man may share his wealth or his liquor or the names in his address book; but there are some things—a pet grouse cover, a favorite piece of trout water—that he does not tell. All these years I had remembered it as the finest dry-fly stream in America. And now I had flown two thousand miles across the country to find the coffeepot boulder, to drop a fly once more on the secret pool that no one knew about except myself.

I rented a car at the airport, and as I drove south the sagebrush hills unrolled before me in a familiar pattern. I had not bothered to bring a map; the white Tetons stood against the sky, and I knew where I was going. The bumpy road would wind through the foothills and cross a narrow bridge, and there would be a little country store and a gas pump on the left. Across the road, under some pines, would be a few log cabins for rent. The cabin where I used to stay was on the very bank of the stream, and at night after supper I could wade out into the flat stretch beside it, when the evening hatch was on, and see the concentric circles of rising rainbows everywhere. I never met any other fishermen. Muskrats scurried silently up and down the banks, and once I watched a cow moose browsing on the opposite shore, her head under water to the nape of her neck.

The Tetons were looming larger ahead, and I began to wonder. The road was smoother than I remembered it, and very straight. Instead of skirting a hill it plunged right through, leaving a wake of uprooted stumps and tumbled earth. Now and then, looking down from a high embankment, I could see a section of the abandoned road below me, winding off through the trees in search of a less efficient and more leisurely past. Cars zoomed by, but I drove slowly, looking for the little store and the gas pump. Maybe this new highway would miss it altogether. Then before I knew it I was crossing the bridge—a wide concrete one now—and I halted beside the finest dry-fly stream in America.

There were no cabins under the pines. In their place was a modern double-decker motel, and behind it the trees had been cleared to make room for a sizable trailer camp. Across the highway, where the country store had been, was an up-to-date shopping center the length of a city block, with its own post office, garage, butcher shop, supermarket, restaurant and glass-fronted bar with neon lights. Cars were parked fender to fender, and I had some trouble in finding a vacant slot at the far end. I walked back along the paved sidewalk, elbowing my way past women vacationers in slacks, and entered a door marked Rental Office.

The man behind the counter told me I was lucky. There was only one room left tonight, on the second floor. This was the height of the fishing season, he reminded me, and people usually made their reservations away ahead. "First time you're here?"

I explained that I had been here a long time ago, before the war.

"I guess you'll notice a lot of improvements since then," he said as I paid for my room in advance. "It's been a big development of this stream."

He turned to ring up the cash register, and I stole a glance at the fishing equipment around me. A number of shellacked wooden poles were stacked in a corner, and the walls were hung with long-handled dip nets and metal gaffs and minnow buckets. On the shelf above the counter was a complete assortment of spoons and plugs, spinning tackle, lead sinkers, jars of salmon eggs and a small tray of artificial lures—mostly grasshoppers and rubber hellgrammites. The showcase was filled with souvenir ashtrays decorated with trout, and a revolving rack offered a selection of comic postcards showing fat anglers falling in the water or catching mermaids. "How's the fishing?" I asked, pocketing the change.

"Oh, they been taking quite a few," the man behind the counter said, "up to eight or ten inches. That's the size of trout the state is stocking now."

It was late afternoon, and still time for the evening hatch. I changed to my waders and hurried down to the stream along a gravel path bordered with cut logs. It led past the trailer camp to the flat stretch I used to fish at night after supper. The bank was lined with people plopping spinning lures from shore, and I could see the silhouettes of others along the concrete bridge, dangling their hooks below. Children scurried up and down the bank, tossing out sticks for a dog to fetch, and on the opposite side of the stream, where I had watched the cow moose once, a middle-aged woman was washing her hair. Her neck was craned over the water, and a trail of white suds drifted below her in the slow current.

I thought I saw a rise, though it might have been a pebble tossed by one of the children, and I waded out toward it. A couple of paper cups and a crumpled cellophane cigarette wrapper bobbed downstream past me; the evening hatch had started. As I lengthened my line I heard the steady thudding of an outboard motor, and a rowboat rounded the point, with three men and a woman trolling in its wake. They passed directly over the spot where I had seen the rise, and waved to me cordially.

I reeled in again and waded ashore, then strolled back up the path to the bar. All the tables were taken, and I planted a felt-soled wading shoe on the brass rail. The television set behind the bar was broadcasting a quiz program, and a jukebox across the room blasted a rival rock-and-roll. The tune was familiar, but I couldn't place it for the moment. A young man in knee-length rubber boots was standing beside me, his elbows hooked on the counter; he noticed my waders and sidled closer, drawn by a common bond of brotherhood. "Catch anything?" he asked me.

I shook my head. It was hard to talk above all the noise.

"I caught one the other day," he volunteered, "went better'n a pound."

I nodded absently. I had just recognized the tune on the jukebox; it was called the "Tea for Two Cha-Cha." They had been playing the same tune twenty years ago. My companion was saying something, and I bent toward him. "I'm sorry, I didn't hear you."

". . . have on?" he repeated, his lips beside my ear. "What were ya using?"

"Fly," I shouted back.

"And now for five hundred dollars, Mrs. Nussbaum," the quizmaster on the television screen was asking, "can you name three Presidents of the United States with beards?"

"Flies ain't any good around here," my brother angler confided. "I tell ya what ya wanna use, if ya wanna catch a big one." He looked around to make sure he was not overheard, and placed a fraternal hand on my shoulder. "This is just between us, see."

". . . and two for tea," the jukebox roared, "and me for you and you for me . . ."

"Ya get some salmon eggs, and ya take and dump 'em in a net, and ya hold the net unna watter so the milk rises offen the salmon eggs . . ."

"Abraham Lincoln is *right*, Mrs. Nussbaum. And now can you name a second one—he was a famous Civil War general."

". . . and ya let a coupla bullheads swim inna ya net, see, and then ya lift it quick . . ."

"Try and think now, Mrs. Nussbaum. His first name was Ulysses."

". . . and ya take and thread ya hook through wunna the bullheads, and ya hang the other one on ya hook so it'll still wiggle, and ya let it way down inna the water, see." He gave me a wink and drained his glass. "Ya'll catch a big one every time."

I thanked him and bought him another drink and left. I wanted to get some sleep; tomorrow I would set out bright and early to find the deep run below the coffeepot boulder. I could find it again with my eyes shut. I would drive along an old lumber road as far as it would go, and hike the rest of the way on foot, then climb down a steep bluff to the stream. No one ever got this far back; I was the only one who knew the secret pool. Across the room the jukebox bellowed, "Nobody near us to see us or hear us . . ."

* * *

Even the lumber road had been improved, I discovered. The brush had been cleared, the sides bulldozed to make it wider, and the surface was packed hard with constant travel. It seemed to go on endlessly, but I noticed a side road to the right, heading in the general direction of the stream. The tire ruts looked fresh as I turned onto it; other cars had used it recently. It terminated in a clearing on a high bluff, and I could hear the roar of the river below me as I climbed out of the car.

In front of me was a wooden sign with carved letters reading STATE CAMP SITE. KEEP THIS AREA CLEAN. Picnic tables and benches had been erected under the trees, and there were conveniently located metal wastebaskets to hold trash, and a public latrine at one end of the clearing. Several trailers were parked at the edge of the bluff, and their occupants in various stages of undress were performing their morning ablutions. A small sign said COFFEEPOT RAPIDS and pointed to a steep trail leading down the side of the bluff. Steps had been cut here and there in the dirt, and there was a rustic handrail to make the descent easier.

The grass beside the stream was trampled, and I noticed some empty salmon-egg jars and a tangled length of monofilament line caught in a snag. I followed a well-worn path along the bank, and the river made a bend to the right, and at the head of the pool was the boulder. The stream parted around it, and the main channel hugged the far bank. The run looked shallow, and somehow the whole pool had gotten smaller, the way an old person shrinks with age.

I put on a No. 16 Quill Gordon and made a long cast across the stream. The fly brushed the grass and dropped onto the slick, and a fish struck it. He broke water as I lifted the rod, and for a moment I had a picture of Old Faithful hanging there in space, halted at the height of his leap. I could see the drops of water standing in the air, the blue heron motionless in midflight, the marmot still frozen on the bank.

I reeled in. A little trout skittered toward me on top of the water, and I slipped a wet hand around him and lifted him gently. He might have gone 8 or 10 inches; I didn't measure him. He had a hatchery pallor, and his breath smelled strongly of liver. I removed the fly from his upper lip and put him back, holding him upright in the water until he regained his strength. He did not dart away at once but swam around my feet, reluctant to return to the stream. I knew how he felt.

I heard steps behind me. My brother angler of the night before was floundering up the path, his knee-length rubber boots dislodging an empty beer can that rolled into the stream with a clank. "Catch anything?" he asked me.

"I caught a 6-pound rainbow," I said.

He didn't believe me, of course. I think he was a little hurt because I was making fun of him. "Yeah? Where?"

"Right there," I told him, and pointed to my secret pool. "Over by that far bank."

It didn't matter now. Why keep my secret any more? No one else could find the pool but myself. It would always be there in my mind, the way it used to be, and Old Faithful would be waiting for my fly. I could take him again whenever I closed my eyes.

How to Become
a 20/20 Angler

ARNOLD GINGRICH

The challenge—and rewards—of taking trout over 20 inches long on a #20 or smaller fly. (December 1959)

A quarter century ago I fished frequently with Ernest Hemingway out of Key West and in the Gulf Stream off Bimini. They say that the human memory tends to enlarge upon pleasure and to minimize pain, but about all I remember of that fishing now is the agonizing backache. I'd pump and reel for the better part of an hour to get a big tuna up to the boat, only to have him sound like an elevator with a snapped cable. Then I'd pump and reel again for the better part of another hour before losing him, finally, to the sharks.

Even when I caught a giant bluefin, I can't say that it was any satisfaction to me. And now, with marine engines souped up, the modern game is more of a joint operation, the skipper and his boat doing the important work. I have the team spirit, but that's not what I look for in angling.

In those days the only other fishing I'd ever done had been plug casting for bass, pickerel, and pike—though in the latter case always in the hope of meeting up with a muskie. I thought that fishing was something you do from a boat. I liked it, and I suppose I'd even do it again if it were the only kind of fishing I could get. For that matter, I'd fish from a pier for perch, with a pearl button for bait, if that were the only kind of fishing to be had. I feel now, as I felt then, that any kind of fishing is better than no fishing.

But I know now, as I didn't know then, that the finest fun in fishing is qualitative—and that all that fishing I used to do, whether trolling for bass in Pistakee Bay or for big fish on the blue water, was merely quantitative. Like most Americans, I started out in fishing by Thinking Big. I didn't know that the added dimension of fishing fun begins only when you start Thinking Fine. Except to heft my father's fly rod as a kid in Michigan, I'd never even held such a rod in my hand, much less waded a stream. And while I thought I'd done a lot of fishing, I didn't even know that real angling begins where mere fishing leaves off, the moment you step into a stream with a fly rod in your hand.

Since 1939, when I first crossed that great divide between fishing and angling, I've acquired a baker's dozen fly rods, including some fairly stout sticks intended for salmon, but for the past five seasons I've hardly ever had occasion to use any of them but one, a custom-made bamboo job measuring just over 6 feet long and weighing just under 1¾ ounces. It's called the Midge, as it's primarily intended for use with tiny midges of size 20 or smaller, but it's such a versatile rod that I've used not only bucktails and streamers of sizes 10 and 12 on it but even salmon flies up to size 4.

On a rod like that, even an 8-incher can put up a very respectable fight, and anything bigger begins to take on proportions that are positively heroic. But you're liable to come in for a lot of kidding about having stolen some kid's toy. That's one of the penalties of Thinking Fine, but there are pleasures in it that more than compensate. Now your eyes are on another target, as it were, and where formerly all that mattered was How Much, now it has become a matter of How Well.

You're in another league, you might say, and its standards are infinitely higher. Your new par for the course is 20/20, and the thrill of making it, even if you manage to bring it off no more than once or twice a season, is greater than that of hauling in a boatload of fish by the old chuck-and-chance-it and troll-and-pray methods. Of course, 20/20 means getting a fish of 20 inches or more on a fly of size 20 or less. Every time you do it you are entitled to give yourself the secret grip of the exclusive society of veritable anglers, as distinguished from ordinary fishermen.

Now, there's a seeming paradox in this Fishing Fine: although it gets you more strikes in the overfished and overcrowded waters near our big cities, where most of us have to do our fishing nowadays, it is also very likely to get you strikes from *bigger* fish. Even if this sounds peculiar, like sailing west to arrive east, you will see on reflection that there is no real contradiction at all. Old saws about "Big bait, big fish" to the contrary, it stands to reason that fish which have managed to survive to any real size in the face of the rising fishing pressure are bound to be too wary to strike at ordinary lures tied to lines or leaders of conventional size. That gives you a great advantage when you start fishing fine. You get big ones.

A small rod naturally calls for a fine line—HEH or HDG. (You'll get still more strikes, and from bigger fish, if it's IHI, which means going back to the English No. 1 silk line, since none of our American line makers has yet seen fit to put a true IHI on the market.) And for the same reason that you must use a fine line, to avoid a fish-scaring slap on the water, you must also use a long leader with a fine tippet. The leader should be at least ten feet long, and longer than that if you can manage it without bird's-nesting it. At the butt end you can use .0185, or .0197 if you find that you need more weight in the butt to enable you to get out its full length. The leader should taper down to a tippet of .0059 for early season, .0047 for mid-May through June, and .0039 after the Fourth of July, when the low water on sunny days makes the shadow of any leader look like that of a telephone trunk line.

It's axiomatic that the longer and finer the leader the more fish you'll move, but this holds true only when you lay that leader out to its full length and drop it on the water quietly and in a straight line. If it lands in a tangled heap, move on to the next pool, because you'll have scared away every fish worth hooking. To help avert pileups of fine leader, use a piece of rubber to rub the full length of your leader several times, thus eliminating twists, curls, or kinks. I learned this long ago from your Fishing Editor, and it has meant more to my own angling success than any other single thing. The rubber ring from a Mason jar, or an old piece of inner tube, or even an eraser or a big rubber band—anything of the sort will do.

Except in very low water, the length of your cast doesn't seem to matter much as long as you're fishing upstream and are deliberate in your movements. A pause to smoke a cigarette, once you've arrived at a spot where you intend to make a cast, is enough to rest the stream after any slight disturbance caused by your wading.

Now that you're there, what fly? When you're fishing as fine as this, it doesn't seem to make a great deal of difference. If it's a size 20 or smaller, I honestly think it could be sky-blue-pink and you'd still get a strike on it. Also, flies this small are very tolerant of slight errors of presentation that might be fatal in the conventional sizes. Drag, for instance, which is supposed to be so terrible on an upstream cast with a dry fly, sometimes seems to be an added attraction in a midge that's floating on or in the surface film. When you see your fly starting to drag, give it an occasional 6-inch twitch, and more likely than not you'll produce an answering explosion.

Then what? Chances are you'll lose him—but have a picnic in the process. If he's a big rainbow or brown, about 18 inches long, you'll probably find he's no longer with you after the second or third jump, assuming you have him on .0047 or .0039. But after you've lost your first few big fish you'll be surprised how well even .0039 will hold. Your chances of hanging onto the big ones get better all the time, as you become more aware, with each successive loss, of the limits of your equipment. Actually, it's only the fine leader that's working against you, since the light little rod is an advantage rather than a handicap, giving ground rather than allowing the fish something stiff to pull against.

As for the leader, just remember that you wouldn't have got the strike at all on a heavier one, and you'll hardly bemoan a certain percentage of breakoffs. You soon learn to play the fish so gently that you're almost afraid to draw a breath while he's on. Once you've developed that attitude, you find that each big fish is on longer than the one before, until finally, to your surprise and pleasure, you begin landing some of those lunkers. In the past three seasons I've had .0039 hold fish up to 3 pounds, .0047 up to 5, and .0059 up to 8.

If you long ago stopped using a landing net, your first experiences with fine tippets may make you want to go back to it. But if you play the fish until he's belly up, you can easily hold him head up with your rod, then grasp him gently from behind and release the hook without exciting him into breaking off the fine tippet.

Fishing fine is a relative thing. When the stream is up to your waist or higher, .0059 is plenty fine, and you can take fish readily on size 14 nymphs and size 12 streamers and bucktails, fishing both downstream and up.

The most consistent fun I have is with a size 14 hairwing streamer called the Betsy—it's really only a hairwing peacock-bodied wet Coachman—that I dress heavily with dry-fly oil, cast across stream, and let float down like a little sailboat. On the down float it often takes fish, but even when it doesn't it serves as a marvelous locator, producing curiosity bursts and bunts. I then try to bring it back over those places where fish have made passes, retrieving it in quick, short jerks that make it pull under and then bob up.

Almost invariably one of the fish that poked at it on its way down will chase it frantically on its way back up—often seizing it within twenty or even fifteen feet of where I'm standing. They seem so engrossed in catching this bobbing little object that they fail to notice me and grab it almost at the moment I'm lifting it from the water for another cast. This happens again and again, not merely with the silly little jaspers under 9 inches long but with fish old enough to know better—big ones by eastern standards that perforce measure fish in inches rather than pounds.

When the water level is about knee-high, better fine your tippet down to .0047, with about thirty inches at the hook end of your leader. With this tippet you get a very lifelike descent to the water on size 16 or 18 dry flies, particularly spiders and hairwings like the Quack Royal Coachman. It's only in low water, barely over your ankles, that you must go down to an .0039 tippet and stick to flies of size 20 or smaller. And it's really only then that you must limit yourself to upstream fishing. For at such times you must fish not only fine but far-off too, or you'll move very few fish.

You will be much better off, when the time of low water comes, to crouch down out of sight as much as possible. If you won't go on your knees for any fish, your only alternative is to make casts of better than forty-five feet upstream, because otherwise you might just as well spare your casting arm. To make that kind of cast with a short, light rod and fine-gauge line, you must use the booster technique known as the double-line haul. The best way to learn it is from somebody who knows it and will teach it to you. The only place it has ever been adequately described in print is in *The Practical Fly Fisherman* by Al McClane.

The fair rewards of fishing fine are a soothing balm to the ego. Your greatest moment will come when you move into a pool that has just been abandoned by a couple of spin fishermen who have tossed several hundred pounds of assorted hardware through it between them, only to reach the disgusted conclusion that it has been fished out. Just watch their faces as you move fish in the very spots they've combed to no effect.

Aside from a few cheap triumphs like that, the biggest reward is a purely inner satisfaction, when you find your whole attitude toward angling changing as you become more and more devoted to the question of How Well as opposed to How Much. We all start out as fish hogs at heart, I suppose, but if we stick to it long enough we finally educate ourselves out of it. Fishing with light tackle becomes a thing that is fun in and of itself. As in the case of the idiots with the swimming pool, you'd enjoy it almost as much even if there weren't any water at all. The satisfaction of making a long, smooth, quiet cast that settles on the water as softly as the fall of snow, and of watching the thistledown way your tiny fly hovers down onto the water on that fine filament—why, you begin to enjoy even the casts that don't provoke strikes.

You find yourself keeping score, rather than keeping fish. Oh, sure, if you've promised somebody some fish, you'll keep as many as you feel you must. But you'll also find that your enjoyment goes up the minute you realize that, having kept enough to fulfill the obligation, you now *don't have to keep any more*. This feeling may well surprise you, the first time it comes over you, but come over you sooner or later it certainly will.

The ironical part of it all is that your headiest success as an angler only begins when you start caring more about the fishing than the fish. It's something like the gambling axiom, "Scared money never wins"—greedy fishing never produces. Or maybe fish are like cats; they won't come to you if they know you want them, but swarm over you if they know you don't. To sum up, you give all the good cards to the fish, then win more handily than you ever did before.

Of course, I must warn you that going in for fine tackle is a case of doing it the hard way. You will get snarled, not only in your leader but in the forepart of your line, and the nests will be pesky to pick loose, because of the very fineness of your tackle. You must be temperamentally inclined toward getting a kick out of doing things the hard way, or this fishing is not for you. My wife says that a tape recording of me "enjoying myself" on the stream would strike fear into the hearts of a riot squad. The slightest unexpected trick of the wind or a lapse in your own timing can make you goof into an unholy mess, and you'll cuss yourself to high heaven. But when that little coil of oiled silk shoots out there ahead of you the way it should, as it does about nineteen times out of twenty, the joy of fishing fine is an unexampled thrill.

Ants Can Make Trout Say Uncle

ERNEST G. SCHWIEBERT

*A leading angler/entomologist reveals how to tie, and when to use,
the most common and killing of all terrestrials.* (May 1961)

Few fishermen ever think of the ant as a trout lure. For one thing, we've conditioned ourselves to flies that imitate aquatic insects, such as the exquisite mayflies. Second, we rarely, if ever, see ant artificials in tackle shops. Hence we tend to overlook a most productive lure. All fishermen have seen ant-eating trout in the hot afternoons of midsummer, but few realize what the fish are taking as they bulge in the surface film or flash in their feeding lies.

Ants are, of course, land insects, but large numbers of them find their way into the water. This happens constantly in all seasons but winter, quite unlike the brief, cyclic aquatic hatches along our trout streams. Like most terrestrial insects, ants are active in the warm, sunny hours of midday, when wading a stream and fishing a fly is pleasant work.

I was painfully slow myself in recognizing the importance of ants in the trout diet, even though I had my first experience with ant-eating fish when I was a boy in Michigan. The brook I fished flowed through a meadow, and usually provided me with several trout. But this day no fish would touch my grasshopper bait, even though I could see brookies bulging regularly at the surface.

When I finally did hook and gut a foolish young fish, I found its stomach crammed with minute black ants less than ⅛ inch long. That was bad news for me. I couldn't use them for bait; my hooks were bigger than the little insects. Today, though, you can buy extremely small hooks—sizes 20, 22, and 24. And there is featherweight tackle to make them usable. With such gear, taking those ant eaters would have been relatively easy.

Many years passed before I noted another ant-eating orgy, this time on the big water of the Gunnison River in Colorado. Our party encountered a vast mating swarm of ants over the river, and the trout were feeding heavily at the surface. There were scattered hatches of pale mayflies coming off the long, milk-colored riffles, but the heavy browns and rainbows ignored them and gorged on the ants.

Desperately we tied some ant imitations, and took a few fish, but on the whole our efforts were fruitless. That afternoon we tried again with orange-bodied flies tied into bulbous sections suggestive of the ant. When the bodies were soaked in lacquer, the orange silk assumed a rusty-reddish sheen suggestive of the naturals. These worked reasonably well as wet flies but were largely failures when fished on the surface. The reason was simple, though it escaped us then. The winged ants that fell into the river struggled along in the surface film, whereas our lacquered imitations sank quickly. The fish ignored them except in broken water, where the naturals sank quickly too. We tried adding hackle, but then the flies rode too high, creating a false silhouette.

What we needed, of course, was a fly that was neither wet nor dry—one that floated in the surface film and not on it, and certainly one that would not sink. Later I studied ants carefully under a microscope and discovered that their bodies were not lacquer-smooth, as I'd thought, but rough with hairlike filaments. Experimenting, I tied some antlike flies with dubbed-fur bodies and sparse, stiff hackles. Fur seemed to be the answer, for it had the proper light pattern and imparted the right floating qualities. That was lesson No. 1.

I got my second lesson several summers later on Penns Creek in central Pennsylvania. I was fishing with Charlie Wetzel, author of the book *Practical Fly Fishing*, and the high priest of the Weikert water on the Penns. The day was hot and windy when we began fishing below a small feeder brook, where cold water entered the river. We saw no rises or insects in the air. While Charlie worked the run along the rocks I fished big variants and streamers in midriver, hoping to pull up an occasional fish. My efforts were fruitless, though Charlie was getting browns with disturbing regularity. Finally I swallowed my pride and asked him what he was using. Laughing, he pulled in his line.

At the end of his 12-foot leader were two large lacquered-silk ants tied on heavy hooks so they would sink quickly and ride deep in the swift Penns Creek current.

Searching through his jacket, Charlie found a fly box and gave me two of the imitations.

It seemed Charlie was getting action because the trees beside the stream were full of carpenter ants, big *Camponotus* workers, and the wind was blowing many into the water, where they sank. My first drift through the run produced a foot-long brown that bounced out and bolted when he felt the pull of the line. From that time on, ant artificials have had a prominent place in my thinking and in my collection of fly boxes.

If you wonder why, consider that there are about 3,000 different species of ants in the family *Formicidae*, and they commonly get into water. I have found ant-eating fish in many waters, both here and in Europe. In time I selected ten species as prototypes and tied imitations of them after considerable experiment and research. Now, these ten don't suggest all the 3,000 species, but they are sufficiently representative of the many well-distributed kinds, and on the whole they rarely fail when trout are feeding on ants.

Formicas are medium-sized ants that are widely distributed and extremely important to the angler. These reddish-brown ants are often present along trout waters; the mating swarm we'd seen over the Gunnison had been composed of them.

A more recent experience with the *Formica* was on the marvelous Gros Ventre River in Wyoming. That day I was fishing the heavy water below Kelly that is known as the Beaverhouse stretch. The first pool was deep and strong, with jade-colored ledges down in the heavy holding water at its head. Since I had found *Formica* ants in the stomach of a large cutthroat I'd killed the afternoon before on a side channel of the Snake, I tied on an imitation and tried it over a feeding fish. The trout rose slowly but without hesitation, took my ant softly, and bolted deep into the pool. Five minutes later he came to net—2 pounds of strong, bright-colored cutthroat.

Other trout came just as easily during the morning. They were concentrated in some stretches, absent in others. I'd just finished fishing one of the barren spots and moved up to the next good-looking piece of water when I noticed rain clouds building over the Wind River foothills.

The main flow came down against a heavily willowed far bank, then angled across the length of the pool. Brush piles had built up in the deep water against the willows, and they interested me, for a local angler had told me that big trout hereabout stay around brush piles, where they are protected from otters. Easing out waist-deep into the tail of the pool, I cast my ant imitation near the cover. It settled softly into the current and drifted awash along the sheltering brush.

Suddenly a long bright-gold fish eased out into the river to intercept my lure.

His take was soft. Then, without breaking the surface, he writhed and stripped line deep into the heaviest current at the head of the pool. After that first frightened bolt he put on two strong runs, each of which threatened to carry the fight over the long chalk-colored shallows into the broken water below. The fish was already tired when he probed the brush that had sheltered him from otters, and I was able to turn him away from the snags.

Large rain drops were falling when I forced the cutthroat back into the open pool. He porpoised now, some twenty yards out, but I soon got him close enough to put my fingers on the leader knot. In a few moments I had measured the trout—23 inches—and released him. By that time I was thoroughly soaked and completely happy.

Another group of small brownish-black ants—*Tetramorium*—is important to the angler. These ants are well distributed and sought after by trout. The imitations I have tied on sizes 16 and 18 hooks have provided me with exciting low-water fishing; these flies have fooled so many selective fish that I cannot recommend them too highly.

I recall an instance on beautiful Slate Run, in the forest-covered mountains of north-central Pennsylvania. In a little meadow there is a small flat-water pool; its head is a fast, rocky chute, and most of it is exposed to the sun. Its tail is sheltered by a tree, and every pebble, root, and stick on the bottom is clearly visible. I always found several decent fish in this pool, and they would often free-rise through the midday hours in a tantalizing and puzzling fashion.

I had spent a midsummer afternoon on the shale pools below the meadow—two hours of poor fishing. At the meadow pool I was surprised to find trout feeding in the flat, ten of them working quietly over the bright gravel, not big but respectable. They rolled slowly, exposing their heads and dorsal fins. I studied the way they rose, then tried a size 16 nymph that suggested the mayfly hatch of that morning. A foot-long fish beneath the tree took the nymph on the first drift. But the others were not so easy; they refused the mayfly.

After I'd studied their rises again I decided they were not nymphing. The tiny green midge larva I tried next was not even inspected. Then I tied on a No. 18 black fur-bodied ant—and suddenly those supercilious browns became ridiculously easy. The best fish was not quite 15 inches, but I will always remember that meadow as a classic case of low water, light gear, minute flies, and the skittish brown trout of midsummer.

My first information about the red-and-black *Formica* ants came from an oldtimer who said he'd seen them on the timberline lakes just after ice-out. But not until I fished Hermit Lake, Colorado, did I have occasion to remember this fishing lore. The lake was about 10,000 feet high, and many snowdrifts still dotted the area.

Fly fishing was slow until midday, when the wind grew harsh. Then feeding activity started along the west shoreline. The trout came up sporadically as they cruised along the edge of the choppy water, but their rises were so infrequent that it was difficult to determine which way the fish were going after each flurry of feeding.

Since we were having poor luck, I decided to walk around the lake to where some spin fishermen were cleaning their trout. On examining the fish's stomachs I found most of them filled with cheese, which the spinners had been using as bait. One fish, taken near the surface, was an exception: it was stuffed with red-and-black ants.

Hurrying back to my friends, I told them of my discovery. We tried ant imitations on the cruising trout along the inlet and soon were into good fish. The technique was simple. With partially greased lines and leaders, we'd cast out into the general rise area and let the ants hang motionless just under the surface. Cruising brookies would swim by and pick up the drifting lures. The method was a low form of fly fishing, but it caught more fish in less time than our random, guesswork casting to the intermittent rises.

I once had two days of the most astonishing fishing I've experienced with *Monomorium* imitations. This was above Moose Crossing, Wyoming, on a small feeder channel of the Snake River. The holding water was brief and mirror-smooth—a hundred yards of it, at most—but it had an astonishing population of big, wild cutthroats and rainbows. My first morning there was both impressive and exhausting, and my nervous system barely outlasted the first full day.

The contest ended in a draw. I raised five trout and landed two; one was a rainbow of 20 inches, the other a bulky cutthroat of 22. Two other fish broke my delicate nylon tippets when my line tangled in the grass.

The fifth took my ant in a shoal channel and cruised calmly up the current for sixty yards. I was helpless; the line hung slack as I tried to pamper my fragile leader by holding the rod high above my head. Then the trout dropped back downstream, opened his jaws, and spit out the tiny No. 22 lure. My mouth hung open. That fish must have been 30 inches long!

The large black carpenter ants that were present on Penns Creek that afternoon I fished with Charlie Wetzel belonged to the important *Camponotus* genus. Most adults measure about ⅝ inch; the infertile female workers may be longer. Very large trout can often be taken with big carpenter-ant imitations. My best fish was a heavy 26-inch brown trout from famous Spring Creek in Pennsylania.

The little *Monomorium* ants that I first encountered many years ago in that Michigan meadow later provided good fishing elsewhere. Measuring less than ⅛ inch, their impressive role as an important trout food is in startling contrast to their diminutive size. Imitations must be dressed on tiny size 22 and 24 hooks. Many fishermen doubt the value of hooks so small, but in the hands of experienced light-tackle anglers they will hold fish of trophy dimensions.

The late Edward Ringwood Hewitt tasted ants, and concluded, in his book *Telling on the Trout*, that their tartness was the secret of their trout appeal. Perhaps the fish savor ants as we do the sourness of dill pickles. Whatever the reason, trout take ants—sometimes in remarkable numbers.

Between feeding periods (when the attention of the trout is focused on the traditional aquatic hatches) and late in the season (when many of these hatches have lived out their brief lives), terrestrial insects are important to the angler. Since that long-ago summer when I first found trout feeding on the minute black ants, my experience has taught me that ant imitations, like any other artificial flies, are no miraculous day-in-day-out panacea but should occupy a major place in streamside literature and angling.

Because of their incredible numbers and constant presence, ants are the commonest insects available to the trout. Ant feeding is far more common on all trout waters than most anglers realize, but those who know the secret of the soft midsummer rises under wind-tossed willows sing the praises of the lowly ant.

Ant Patterns

BLACK ANT (*Tetramorium caespitum*)

Head:	Black-dyed seal fur
Thorax:	Black-dyed seal fur on brown silk
Legs:	Iron-blue-dun hackle tied sparse
Gaster:	Black-dyed seal fur
Silk:	6/0 black
Hook:	16 or 18 down-eye

HONEY ANT (*Solenopsis molesta*)

Head:	Honey-yellow nylon wool dubbed on yellow silk
Thorax:	Honey-yellow nylon wool dubbed on yellow silk
Legs:	Pale-honey hackle tied sparse
Gaster:	Honey-yellow nylon wool dubbed on yellow silk
Silk:	8/0 white
Hook:	20 down-eye

CINNAMON ANT (*Lasius niger*)

Head:	Dark reddish-brown fur dubbing
Thorax:	Dark reddish-brown fur dubbing
Legs:	Dark furnace hackle tied sparse
Gaster:	Dark reddish-brown fur dubbing
Silk:	8/0 white
Hook:	20 down-eye

RED-AND-BROWN ANT (*Formica subintegra*)

Head:	Reddish-brown seal fur on red silk
Thorax:	Reddish-brown seal fur on red silk
Legs:	Light furnace hackle tied sparse
Gaster:	Dark-brown fur dubbing
Silk:	6/0 black
Hook:	12 or 14 fine-wire down-eye

RED ANT *(Formica schaufussi)*

Head:	Reddish-brown seal fur on brown silk
Thorax:	Reddish-brown seal fur on brown silk
Legs:	Light-brown hackle tied sparse
Gaster:	Reddish-brown seal fur on brown silk
Silk:	6/0
Hook:	12 or 14 fine-wire down eye

RED-AND-BLACK ANT
(Formica rubicunda)

Head:	Dark reddish-brown seal fur on red silk
Thorax:	Dark reddish-brown seal fur on red silk
Legs:	Dark fiery-brown hackle tied sparse
Gaster:	Black-dyed seal fur on brown silk
Silk:	6/0 black
Hook:	12 or 14 fine-wire down-eye

CARPENTER ANT
(Camponotus herculeanus)

Head:	Black-dyed seal-fur dubbing
Thorax:	Dark-brown fur dubbing
Legs:	Iron-blue-dun hackle tied sparse
Gaster:	Black-dyed seal-fur dubbing
Silk:	6/0 black
Hook:	8 or 10 fine-wire down-eye

MINUTE BLACK ANT
(Monomorium minimum)

Head:	Black-dyed seal-fur dubbing
Thorax:	Black-dyed seal-fur dubbing
Legs:	Iron-blue-dun hackle tied sparse
Gaster:	Black-dyed seal-fur dubbing
Silk:	8/0 black
Hook:	22 or 24 down-eye

Hatch of the Coffin Flies

HUGH FOSBURGH

On a very, very few evenings a year, a glut hatch of these huge mayflies triggers an unforgettable feeding frenzy. (June 1961)

Early in June on Big River there is an occurrence that sets all the trout crazy with pleasure, and the trout fishermen, too, if any happen to be there, which is unlikely. This is the hatch of the coffin flies. It occurs just before dark, abruptly and without warning, and it may happen two evenings in a row, or three at the most, and then it is over.

Coffin flies are fat, awkward, nondescript things—delectable mouthfuls for the very largest and most discriminating brown trout—and on Big River they hatch in incredible swarms. They have little of the delicate beauty of some mayflies, and they are unlike them in another respect that is important to the trout and fishermen. When the usual mayfly nymph rises from the river bottom to the surface, it sits there awhile, freeing itself from the nymph casing and drying its wings—apparently in no hurry to get off the water and go about its business. A trout knows all about this serene complacence and comes rolling up with leisurely confidence to suck in the fly. There is just a little boil on the surface, and maybe a couple of bubbles, to show what has happened.

Coffin flies are different; they're in a frantic rush to be free of the water. The nymphs come fighting up from the bottom, and by the time they reach the surface

230

they are no longer nymphs; they are flies that erupt from the water and go lumbering into the air.

Trout know about this, too, or at least learn very quickly, and their usual polite, dignified manner of feeding goes to hell in a hurry. They turn hog-greedy, lose all sense of caution, and go slashing about like sharks, grabbing up almost anything that looks like a coffin fly. They have an orgy.

A fisherman wise to this situation can have an orgy too. He will know the approximate time of year to expect the hatch, and he will have his location picked out—preferably a slick just below some fast water. Each evening, just at sundown, he'll station himself there. He may use a wet fly imitation of the coffin-fly nymph, but probably he will fish with a big fanwing—a Royal Coachman is very good —or perhaps a smoke-colored hair fly, which is easier to keep afloat than the feathered kind.

However wise the fisherman, the coffin-fly hatch, when it starts, will take him by surprise. He will fish two evenings perhaps, and he may catch some trout or he may not, but in either case there will be no sign of the coffin flies. The third evening he is there again. The river, so far as he can see, is lifeless—there are no flies on the water, no sign of rising fish. Then, about 8:15 or 8:30, while he is casting the fanwing (he has to do something while he waits for activity), a trout comes whacking for it and is hooked.

This may or may not mean a thing; sometimes a lone fish will come for a fanwing when no other trout are feeding. But this time it does. It means that the first coffin flies are coming up and that the fish are alert to them and are grabbing the nymphs before they reach the surface. Chances are, when the fisherman nets his fish and casts again to the same place, another trout will stab for the fly and be hooked. A trout taking what he presumes to be a coffin fly is easily and firmly hooked because in his rush to get it he engulfs the imitation.

About this time the fisherman will begin to notice an occasional swirl or boil or dimple at various places—trout taking the still-submerged nymphs. Finally, up where the fast water dumps into the slick, the first unmistakable coffin fly will pop up and go zooming toward the sky. Then, for certain, the hatch is coming off, and the orgy is under way.

Well, if the fisherman is an excitable type, he will very soon be in a frenzy. Here is the situation for which he has long waited, the dream come true. Coffin flies are exploding from the water in droves, trout have the whole slick in a turmoil—and it is almost dark. He must work fast; each minute counts; night is settling down like a curse.

He works too fast, of course. In his haste to net a fish, he breaks the leader. Or his fumbling, bumbling fingers take an agonizing eternity to put on a new fanwing. Or he loses the bottle of floater liquid. Or his meticulous preparations for this event have neglected one thing—he has forgotten to smear himself with fly dope. Now the midges are a relentless torture about his face and collar and wrists.

And finally, just before total dark—when there is still a chance for one last cast—the line and leader will become an infuriating bird's nest that only daylight and a return of patience can solve.

The fisherman will go ashore then. If he has come merely to catch trout he will go home immediately, to gloat over them and show them to the boys. If he has come for other reasons besides, he will sit awhile on the bank, listening to one of the most exciting sounds in the world—the sucking slurp of rising trout. It is a small sound, yet strangely and distinctly audible above the murmurous flow of the river.

All About Worm-Fishing

ED ZERN

With tongue firmly in cheek, a top humorist describe the calamities that can result from dunking the "garden hackle." (July 1965)

I met Malcolm Wheatly on 45th Street the other day, and when the subject of trout fishing came up, I found him no less vehement on the matter of worm fishing than he has been, more or less, for the past thirty years. "Mal," I said finally, "I think you exaggerate. Personally I'm a fly fisherman, and think it's the best way to fish for trout, but I can't believe that worm fishermen do as much damage to streams as *you* seem to believe."

"Ye gods, man!" shouted Mal, who's excitable. "You can't be serious! I can cite you dozens of cases where streams have been RUINED by worm fishermen!" "Name one," I said. Mal spluttered for a moment, then dragged me into a coffee-shop and flung me into a booth. "All right, buster," he snarled, "you asked for it. Just one case? Okay, you know the Lackawaxen, in Pennsylvania?" "Certainly," I said. "Well, sir," said Mal, "just about five years ago this month a worm fisherman from New Jersey went there fishing with his fiancée. It so happened she was from Barnegat, and had an almost insane passion for orderliness. One of those people who go around straightening pictures that are already straight and empting ashtrays with one burnt match in them." "I know the type," I said, "but what about worm fishing?"

"I'm coming to that," Mal snarled at me. "When this worm-fishing s.o.b. asked her to pick him out a wiggler from his bait can, where he had them in sphagnum moss, she opened up the can and then let out a helluva shriek. 'THE KELP!' she yelled. 'IT'S ALL TANGLED!' It wasn't kelp, of course, but to anybody from Barnegat it looked like seaweed. And naturally it was kind of messed up, which on account of this thing she had about orderliness caused her to scream." "Naturally," I had to admit.

"Well," said Mal, "a native walking by on the road alongside the river heard her scream—matter of fact, he'd seen them going down the bank and had figured they were up to no good—and then heard her holler what he thought was 'HELP! I'M BEING STRANGLED!' " "That figures," I conceded.

"Okay," said Mal. "When the native heard that, he ran out in front of a passing car to stop it and get help. Unfortunately he jumped right in front of the car and it hit him and killed him stone-dead." "For goodness' sakes," I said. "What a pity." "Ha!" said Mal. "That's nothing! True, the guy was penniless and had an invalid wife and no insurance—but the lady driving the car that hit him jammed on her brakes, and the truck behind her hit *her*. It so happened she was a destitute widow with seven children, and the whiplash injury she got when the truck slammed into her left her paralyzed from the eyeballs down—a hopeless case. The children were all farmed out to orphanages, and are growing up bitter and neurotic at the trick fate played on them." "It *was* a tough break," I agreed.

"You ain't heard *nothin'*, pal," Mal said darkly. "The bird driving the truck bumped his head into the windshield, and although nobody thought much about it at the time, he complained of pains in his head for six months afterwards, and then went berserk one day and killed six people with a meat cleaver before they gunned him down like a dog." "You can't blame them too much," I said. "After all, six—"

"Never mind them!" Mal screeched, his face contorted with fury. "I haven't even come to the bad part! While the truck was standing there a deputy sheriff with a wife and five children came roaring down the road in a high-powered car—he'd had a call from a nearby farmhouse—and smashed into the truck, kapow! In fact, he hit the truck so hard that the car bounced off it and down the bank into the creek, drowning the driver." "Gosh," I said, "what a terrible tragedy!"

"Listen!" yelled Mal. "Here's the payoff! This deputy had a house and a rose garden and a nice lawn and all that, and loved gardening, and when he took off to answer the accident call he had a gallon jar of weedkiller in the back seat, and when the car rolled down into the creek the jar broke and the weedkiller ran out into the current. Every last drop—right into the river!" "What about it?" I said.

"Great balls of fire!" Mal screamed. "Holy saints in heaven! *That gallon of poison killed nearly one hundred trout in the next quarter mile of river—including a dozen or so that would go over three pounds!* AND YOU ASK WHETHER WORM FISHING DAMAGES A TROUT STREAM? HA!"

I had to admit he had a point, and so I paid for the coffee.

First Trout, First Lie

NICK LYONS

A dyed-in-the-wool fly-fisher confesses to the criminal capture of his first trout. (February 1969)

Since I began to fish in the days before memory and have no consciousness of ever not fishing, the evidence is clear that I was born a fisherman. And though I did not catch my first trout until I was eight, it seems equally clear that I was born to angle for the trout, especially with flies only—which is what I now do.

My first experiences were in the lake that bordered the property my grand-father owned when the Laurel House in Haines Falls, New York, was his. At first no one gave me instruction or encouragement; I had no fishing buddies; and most adults in my world only attempted to dissuade me: they could only be considered the enemy. It was a small, heavily padded lake, little larger than a pond, and it contained only perch, shiners, punkinseeds, and pickerel. Invariably I fished with a long cane pole, cork bobber, string or length of gut, and snelled hook. Worms were my standby, though after a huge pickerel swiped at a small shiner I was diddling with I used shiners for bait also, and caught a good number of reputable pickerel. One went a full 4 pounds and nearly caused my Aunt Blanche to leap into the lake when, after a momentous tug, it flopped near her feet, which were in open sandals. She screeched and I leaped toward her—to protect my fish.

I also caught pickerel as they lay still in the still water below the dam and spillway. It was not beneath me to use devious methods: I was in those days cunning and resourceful and would lean far over the concrete dam to snare the pickerel with piano wire loops. It took keen discipline to lower the wire at the end of a broomstick or willow sapling, down into the water behind the stick-like fish, slip it abruptly (or with impeccable slowness) forward to the gills, and yank.

After the water spilled over at the dam it formed several pools in which I some-times caught small perch, and then it meandered through swamp and woods until it met a clear spring creek; together they formed a rather sizable stream, which washed over the famous Kaaterskill Falls behind the Laurel House and down into the awesome cleft.

Often I would hunt for crayfish, frogs, and newts in one or another of the sections of the creek—and use them for such delightful purposes as frightening girls. One summer a comedian who later achieved some reputation as a double-talker elicited my aid in supplying him with small frogs and crayfish; it was the custom to have the cups turned down at the table settings in the huge dining room, and he would place my little creatures under the cups of those who would react most noticeably. They did. Mainly, though, I released what I caught in a day or so, taking my chief pleasure in the catching itself.

Barefoot in the creek, I often saw small brightly colored fish no more than 4 inches long dart here and there. Their spots—bright red and gold and purple— and their soft bodies intrigued me, but they were too difficult to catch and too small to be worth my time.

That is, until I saw the big one under the log in the long pool beneath a neglected wooden bridge far back in the woods. The fish seemed to be of the same species from his shape and coloration, and was easily 16 or 17 inches long. It was my eighth summer, and the fish completely changed my life.

In August of that summer, one of the guests was a trout fisherman named Dr. Hertz. He was a big, burly, jovial man, well over six-foot-three, with kneecap difficulties that kept him from traveling very far by foot without severe pain. He was, quite obviously, an enthusiast: he had a whole car-trunk full of fly-fishing gear and was, of course, immediately referred to me, the resident expert on matters piscatorial. But he was an adult so we at once had an incident between us: he refused, abjectly refused to believe I had taken a 4-pound pickerel from "that duck-pond," and when he did acknowledge the catch it was condescending, unconvincing. I bristled. Wasn't my word unimpeachable? Had I ever lied about what I caught? What reason would I have to lie? Yet there was no evidence, since the cooks had dispatched the monster—and could not speak English. Nor could I find anyone at the hotel to verify the catch authoritatively. Aunt Blanche, when

I recalled the catching to her in Dr. Hertz's presence, only groaned "Ughhh," and thus lost my respect forever.

Bass there might be in that padded pond, the knowledgeable man assured me: pickerel, never. So we wasted a full week while I first supplied him with innumerable crayfish and he then fished them for bass. Naturally, he didn't even catch a punkinseed.

But it was the stream, in which there were obviously no fish at all, that most intrigued him, and he frequently hobbled down to a convenient spot and scanned the water for long moments. "No reason why there shouldn't be trout in it, boy," he'd say. "Water's crystal clear and there's good streamlife. See. See those flies coming off the water." I admitted that yes, I did see little bugs coming off the water but they probably bit like the devil and they were too tiny to use for bait anyhow. About the presence of trout—whatever they might be—I was not convinced. And I told him so.

But Dr. Hertz got out his long bamboo rod, his delicate equipment, and tried tiny feathered flies that floated and tiny flies that sank in the deep convenient pools where the creek gathered before rushing over the falls and down into the cleft. He caught nothing. He never even got a nibble—or a look. I was not surprised. If there *were* trout in the creek, or anywhere for that matter, worms were the only logical bait. Worms and shiners were the only baits that would take *any* fish, I firmly believed, and shiners had their limitations.

But I did genuinely enjoy going with him, standing by his left side as he cast his long yellow line gracefully back and forth until he dropped a fly noiselessly upon the deep clear pools and then twitched it back and forth or let it rest motionless, perched high and proud. If you could actually catch fish, any fish, this way, I could see its advantages. And the man unquestionably had his skill. But I still had not seen him catch a fish.

As for me, I regularly rose a good deal earlier than even the cooks and slipped down to the lake for a little fishing from the shore. I had never been able to persuade the boat boy, who did not fish, to leave a boat unchained for me: unquestionably, though he was only fourteen, he had already capitulated to the adults and their narrow, unimaginative morality. One morning in the middle of Dr. Hertz's second, and last, week, I grew bored with the few sunfish and shiners available from the dock and followed the creek down through the woods until I came to the little wooden bridge.

I lay on it, stretching myself out at full length, feeling the rough, weathered boards scrape against my belly and thighs, and peered down into the clear water.

A few tiny dace flittered here and there. I spied a small bull frog squatting in the mud and rushes on the far bank—and decided it was not worth my time to take him. Several pebbles slipped through the boards and plunked loudly into the pool. A kingfisher twitted in some nearby oak branches, and another swept low along the stream's alley and seemed to catch some unseen insect in flight. A small punkinseed zigzagged across my sight. Several tiny whirling bugs spun and danced around the surface of the water. The shadows wavered—auburn and dark—along the sandy bottom of the creek; I watched my own shimmering shadow among them. And then I saw him.

Or rather, saw just his nose. For the fish was resting, absolutely still, beneath the log bottom-brace of the bridge, with only a trifle more than his rounded snout showing. It was not a punkinseed or a pickerel; shiners would not remain so quiet; it was scarcely a large perch.

And then I saw all of him, for he emerged all at once from beneath the log, moved with long swift gestures—not the streak of the pickerel or the zigzag of the sunfish—and rose to the surface right below my head, no more than 2 feet below me, breaking the water in a neat little dimple, turning so I could see him, massy, brilliantly colored, sleek and long. And then he went back under the log.

It all happened in a moment; but I knew. Something dramatic, miraculous, had occurred, and I still feel a quickening of my heart when I conjure up the scene. There was a strong nobility about his movements, a swift surety, a sense of purpose—even of intelligence. Here was a quarry worthy of all a young boy's skill and ingenuity. Here, clearly, was the fish Dr. Hertz pursued with his elaborate equipment. And I knew that, no matter what, I had to take that trout.

I debated for several hours whether to tell Dr. Hertz about the fish, and finally decided that, since I had discovered him, he should be mine. All that day he lay beneath a log in my mind while I tried to find some way out of certain unpleasant chores, certain social obligations like entertaining a visiting nephew my age—who hated the water. In desperation, I took him to my huge compost pile under the back porch and frightened the living devil out of him with some giant night crawlers—for which I was sent to my room. At dinner I learned that Dr. Hertz had gone off shopping and then to a movie with his wife. A good thing, I suppose, for I would surely have spilled it all that evening.

That night I prepared my simple equipment, chose a dozen of my best worms from the compost pile, and tried to sleep. I could not. Over and over the massive trout rose in my mind, turned, and returned to beneath the log. I must have stayed awake so long that, out of tiredness, I got up late the next morning— about 6:00.

I slipped quickly out of the deathly still hotel, too preoccupied even to nod to my friend the night clerk, and half ran through the woods to the old wooden bridge.

He was still there! He was still in the same spot beneath the log.

First I went directly upstream of the bridge and floated a worm down to him six or seven times. Not a budge. Not a look. Was it possible? I had expected to take him, without fail, on the first drift—and then march proudly back to the Laurel House in time to display my prize to Dr. Hertz.

I paused and surveyed the situation. Surely trout must eat worms, I speculated. And the morning is always the best time to fish. Something must be wrong with the way the bait is coming to him. That was it. I drifted the worm down again and noted with satisfaction that it dangled a full 4 or 5 inches above his head. Not daring to get closer, I tried casting across stream and allowing the worm to swing around in front of him; but this still did not drop the worm sufficiently. Then I tried letting it drift past him so that I could suddenly lower the bamboo pole and provide slack line, thus forcing the worm to drop near him. This almost worked, but, standing on my tiptoes, I could see that it was still too high. Sinkers? Perhaps *that* was it.

I rummaged around in my pockets, and then turned them out on a flat rock: pen knife, dirty handkerchief, two dried worms, extra snelled hooks wrapped in cellophane, two wine-bottle corks, eleven cents, a couple of keys, two rubber bands, dirt, a crayfish's paw—but no sinkers, not even a washer or a nut or a screw. I hadn't used split shot in a full month, not since I had discovered that a freely drifting worm would do much better in the lake and would get quite deep enough if you had patience—which I was long on.

I scoured the shore for a tiny pebble or flat rock and came up with several promising bits of slate; but I could not, with my trembling fingers, adequately fashion them to stay tied to the line. And by now I was sorely hungry, so I decided to get some split shot in town and come back later. That old trout would still be there. He had not budged in all the time I'd fished over him.

I tried for that trout each of the remaining days that week. I fished for him early in the morning and during the afternoon and immediately after supper. I fished for him right up until dark, and twice frightened my parents by returning to the hotel about 9:30. I did not tell them about the trout either. Would *they* understand?

And the old monster? He was always there, always beneath the log except for one or two of those sure yet leisurely sweeps to the surface of the stream.

I brooded about whether to tell Dr. Hertz after all, and let him have a go at my trout with his fancy paraphernalia. But it had become a private challenge of wits between the trout and me. He was not like the huge pickerel that haunted the channels between pads in the lake. Those I would have been glad to share.

This was my fish: he was not in the public domain. And anyway, I reasoned, Dr. Hertz could not possibly walk through the tangled, pathless woods.

On Sunday, the day Dr. Hertz was to leave, I rose especially early—before light had broken—packed every bit of equipment I owned into a canvas bag, and trekked quickly through the woods to the wooden bridge. Water had stopped coming over the dam at the lake the day before, and I noticed that the stream level had dropped a full 6 inches. A few dace dimpled the surface, and a few small sunfish meandered here and there. The trout was still beneath the log.

I tried for him in all the usual ways—upstream, downstream, and from high above him on the bridge. I had by now, with the help of the split shot, managed regularly to get the worm within a millimeter of his nose; in fact, several times that morning I actually bumped his rounded nose with the worm. The old trout did not seem to mind. He would sort of nudge it away, or ignore it, or shift his position deftly. Clearly he considered me no threat. It was humbling, humiliating.

I worked exceptionally hard for about three hours, missed breakfast, and kept fishing on into the late morning on a growling stomach. I even tried floating grasshoppers down to the fish, and then a newt, even a little sunfish I caught upstream, several dace I trapped, and finally a crayfish. Nothing would budge that confounded monster.

At last I went back to my little canvas pack and began to pack together my scattered equipment. I was beaten. And I was starved. I'd tell Dr. Hertz about the fish and if he felt up to it he could try it.

Despondently, I shoved my gear into the pack. And then it happened! My finger got sorely pricked with a huge Carlisle hook, snelled, that I used for the largest pickerel. I sat down on a rock and looked at it for a moment, pressing the blood out to avoid infection, washing my finger in the spring-cold creek, and then wrapping it with a bit of shirt I tore off—which I'd get hell for. But who cared.

The Carlisle hook. Perhaps, I thought. Perhaps.

I had more than once thought of snaring that trout with piano wire lowered from the bridge, but too little of his nose was exposed. It simply would not have worked.

But the Carlisle hook! Carefully I tied the snelled hook directly onto the end of my 10-foot bamboo pole, leaving about 2 inches of firm gut trailing from the end.

Then, taking the pole in my right hand, I lay on my belly and began to crawl with immense slowness along the bottom logs of the bridge so that I would eventually pass directly above the trout. It took a full fifteen minutes. Then, finally, there I was, no more than a foot from the nose of my quarry, directly above him.

Now I began to lower the end of the rod slowly, slowly, slowly into the water, slightly upstream, moving the long bare Carlisle hook closer and closer to his nose.

The trout opened and closed its mouth just a trifle every few seconds.

Now the hook was fractions of an inch from its mouth. Should I jerk hard? Try for the underlip? No, it might slip away—and there would be only one chance.

Instead, I meticulously slipped the bare hook directly toward the slight slip that was his mouth, guiding it behind the curve of his lip. He did not budge. I did not breathe.

And then I jerked abruptly up!

The fish lurched. I yanked. The rod splintered but held. The trout flipped up out of his element and flopped against the buttresses of the bridge. I pounced on him with both hands, and it was all over. It had taken no more than a few seconds.

Back at the hotel I headed immediately for Dr. Hertz's room, the 17-inch trout casually hanging from a forked stick in my right hand.

To my immense disappointment, he had left.

I wrote him that very afternoon, lying in my teeth.

> Dear Doctor Hertz:
> I caught a great big trout on a worm this afternoon and brought it to your room but you had gone home already. I have put into this letter a diagram of the fish that I drew. I caught him on a worm.

I *could* have caught him on a worm, eventually, and anyway I wanted to rub it in that he'd wasted two weeks of my time and would never catch anything on those feathers. It would be a valuable lesson for him.

Several days later I received this letter, which I found several weeks ago in one of three closets crammed with clipped trouting articles, fly-tying equipment, Thomas and other bamboo rods, innumerable fly boxes, sinking and floating fly lines, and all that other elaborate and delicious paraphernalia of a discipline no more exhaustible than "the Mathematicks":

> Dear Nicky:
> I am glad you caught a big trout. But after fishing that creek for a whole two weeks I am convinced that there just weren't any trout in it. Are you sure it wasn't a perch? Your amusing picture looked like it. I wish you'd sent me a photograph instead, so I

could be sure. Perhaps next year we can fish a *real* trout stream together.

> Your friend,
> Thos. Hertz

Real? Was that unnamed creek not the realest I have ever fished? And *your friend*. How could he say that?

Let him doubt: I had, by hook and by crook, caught my first trout.

Winning Steelhead River

CHARLES F. WATERMAN

On a river where the average *fly-caught fish weighs 15 pounds, the author takes a 26½-pounder and doesn't come near the record.* (February 1970)

I never thought of a FIELD & STREAM Fishing Contest as eyeball to eyeball confrontation until we camped on the Kispiox River one September and found ourselves within 100 yards of three winners for fly-caught western rainbow trout. But when you consider that in the past fifteen years, only two first places in that classification came from any other river, you can understand why they were on this British Columbia water.

Of course, on the Kispiox, rainbow means steelhead, and where fly-caught steelhead average 15 pounds, things may move a little strangely. Undaunted by our celebrity neighbors, my wife Debie and I waded in near camp and began casting sinking lines. There were dead salmon along the shore, and when Debie felt a slow and heavy something in midstream 20 minute later, she drew quick conclusions.

"Can't be a steelhead," she said. "It won't do anything. Must be a spent salmon. I'll just drag him in."

She pumped until her leader butt was almost to the rod tip, and then a giant steelhead blew into the air and broke off. It was the only one she hooked on that whole trip. Fishing for records isn't apt to be fast.

John P. Walker of Great Falls, Montana, won the 1968 western rainbow fly division with a Kispiox fish that went 27 pounds 10 ounces. Jack M. Jones took second on the Babine just a few miles away, and Forrest Powell was third with a Kispiox entry. That's about typical—in the past fifteen years, thirty-two of the forty-five winners of the first three places have come from the Kispiox. Walker has been high on the list almost annually since he started going there. Powell won in 1967 and has been in the top three *five times* since 1962. The world record fly fish, a 33 pounder, was caught there by Karl Mausser in 1962, and Mausser was first again in 1965.

I don't know if any fly-fisherman really gets used to such large trout. I leaned on one for a long while and he simply hung in midstream and sent up enormous boils and booming splashes. I never saw him and, to my shame, the leader broke up in the heavy section, obviously damaged previously.

Dr. Andrew Jordan of Choteau, Montana, has the second largest all-time fly fish, a 30-pound 2-ounce steelhead he won with in 1966 (you know where), and in 1967 he made a good try. The day Jordan made his bid for a second record, he was to meet Walker, and when he didn't show up Walker went looking. He found Jordan in a pool on serious steelhead business. The fight between man and fish went on for 6 hours and 55 minutes before the leader gave way, and for the time being, at least, Jordan was glad of it.

Plenty of other anglers visited the pool where he was doing his thing. When the monster dogged it behind a boulder, volunteers would throw rocks to get him moving again; one Samaritan nearly drowned when he stumbled with his wader front full of stones. The fish was plainly seen and everybody says it was more than 40 pounds.

Although the Kispiox is the winning river, the Babine, which also empties into the Skeena River system, has equally large strains of fish, according to Les Cox, a Smithers, British Columbia, game warden and steelhead expert. But it's harder to get to the Babine, and fly-fishermen don't work it so much.

A fly-caught steelhead from the Kispiox first entered the FIELD & STREAM contest win column in 1954, and in 1955 George McLeod set a record with a 29-pound 2-ounce fish. Since then the river has continued to dominate the western rainbow fly fishing division. Although there are more lure-fishermen than fly-fishermen, steelhead caught on lures must compete with the big resident rainbows of lakes like Pend Oreille, and except for a few years when "steelhead" were classified separately from "western rainbow," the deep-going lake fish generally have taken honors in the lure classes.

To get to the Kispiox, you drive to Hazelton, its hometown, from Prince George on a hard-surfaced road. Then from Hazelton you continue on good gravel alongside the river after passing the Indian village of Kispiox. Riverside camping costs a dollar a night, and partly furnished cabins are inexpensive. You're beyond the electric lines, and the regulars stay in travel trailers or truck campers for the most part. A travel trailer is ideal because it can be parked and the car or truck used for commuting to the various "drifts" (steelheader rhetoric for "pool"). The area is about 200 miles from where the fish must start their upstream migration from the mouth of the Skeena at Prince Rupert, over on the Pacific coast.

Drifts are named and access is easy, but it takes a long time to learn just exactly where the fish lie, and first-timers cast over lots of barren water. But if you keep at it, you're bound to get lucky. In 1966 I temporarily gave up the Kispiox and went over to the nearby Bulkley to catch a smaller fish. Then when I came back to the Kispiox I got into trouble with a Skykomish Sunrise fly just above Wookey's Camp where our tent sat damply in a normal Kispiox drizzle.

The heavy fly stopped as it had done a thousand times before on bottom boulders, and in seconds a great, red-sided fish was making plunging jumps in white water above me, the line sagging far back in the current.

It's a good thing, I thought, to have a fish jump eight times in fast water; should tire him out fast. But he tired *too* fast and let go suddenly, carried downstream with much of my line, and I wallowed almost a quarter mile after him before I beached him in front of camp. He weighed 22 pounds and it had been a pretty grim tussle, but I was embarrassed the following morning when Forrest Powell cast from the same place and landed a 20-pounder in five minutes. Powell made me feel better by telling of Kispiox steelies that never do stop and claimed his was an easy one.

A fresh-run steelhead, silvery from the sea and not far upstream, is probably the roughest customer of all, but when he gets to the Kispiox he will be tired from his travels. Later, after being in his home stream for a while he begins to take back true rainbow colors, embellished by spawning brilliance, and is his violent self again.

Trophy fish are caught mainly in September and October, although some are present in August. Late October may have severe weather, and Walker's 1968 winner was caught on a snowy November 8. Les Cox says there are more late-season fish simply because of the accumulation of earlier runs. They're winter fish, and catching one on a dry fly is almost unheard of, although summer-run fish in nearby streams may perform like resident rainbows.

This river doesn't carry the booming torrent of some Canadian steelhead streams. It is not especially clear and goes up and down "like a yo-yo," as restless anglers say while they watch their vacations dwindle into a chocolate flood. The official government depth gauge is used dozens of times a day. Water is more consistently clear late in the fall when it is unlikely that sudden warm spells will melt snow in the mountains.

Some of the steelhead migrations are predictable, and members of the Seattle Steelhead Club, who keep careful records, speak freely of the "Labor Day Run." But with so much overlap and so many varieties of weather, any time in September or October can be good.

Steelheading can continue through the entire winter. The river also has one of the best spring salmon runs in the Northwest. Chinooks (spring salmon) are caught with spoons and run up to 50 pounds. The coho, or silver, salmon run around August 1 taking flies or lures, and hump-backed salmon show up early in August.

All Kispiox rainbows are potentially steelhead although some spend two or three years in fresh water before going to sea. The big contest fish are usually from 6 to 8 years old. Most of them have spawned more than once, although the odds and hazards are against a given fish making it home a second time.

Within an 80-mile radius of the Kispiox are the Copper, Skeena, Bulkley, Telkwa, Morice, and Babine, all famous rivers in their own right.

A long cast will get across the Kispiox in a few places. Most wading is fairly easy, but in order to work a fly all the way around downstream it's good to get in as far as convenient, and intrepid waders with felt soles have an advantage.

Most of the veteran lure fishermen use turning-spool reels; monofilament line; conventionally long, light-action rods; and pencil sinkers carefully adjusted to keep their bobber-type lures just above the bottom. Spoons and spinners catch fish too but are less popular among the regulars.

Fly-fishermen use sinking lines, most of them employing shooting heads. Some of the most successful, such as Walker and Jordan, use complete lines with stripping baskets. Powell, unlike most of the regulars, sometimes uses a medium sinking line instead of a fast sinker and says he doesn't keep his fly as near the bottom as the rest do. One year when he and Mausser fished together he caught more fish, but Mausser, using a fast sinker, caught bigger ones. There may be something here.

Walker doesn't manipulate his fly but lets it swing down "dead" with the current. Mausser frequently gives his fly action of some sort.

Many of the flies are orange or orange and green and often are made with fluorescent materials. They are simply tied and few are well-known or conventional patterns. If there is one most popular pattern, I suppose it is the Skykomish Sunrise, an orange-bodied fly with white hairwing and tinsel or Mylar wrapping. The McLeod Ugly, a nearly all-black number, is good too.

Most popular fly sizes are Nos. 1 and 1/0, and most fly anglers say that if you don't lose flies, you're too shallow. I generally leave four to five a day in the river. The constant boulder-bouncing dulls hooks rapidly, so a sharpener may save a fish. If you get no more Kispiox strikes than I do, you should play all the angles.

In 1967, Powell caught his winner on a Sam 'n Daisy Special, named for Sam and Daisy Langlois, retired couple and exceptional steelheaders, who visit the Kispiox annually.

When the real Sam offered me one (it's a simple, multicolored yarn tie) I grabbed with alacrity. Sam and Daisy don't fish with flies, doing a successful job with casting outfits, but they were steering me around a little.

Anyway, after that three days without a strike except from a single midget rainbow that may never have been to the ocean, I stood up to my belt in the tail of a good drift and cast a Sam 'n Daisy fly against a steep bank. Its namesakes were nearer shore and had caught a couple of fish when I decided my new fly wasn't hung after all and watched it move off upstream with nerve-racking steadiness.

That fish never jumped at all. He moved straight upstream for 50 feet, then came back and made a complete circle around me while I tried to gather line. He went clear around me twice, the second time within 6 feet of my waders in a tight turn, almost lazily, and a glimpse of nearly 4 feet of steelhead didn't contribute to my cool.

The river split below me, both sides turning into curving rapids with jutting snags and boulders. Where the split began was a down tree, the branches downstream and the ragged roots waving derisively where they broke the current and seemed to reach for my leader.

Another Sam, this one named Olson, waded up from below and stood guard over the tree roots, prepared to drive the fish off.

The fish headed into the mainstream again and moved far into the upstream pool, 200 yards of evenly moving water, and there he made his fight. When he came back down, Sam and Daisy had cleared out the sticks and other trash that might interfere with beaching in a shallow mud-bottomed backwater.

Anyway, Sam Langlois grabbed my fish for me and it weighed 26½ pounds, earning a moment of glory and a barbecue back at camp—but it never even showed on the winner's list.

That's the kind of steelies they have on the Kispiox.

A Return to the Roaring Kill

PETER BARRETT

Who in the world would drive for several hours to fish for four to seven-ounce trout? Probably you *would after reading this.* (May 1971)

It was John McLain's turn at the rod. He lifted it, got the worm swinging well, and then carefully lobbed it to the head of the next pool. As the current swept the worm along, McLain lowered the rod so the line would flow easily through the guides.

Ed Lyon and I watched. We were sprawled on a bank of the stream drinking beer and smoking. The May sun warmed us and scented the air with the fragrance of fallen spruce needles. Somewhere downstream a ruffed grouse drummed because it was a lovely spring day.

It had been about twenty years since we three had fished this brook in the Catskill Mountains of New York, and little had changed up here on the lonely Roaring Kill. Nor had the old house overlooking it. McLain, Lyon, and other school friends of their Goose and Gander Club had scraped together $500 in the middle thirties to buy the long-empty house and acreage, and we had all become graduate worm fishermen on the "Kill," which ran only 20 yards from the back door.

"The back porch looks good," I remarked to Ed. "Must have been patched up."

Some pretty good beer parties used to get thrown here. As a consequence, beer, food, coffee, and whatnot got spilled on the weathered wood of the back porch. This proved to be a strong attraction for porcupines and they practically ate the porch out from under us in a few years. But now it had been fixed.

"We have a big woodchuck living under the front porch. Maybe he keeps the porcupines away," Ed told me.

Just then McLain gave a yell and whipped his worm into overhead branches. This was always a problem up here near the Notch—the brook is so overgrown with trees that you just about *have* to fish a worm. We were doing this out of choice, however, because it had long been the custom. I'd even bought a wicker creel for the occasion, which McLain was now wearing as sloppily as when he was a school kid.

"Big one!" he shouted at us over the splashing of the brook.

A few moments later, McLain derricked a fish from the Roaring Kill. We crowded close to admire the first catch—a brook trout about 8 inches long and vibrantly colored. "He was as fussy as a salmon," McLain declared. "I had forgotten how careful you have to be to let the worm float freely."

Ed Lyon now took up the rod and creel and bait box. I fished a beer from the Kill and handed it icy-cold to McLain. We lit our pipes and lay back on the bank, half watching Ed.

"Remember the first meal I cooked on the old stove?" John was recalling a startling occasion. He and Ed and I had driven north to the old house shortly after it was first bought. It was late in the fall and a drift of snow lay across the kitchen floor, fallen in through a hole in the roof. We were so famished we decided to have a meal immediately and forget about the snow.

We stuffed the cast-iron range full of wood which happened to be somewhat damp. The fire wouldn't catch so John poured a liberal dose of kerosene on the wood and replaced the stove lid. Nothing happened. We were sitting in three rickety chairs facing the stove, waiting for warmth.

"You were pretty mean with that kerosene," Ed Lyon remarked.

McLain removed two stove lids this time and really sloshed kerosene around. Meanwhile, a tiny flame was working up through the kindling.

Suddenly there was a roar and the heavy iron lids flew upward, turning lazily end over end like tossed pancakes. We fell over backwards onto the snow. The fire had started at last.

"What did we do about the snow?"

"We let it melt and then mopped it out the back door."

Ed Lyon looked around at us with a wide grin.

"He's got one on," John said. "I never saw a more thorough worm fisherman."

Presently Ed flicked the rod to set the hook and drew a small trout splashing from the Kill. "He's too small," Ed said. The trout was only about 5 inches long.

"There's no minimum length in New York anymore," I remarked. "Let's keep it for breakfast."

I took the rod and paraphernalia, reflecting that I still had some Thomas rods and a Garrison, even, with black dots applied with India ink then varnished over, exactly 6 inches apart. Later, when the minimum went to 7 inches, I added a bar with the number 7 above it. Perhaps it was the effect of the Great Depression, but every keepable trout got kept when I was a youngster, and usually got listed by exact measurement in a journal besides.

I threaded on a worm, started at the head (how long ago *that* had been!) and swung the bait toward a dark, swirly bit of water at the beginning of the next hole.

If my fly-casting friends could only see me now, I thought with a grin, and lifted the rod gently to check for the throb of a trout worrying the worm.

Suddenly I recalled an anguished moment of my youth at a deep pool on the West Branch of the Croton River in southern New York. A night crawler I was using had washed unexpectedly to the surface and I raised the rod sharply in annoyance to make a fresh cast. Just as the worm left the water a brook trout of astonishing length and depth made a pass at the worm and missed.

And then I remembered standing beside a tiny brook in the Adirondacks and idly dunking a worm in a pool with an overhung, grassy bank at my feet. The brookie that swept out, engulfed the worm, and disappeared was a foot long— a giant for that rivulet. I can still recall the spooky feeling I got when I put a little pressure on the line to see if the trout was still on, then the thrill as a hard rod yank stung the hook home and the unseen trout splashed mightily under the bank before being drawn clear, to swing glittering like a rare jewel to the turf.

Now I raised the rod to bring the worm to the surface so I could check its progress. There was a lively boil behind the bait and my line snaked toward a rock. With my heart ticking over, I waited long seconds, then struck. I had caught a good one for the Roaring Kill—9 inches of wild brook trout.

I gave the rod to John McLain, retrieved my beer, and rejoined Ed on the bank.

I took a swig of beer, lit my pipe, and then lay on my back watching the puffy white clouds drift by. Some way I got to thinking about the house.

During Prohibition, the late Legs Diamond had a still put in the barn that went with the place, and the bootleggers who worked the still lived in the old house. Their lookout was a woman who lived down the dirt road. Lookout or not, the revenuers came one day, burned the barn, smashed the still, and ripped apart the house somewhat, looking for money perhaps. Ed Lyon and friends became the new owners after the house had lain empty for some years.

Today it is as isolated as the day Legs Diamond first saw it—more so, perhaps, since the orchard is grown up with birch, maple, and hemlock now. The Catskill Mountains crowd down on this tiny valley—called Mink Hollow—cut on one side by the Roaring Kill and presided over by the old house.

"Did you guys ever use the power plant?" I asked.

"Nope. After we got it in, we decided it was too civilizing."

At considerable effort, a concrete slab had been poured for the foundation. Then the powerhouse was built. Finally a secondhand generating plant of considerable weight and age was jackassed into position and a cable was buried leading to the house some 50 feet away. There is still some crude wiring in the house which, by the way, is a narrow two-story clapboard affair with a brick chimney somewhat out of plumb. The kitchen is at the back in a shedlike room.

From the beginning, the house was lit by kerosene lamps and it still is. The house has resisted change rather successfully. Repairs were made only from absolute necessity, as when frost-heaves tumbled in part of a fieldstone wall in the dirt-floored cellar.

John McLain came over to join us. "I must be losing my touch. A trout cleaned me three times running. We're out of worms."

We began turning over rocks, finding worms and chasing small, lively salamanders which also make excellent trout bait. Presently we had the bait box well stocked and sat back to take it easy.

Absolutely nothing can beat a fine spring day in the Catskills. You cannot imagine clearer air, or greener, fresher buds on the trees, some with that waxy look they take on just before bursting. The Roaring Kill ran as pure and clear as it must have a century ago.

"Look at those wild brookies," I remarked. "There are darn few left in the East now." We could see two diminutive trout finning easily at the edge of a current, their white-edged lower fins poised, their tails cocked in the partial curl of trout ready to dash for an insect.

"How do you know they're wild?"

"Easy. The state doesn't stock them this small. They've always been wild brookies in the Kill."

When we were kids the brook trout was our piscatorial Golden Fleece. To be sure, some rainbows ascended the Roaring Kill from its eventual junction with the upper Schoharie Creek a few miles downstream, but we knew they were fish-truck intruders invading the Kill because of their spring spawning urge.

So it was that catching a "big" brookie—say 10 inches long—was a real event. A fish this size would be fully mature in this brook and able to reproduce. It would also be more than passing wise. To my surprise, I began to remember individual pools where such brook trout had made a fatal mistake, and McLain now approached one. Ed and I crowded behind, kibitzing.

"You're fishing the wrong area," Ed advised. "They're always down at the tail of this pool."

"I can't cast down there without spooking them."

So we let him be, and soon he panicked a fair trout at the tail which shot forward with a zigzag wake. We eased down the brook, leaving no trout hiding place unprobed.

Eventually it was Ed's turn again. "Remember the day we fished Platte Cove?" McLain remarked. "That was a mistake!"

We had climbed down a 45-degree slope to get at a remote brook tumbling over great boulders and foaming into spectacular pools. The trouble was, these falls were just steep enough to prevent trout from ascending and the brook was barren.

It grew hot. McLain opened the creel and there was lunch—withered "rat" cheese and a stale loaf of bread. We choked some down and by evening finally worked our way to the floor of the valley, still troutless.

Then the alpine climb up the road. Unbelievable. At Mike Curran's bar in Tannersville I drank the most beers of my life at one sitting—seventeen. And still I was thirsty.

We talked about the time I made a crazy bet with McLain that I could catch a trout in the Roaring Kill in the dead of winter. I forget what the payoff was to be if I failed. But I do remember the drifts across the dirt road, and the struggle we had getting the car through them and over the last rise before it was downhill to the house.

I also remember the unrelenting cold in the house, with the thermometer at the kitchen-sink window standing at around 15 degrees below zero. We didn't have sleeping bags in those days, and there were never enough blankets in the place. Furthermore, we weren't equipped with clothing that was really warm, and I recall that John wore a football helmet with a towel under it.

Well, I had read somewhere—Jack London, perhaps—that you could catch trout through the ice on uncooked bacon, so off we headed down the Roaring Kill, me with a fly rod, reel, line, and bare hook on a short leader. I kept the bacon in my pocket so it would stay limber.

The big trouble was unexpected; the brook was frozen over! You could hear it chuckling away under the ice, but you could walk right over the main current, sidestepping the drifts. What we were doing was illegal at the time, but we solved this problem by agreeing that if I caught a trout, I would release it promptly.

Down the Kill we stumbled, wishing we had snowshoes but determined to find some open water. I put forward the notion that if the brook was iced over for a mile, we ought to quit and that all bets were off.

McLain would have none of this. "You'll fish if I have to chop a hole in the creek," he said. Relentlessly he led the search for open water.

And eventually, deep among the hemlocks, we came upon an opening in the Kill. It didn't happen to be an opportune place for fishing, being in the middle of a fast riffle, but there was a pool below locked under the ice and just to get the entire shambles over with, I drew the bacon from my pocket and impaled a dirty wad of it on the hook.

The current swept this offering under the ice, drawing it downstream to the pool. I felt what I thought was a nibble and struck, then reeled in interminably. In time a brookie about 5 inches long appeared, so cold it could hardly wiggle. Indeed, I didn't know it was on during the retrieve. We took a picture, released the trout and trudged back, wondering what we were going to do with the rest of that frigid weekend.

It was great being kids in those pre-television days. Time was endless, worries unknown. No one had any money but that hardly mattered. Some of this feeling of absolute freedom came to us now as we entered that part of the Roaring Kill deep in the woods before you reach the old steel bridge. There are long pools here, and some deep ones too. In places it is even possible to cast a fly.

I was fishing again. We had finished our beer and buried the last set of cans. We'd had no lunch and it was now midafternoon, but no one spoke of turning back. The challenge of the little trout, the fun of fishing with worms again after all these years, the ordinary pleasure of walking down the Kill in solitude—these elements drew us on and on.

I came to a certain pool and recalled a time of triumph when I was just starting to fish with flies and had never caught a decent trout on a dry fly. It seemed there was a mystery that I'd never master. Anyhow, I came to this pool fishing by the instruction book—tapered line, a 9-foot leader ending in the lightest wisp of gut, and on the end a No. 12 Dark Cahill.

The pool seemed empty. I made a cast anyhow from the bottom of it, so the fly would float toward me without drag. Midway, over an open gravelly bottom, a trout rose to intercept the fly. It was like a dream as the spotted brookie stuck its nose above the surface and clamped on the fly. How savage that trout was! I could see it run along the bottom, rubbing its jaw against the pebbles as it tried to dislodge the fly.

I spoke out loud to this trout, entreating it to behave. When it made for a sunken bush I just managed to keep the fish clear. And eventually—just as in the books—I drew it swimming weakly to me and beached it on a tiny spit of sand. I had caught a patriarch of the Roaring Kill—a whopping 13-incher—by artificial means in the most sporting tradition, and that one incident, more than any other, made a lifelong fly fisherman of me.

This time, I caught a 5-incher on a worm and dropped it into the creel.

A couple of hundred yards farther along, we quit. Ed Lyon, the most thorough and persistent worm angler I ever saw, drew not a touch from three lovely pools and we decided the Kill had been penetrated from below by others to this point. So we climbed the steep banks, shouldering aside the beeches till we hit the dirt road leading to the old house.

It was cool inside, with front and back doors open. I threw together some sandwiches and we sat around the kitchen table relaxing. A couple of corks had been pulled and that helped.

Above the table hung the antique kerosene chandelier. On the wall behind me reposed the charcoal nude, just a touch suggestive and definitely a work of art, that Hugh Laidman had done so many years ago. The "new" pump at the sink—perhaps 17 years old now—still drew clear, cold water from the dug well directly below in the cellar. And there was still a good wood- or coal-burning kitchen range of about the same vintage as the pump. I glanced out the back door and caught the glint of the Roaring Kill. *How little it changes here*, I thought.

Suddenly remembering the trout, I got up and put them in a big plastic bag and set them inside the icebox. Not a one was over 9 inches long but this didn't matter at all. McLain lit up a twisty, black cigar. Ed Lyon lounged in a rickety chair, twirling his whiskey glass.

"Fishing the Kill with only one rod is the absolute answer," John remarked. "No hurrying to get past somebody. Every pool gets fished. We were together."

That was partly why it had been so great. That and the unchanged Roaring Kill, starting at a spring on the hillside to the left of the Notch and flowing down through the Mink Hollow, clear and just a bit noisy, with just enough wild brook trout to keep you going from pool to pool.

The Chalk Streams
of Olde England

ARTHUR OGLESBY

One of Britain's foremost anglers takes you to the hallowed streams where the dry fly, the nymph—and some claim, even trout—were invented. (March 1972)

The small nymph clutched uneasily to the waving frond of ranunculus. It had seemed a long time since its birth on the riverbed and it was nearly time for that wonderful transformation when it would shed its nymphal case and emerge fluttering on the water to begin another phase of its fantastic life cycle. An old brown trout hovered on the fin nearby. He was well aware that a hatch of fly was due and had positioned himself in a favorite lie where he could take maximum advantage of the feast the hatching flies would offer, with the minimum amount of exertion on his part. The nymph released its precarious hold on the waving weed and made for the surface with surprising rapidity; there, in the glorious sunshine of a June morn, it shed its aquatic trappings, aired its wings, and began its slow drift downstream. David Jacques and I watched as it made its first feeble attempts to get airborne—and then from the depths came the old, fat trout. A snout appeared to ripple the surface, and that little fly was gone. "He's taken a pale watery dun," said David excitedly. Crouching down in the marshy reeds at the river's bank we were able to see the trout quite clearly as first one and then another fly came floating over him. Up he would come to sip them in, apparently oblivious of the fact that the hunter was about to be hunted.

David eased the cast out carefully, pulling line off the reel at every false cast. The placing of his carefully selected artificial had to be right first time, with correct assessment of any drag the current might give to the fly, yet with ample time for the fish to see the manmade offering and accept it as the real thing. Slowly, it seemed, the line was aerialized and then the cast was made. The fly fell like thistledown about 2 feet upstream of the fish. Slowly and loglike, the big trout moved, then made a porpoiselike roll, and the fly was gone. From that moment all hell broke loose. The fish twisted and bored in frenzy, stripping line off David's reel as it sought the sanctuary of a big weed bed. Seconds later it was fast in the weed and David had to resort to hand-lining in order to get the fish free once again. After that the fish continued its fight with a downstream lunge and there were many anxious moments before David could slide the fish over the rim of the waiting net. It weighed 2½ pounds—as nice a brown trout as anyone could wish for.

The duns continued to hatch and other trout were seen rising. The water flowed quietly but ceaselessly, and the lowing cattle in the nearby meadows presented a tranquil scene. The river was gin clear, with abundant weed growth and high alkalinity, for this was a chalk stream—England's famous River Test —and we were opposite the hallowed waters of the Houghton Club.

The chalk streams of England are almost unique. They have their source in the vast chalk strata of the Downs in and around the counties of Hampshire, Berkshire, Wiltshire, and Dorset—the approximate area, in fact, known from feudal times as Wessex when Winchester was the Capital of England. Winchester today still bears the marks of its long medieval history; and its association with anglers is highlighted by the fact that the late Izaak Walton lies at rest in Winchester Cathedral.

North of the Downs there is but one other chalk strata of note and this comes in the eastern part of Northern England in the county of Yorkshire. The chalk springs here produce two other well-known trout streams at Driffield and Foston; but it is the two main rivers of Hampshire, the Test and the Itchen, which have become world renowned for the type of sport they offer. Like all chalk streams, these rivers receive a constant supply of highly alkaline water from the chalk springs. They are rarely subject to flooding and maintain a similar height and temperature throughout the year. Rich in all forms of aquatic life, they provide a feasting parlor for the trout and grayling which inhabit these waters, and challenging fishing for the fortunate few who are privileged to fish these exclusive reaches.

In the year 1877 a young man by the name of Frederick M. Halford secured some fishing on the River Test by gaining access to the famous Houghton Club. Although only in his thirties he already had some ten years experience of dry-fly fishing and was destined to become the world's leading authority on dry-fly tactics in his day. Many of the great American authorities on dry-fly fishing came under the initial influence of Halford, and much reference was made to him by Theodore Gordon and George LaBranche. Perhaps the greatest compliment from an American about Test fishing, however, came from Edward R. Hewitt in his book *A Trout and Salmon Fisherman for Seventy-Five Years*. Hewitt said, "the Test and Itchen fish were the most difficult I have seen anywhere in the world, and for that reason the most interesting. The Houghton Club was the finest sporting place I have ever visited."

Whatever may be said of Halford today, there can be no doubt that he brought sanity and order to the confused thinking of those days. His initial encounter with the trout of the Test disillusioned him somewhat, for he already imagined himself to be quite an expert trout fisherman and he was greatly confused by the Test trout, which were not quite as suicidal as trout on other waters he had fished. From that time on he devoted himself to a detailed entomological study of the fly-life in the Test and he eventually became fully convinced that some form of precise imitation was more or less essential for success. It could rightly be said that he was the first angler to seriously consider the problems of "matching the hatch." That history might accuse him of being overzealous in no way detracts from his positive thinking at that time. Halford, and later Skues, were the products of an era, a time when many anglers were seeking to find a formula in lieu of "chuck and chance it" techniques. Although no formula will ever exist in fishing, there can be no doubts that we owe a great deal to the Halfords, Gordons, Skues, and LaBranches of this world. The angler of today is still striving to find a more reliable recipe for sustained success; but if one is ever found, I suspect that a lot of us will give up fishing in disgust.

As a trout fisherman myself, of nearly forty years experience, I had spent much of my youth in reading the works of Halford and Skues. With the cessation of World War II I took to my fishing with renewed vigor—glad to be alive. During the early fifties, I became the secretary of a small, exclusive club at Foston in the North of England. This small stream is a true chalk stream with all the essential ingredients to make it a miniature Test. The trout were fat and sassy and adopted the same preoccupation in their selective feeding as any trout that swam. There were more years of apprenticeship before I came to terms with those fish and it was during those years that I met many of the well-known British anglers of today. The late Oliver Kite had modeled his thinking on that of Skues and was frequently more content to fish with a nymph than make serious attempts with "exact imitations" of hatching duns. Like myself, he was somewhat sceptical of the necessity for precise matching, believing that dexterity with tackle was perhaps more paramount for success. David Jacques, on the other hand, has emerged as a true disciple of Halford and may well be England's leading authority on present-day tactics for chalk-stream fishing. Following closely in his footsteps is John Goddard, and both of these talented anglers have become Fellows of the Royal Entomological Society through their investigations on aquatic fly life. Both have written books on the subject and have cooperated closely together.

With my experience limited to the northern chalk streams it was not unnatural that I was quick to accept an invitation to fish the classic streams of the south. Not just to fish the Test and Itchen, but also to see the appreciable number of other, lesser-known rivers which abound in that area, all of which, on their day, can provide similar sport—such other rivers as the Kennet, Wylie, and Avon where equally big fish lurk.

My first encounter in Hampshire occurred as a guest of Barrie Welham, the head of Garcia Tackle in the United Kingdom and a very talented angler. He had arranged for me to fish a portion of the lower Test at Timsbury, and although the day was far too hot for comfort there were one or two obliging fish. I did not get any monsters, but there was something challenging about the fishing, particularly with such a bright sun. On subsequent days I was a guest of several hosts and fished many of the legendary beats of various rivers. Fishing techniques were little different from any other form of dry-fly fishing; but it is frequently the custom to spot a good trout and then sit down on a stool until the fish start some rising activity. Then a careful assessment of the natural fly is made, sometimes with the aid of binoculars or a plankton net, and a suitable artificial facsimile is put on the leader.

Fly rods are always singlehanded and about 8½ to 9 feet in length. American floating lines are popular, and the 9-foot leader is generally tapered to around 2- to 3-pound breaking strain. The more serous-minded anglers all tie their own flies and derive as much pleasure from fly identification and matching as they do from catching fish. Indeed, for many of them, a deal of fun would go out of the sport if they did not feel some conviction that matching the hatch was important. They will readily accept that there are a few unsophisticated trout which will take anything reasonably presented, but they prefer to approach all fish as being fully selective.

Much of the fishing comes into the exclusive category; most certainly the Houghton Club does. Other waters are controlled by private landowners, syndicates, and clubs; and if a vacancy does occur, filling it is not merely a question of putting up the money, for the angler's social standing will also come in for close scrutiny. Providing, therefore, that the cap fits in every respect, it is sometimes possible to acquire access to the fishing on payment of around $1,250 a season. Alternatively, the angler may opt for just one day a week of the season and pay the lesser fee of $250. There are only a few places where day tickets are available, and any casual visitor, unless he be the President or a roving Ambassador, is quite likely to have a very tough task in finding suitable access. Just a little information on this may be gleaned from a publication titled *Where to Fish*, published by the Harmsworth Press of 8 Stratton Street, London W.1.

At Stockbridge—the Mecca of Test fishermen—the Greyhound Hotel has some water where the fish average 3 pounds. Charges (when water is available) are around $7 a day. Local enquiries, however, can sometimes lead to access; but a fishing trip to this hallowed area may never be planned with certainty. Most owners and clubs impose strict bag and size limits. Rarely, on the Test, is it permissible to retain trout under 14 inches in length and all smaller fish must be returned to the water. Policies differ slightly, however; some owners prefer the angler to kill every fish he may catch—up to a certain number—on the principle that once a fish has bitten, it is twice shy, and that fish frequently returned to the water will eventually become worthless for sport. The general season extends from April 1 to the end of September with slight variations on different rivers. The extensive weed growth has to be cut at least twice a year and this brings a period when fishing virtually comes to a standstill until the floating weed is removed.

Other fisheries in the area have become very artificial, and a series of manmade lakes, known as "Two Lakes," near Romsey is producing some of the finest rainbow trout to be found in the country. All fish caught have to be killed, and the angler is limited to five fish per day. On a good day, however, they will all average over 3 pounds.

The highlights of my trip came when I was fishing the middle Test near Stockbridge, Bossington, and Marshcourt. This is where the river gives of its best, and to have the benefits of wonderful hosts like Barrie Welham, David Jacques, and John Goddard meant that I would have every opportunity of fine sport, despite the fact that at the time of my visit the sun was beating down on us and it was in the high 80's.

The first noteworthy trout I was to encounter was quietly taking some pale watery duns within a few feet of the bank of the Test at Bossington. I had to get down on hands and knees to make a stealthy approach; but eventually my fly covered the fish, and it took without any inhibitions. As soon as it felt the hook, the fish gave a mighty leap and landed on the bank. Within split seconds, however, it was back in the water, fortunately with the fly, leader, and line still intact. A dingdong battle ensued, and I had all on to keep the fish out of the weeds. It was one of the gamest chalk-stream fish I have ever played and I breathed a deep sigh of relief as I slid its 2 pounds into my net.

On another occasion I was on the Test at Marshcourt, opposite the famous Houghton Club water, when a likely looking fish started rising under an alder tree. It was not an easy cast and it required a bit of care to steer the fly under the overhanging branches. Eventually it did land right and the fish took it with a bang. It did not seem a big fish, but the trout's gallant runs had me straining rod and leader to the limits, and it was quite some time before I had this 1½-pounder subdued and into the waiting net. David Jacques was quickly on the scene and placed his marrow scoop down its gullet. From a glance at the stomach contents it was pretty obvious that my fish had fed on everything that had come its way. There was even the remains of an alder fly—a fly, incidentally, which Halford never found during an autopsy of a Test trout. David dismissed my fish with a grunt. "That fish would have taken anything," he said. "Now go and catch a difficult one!"

Feeling somewhat admonished, I renewed my efforts; but my time in Hampshire was drawing to a close and I could do little more than take in the beauty of the surroundings and reflect that the great Izaak Walton was laid quietly at rest in his nearby cathedral tomb and that the ghosts of Halford and Skues would be looking on. I hoped that the passage of time had not spoiled the sacred shrines of dry-fly purism and that Halford and Skues would approve of present-day trout management, current angling techniques, and the people who fish there.

The Alive and Kicking Dry Fly

LEONARD M. WRIGHT, JR.

The ubiquitous caddis fly, always a treat for the trout, is re-introduced to the angler. (February 1973)

I'm now convinced that the traditional method of fishing the dry fly is all wet. It pains me to say this about the most beautiful and hallowed method of angling: I'm one of the millions who have been fascinated by it for years. But I am now almost certain that fishing the conventional dry fly in a dead-drift manner is dead wrong most of the time on most of our streams.

Not that the floating fly itself is dead—or even dying. Far from it. In fact, I'm predicting new life for the dry fly because more and more fishermen, as they examine the evidence, will begin to fish the floating fly as an alive-and-kicking insect instead of presenting it as a bunch of dead feathers.

I have been a confirmed heretic about both our standard patterns and our conventional ways of fishing them ever since one late-May morning several years ago when I met the perfect fly fisherman. I first sighted him some 100 yards downstream and, even at that distance, his casting and presentation seemed so elegant that I sat down on a boulder out of respect and watched him work up the pool. When he reached the white water that marked the top of that stretch, he reeled in and walked over towards me, giving an informal greeting with his hand. "Any luck?" I asked.

He shook his head. "I've raised only one and he was bait-sized. I didn't expect to do much till late afternoon, anyway, but it's just too great a day to be sitting around the house, isn't it?" Then he wished me luck and walked off slowly upstream and I never even found out what his name was.

I rested the water several minutes and then stepped in—even though his was a hard act to follow. I messed up my first few presentations trying to imitate his crisp, high backcast, then I settled into my normal fishing rhythm and twenty minutes later, when I reached the bottom of the pool, I realized I had raised seven trout and landed four—two of which had been 12-inchers and very respectable fish for those waters.

Admittedly, I'm not considered a duffer—I manage to put in fifty to sixty days on trout waters each season and have for years—but I wouldn't dream of classing myself with the unknown angler who'd preceded me. Yet I had interested far more fish despite his obvious advantage in streamsmanship. Clearly, the difference in our results was due to another factor: he had been casting a standard pattern in the classic, upstream manner, while I had been fishing a new type of floater downcurrent with a highly unorthodox technique.

The perfect fisherman had made each of his presentations flawlessly—by the book. And the book clearly states that the floating fly must approach and pass over the waiting trout dead-drift or drag-free—meaning that the line and leader must in no way impede the fly from floating downcurrent as if it were a completely detached object. Accomplishing this is no mean feat. Casting upstream with carefully executed curves or waves in the line gives the best chance for success, and the ability to outwit the hidden hands in the current is the accepted measure of a dry-fly man's skill.

I, on the other hand, had been breaking two great dry-fly commandments. I had been fishing in a slightly downstream direction. And I had made my fly move, on purpose, just before it reached the likeliest taking-place on each and every cast.

There was a method in my madness, though—a method I'd worked out several years previously after a series of frustrating experiences. On several occasions in close succession I had failed to catch—or even raise—a single fish even though trout were leaping and splashing all around me. And, on each of these occasions, the trout had been feeding on caddisflies that were hatching out and swarming all over the water surface.

These common, but much-neglected, aquatic insects very definitely do not float downcurrent like priceless objects of art. They bounce, crawl, skitter, flutter, and zigzag when on the surface, and always in an upstream direction. Book or no book, I decided, if I were going to catch trout on the dry fly during a caddis hatch, I would have to give my fly some motion and I would have to move it in an upstream direction.

The method I have worked out consists of casting across and slightly downstream, rather than up and across. Soon after my fly hits the water, I give it a small twitch of an inch or less than makes the fly's hackles twinkle in the surface film. My theory is that this telltale motion telegraphs to the waiting trout that a lively caddis is coming downstream, and the trout seem to think so, too.

I soon became so fascinated with this type of presentation that I tried it at odd times of day when no fish were rising. And, to my surprise, I discovered that the twitched-caddis was a dual-purpose weapon: it not only did great execution during the previously baffling caddis hatches, but it was a deadly way to pound up fish during those long hours when few or no fish were showing at the surface.

Further observation soon showed me why this mini-manipulation of the fly raised trout when most of them weren't having any. A fluttering fly not only advertises itself more vigorously to a non-feeding trout, but it is also more realistic since most aquatic insects—whether mayflies, caddisflies, or stoneflies—flutter on the surface before taking off or floating downcurrent.

Once I realized this simple fact, I began to cash in on it with both the fish and the fishermen. While a fishing companion and I would munch soggy sandwiches during the noontime lull, I would start laying bets on the fates of the few straggling insects that occasionally floated downstream. When I spotted a fly struggling on the surface some 50 feet upstream I'd say, "Bet you a quarter a fish takes that fly before he floats down opposite us." And, just to mix it up, I'd bet the opposite way on a fly that was floating downstream inert. Naturally some of the flies crossed me up. Active ones often took off before they reached us and lifeless ones suddenly became active and sealed their own fates. But despite these occasional setbacks, I'd be rich and retired by now if I hadn't run out of takers. Trout preference for a fluttering fly is that predictable.

By this time you're probably wondering: if trout really prefer a surface fly fished with some life to it, why have so many seemingly intelligent men fished the standard floating fly drag-free for so long? After all, many leaders in business, science, and the arts (not to mention two of the last seven Presidents of the U.S.) have been dedicated fly fishers. Have they all been duped and deluded?

The answer, I think, lies somewhere between "Yes" and "Probably." And the reason why such a thing could happen in this age of enlightenment makes a fascinating, though little-known, story.

Dry-fly fishing may have been developed over many years by many men, but it didn't reach the angling world at large till 1886. In that year, *Floating Flies and How to Dress Them* was published, and anglers haven't recovered from its enormous influence to this day. The author was Frederick M. Halford, an English gentleman, who gave up money-grubbing in all its forms at a relatively early age to devote his life to the nobler ideals of dry-fly fishing for trout.

The streams Halford fished are the most fertile in the world. The Test and Itchen in Southern England produce twenty times as much trout food per cubic foot of water, as do most famous streams on this side of the Atlantic. Back in Halford's fishing days, before road-washings, insecticides, and other pollutants had begun to take their toll, the hatches of insects, especially of mayflies, on these waters were incredibly profuse.

Under these conditions, a few fish rose fairly steadily all day long, and for several special hours every day when the glut hatches occurred, every fish in the river seemed to be on the take. It was a fly fisher's paradise and too perfect to be spoiled for other club members by some heavy-handed chap who put down the fish by flailing a team of wet-flies through these clear waters in the hope of taking an unseen trout.

The accepted drill was quite specific. First a rising trout must be located. Then an accurate imitation of the fly on the water—not just some attractive and buggy looking artificial—must be cast upstream of the trout and allowed to float, dead-drift, over the nose of that particular fish. No attempt must be made to cater to its greed or curiosity. The only proper way to take such fish is to convince them that your counterfeit is, indeed, just another of the duns on which they have been feeding with confidence.

Fishermen on both sides of the Atlantic became fascinated by the science, skill, and delicacy of this new method. Halford became the high priest of a cult that spread the true doctrine with fanatical zeal. Soon the wet fly was considered a secret vice and club members caught using it were asked to resign their expensive rod privileges. The dry fly became a moral issue. After all, dammit, a gentleman didn't shoot grouse on the ground, he didn't cheat at cards, and he most certainly did not fish the wet fly, either!

From what I read, we seem to have shaken off most of our old Victorian hang-ups by this time, but the dry fly is still considered holier than the wet and the Halfordian dogma of dead-drift seems to be a vestigial part of this ethical package. The moral origins of this doctrine may be lost in history, as far as most anglers are concerned, but the ritual is still with us.

In all fairness to Halford, though, I must repeat that he was fishing the stately chalk streams of England which teem with small mayflies. And, so even so, he included five highly realistic caddis patterns in his final selection of forty-three dry-fly patterns. But can we, who fish rivers that are mostly rain-fed, acid, and where caddis rival the mayflies for top place on the trout's menu, afford to ignore caddis imitations completely?

For we seem to be doing just that. For example, check the contents of your own dry-fly boxes. How many floating imitations of caddisflies do you carry? Don't count nondescripts or flies like the Adams which are said to duplicate some caddis but which are tied with the characteristic mayfly upwings and tails. I mean true caddis patterns like the English "sedges" with wings tied parallel to their bodies and which show a realistic caddis silhouette. Can you find many— or even any—in your fly boxes?

If you're like most anglers I know or meet—and many of these are advanced fly fishers—you probably don't have a single one. And chances are you can't find any at your favorite tackle shop, either. With the exception of a few terrestrials, nearly all floaters displayed in even the most fully stocked stores are designed to imitate some mayfly or other.

Admittedly, these popular mayfly patterns have proved themselves over and over again—*when there are enough mayflies hatching to start trout feeding regularly and selectively*. But how much of the time do you meet these conditions on the rivers you fish? What do you offer when caddisflies are hatching out in large numbers and trout are feeding on them selectively? What fly do you put on when stoneflies are on the water? Or during those all-too-long periods when nothing is hatching and the trout are taking only the occasional, windfall, land-bred insects like bees, wasps, or houseflies? Is the traditional mayfly silhouette the most appealing to trout at times like these?

I think not. And I think this is the reason why the series of flies I have worked out to represent the most common species of caddisflies have proved themselves as excellent prospecting flies, too. Their silhouettes are more accurate representations of most land-bred windfall insects than are the shapes of the standard mayfly patterns.

Straw, ginger, brown, light dun, dark dun, and ginger-and-grizzly mixed have proved the most useful colors, but there are endless variations. Sizes 16 and 14 seem to cover most common caddis hatches, although I always carry some 18's and 12's just in case. Most of the caddis patterns I use have wings, hackle, and body of the same shade because caddisflies tend to be much the same color all over. My stonefly imitations, tied in the same manner, usually show more contrast, as do the naturals.

If you tie your own flies, or have a friend who ties for you, you may be interested in how these new Fluttering Caddisflies are tied. I start out by winding the tying silk back toward the tail, proceeding a little further than is customary, or just a bit around the bend. The reason for this is that most caddis have slightly down-pointing abdomens and because this fly needs more room at the eye-end of the hook. Tie in, at this point, two, at most three, strands of fine herl (pheasant-tail fibers are a good example) and very fine gold wire. Wind the herl up the shank, being careful to keep the body slim and even, to a point just halfway to the eye of the hook and fasten it down. The wire is then wound tightly to the same place with four or five even turns, but in an opposing spiral so that it binds down the herl and protects it.

Next comes the wing, and this must be put on with great care. Take a good spade feather, shoulder hackle, or the stiffest fibers on the neck that you usually reserve for tail materials, even up the points, and twitch off a section about three-fourths of an inch wide. Position this bunch on top of the hook so that from the tying-in point to tips it is about twice as long as the body, and bind it down with one full, firm turn of tying silk. If the fibers lie absolutely flat along the shank, you're in business. If not, take them off and build up the wingbed with thread until it is even with the hard portion of the herl body. When you have wound the body correctly with a suitable, small herl, this is seldom necessary, but these extra turns of silk can remedy any small error.

Once these top fibers are properly set, place two more bunches of the same bulk and length, one on each side of the hook, and tie them in with one turn each. Now half-hitch or weight the tying-silk and examine the wing from all angles. When viewed from the rear, it should look like the upper half of a small tube, only slightly larger in diameter at the tail end than it is at the tying-in point. It should also veil the body a bit when viewed from the side. At this point you can still make minor adjustments by pinching and cajoling the fibers where they join the hook. Once you are satisfied with the overall appearance and symmetry, bind down firmly and finally with three or four turns of silk placed in tight sequence toward the head of the fly.

Take a fine, sharp pair of scissors and trim the wingbutts to form a gradual inclined plane, heaviest near the tying silk and coming to a point just back of the eye of the hook. It's a good idea to hold the wings firmly with your left thumb and forefinger right at the tying-in point while performing this delicate process so that the wing is not jostled out of position at this crucial stage. When the taper is absolutely even, take some varnish or cement and work it into the exposed butts to keep the slick hackle fibers from pulling out during the punishment of fishing. When the head becomes tacky, tie in two hackles of the usual size for that hook and wind them on in the conventional manner, being careful to bunch the turns tightly so they don't slide loosely down the inclined plane toward the eye of the hook. Whip finish, varnish the head, and the fly is finished.

Each caddis represents a larger than average investment in choice materials and in effort, but it's worth it in the long run. If properly tied, it will float higher and take more punishment than any other dry fly in your box. And, I've found, it will take more fish, too.

Even if you're not a tyer, or don't know any, you should be able to give these new patterns a tryout next year because several tackle companies tell me they're going to offer this series of flies soon.

I know this is not the perfect dry fly for every single situation although I, myself, now use it the majority of the time. Of course I still fish standard mayfly imitations when those naturals are on the water—though I often give even these easily sinkable patterns a tiny twitch when a steadily rising fish continues to ignore my artificial.

I also know that this new method will never make me into the perfect fly fisherman, either. But with these new patterns and this unorthodox presentation, I am now catching several times as many trout from hard-fished waters as I did a few years ago. Try them yourself this coming season during a caddis or stonefly hatch or during those all-too-long "non-hatches." I think they'll do the same for you.

The Fishing Story
Life Missed

ROBERT TRAVER

The best-selling author of Anatomy of a Murder *and* Trout Madness *tells how America's largest magazine missed a big story by focusing on the celebrity.* (October 1974)

After writing three books the cheering throngs of readers of which I could have accommodated nicely in a two-car garage—no, better make that one—I wrote my first novel, and all hell broke loose. While I still wonder what *that* book had the others didn't, the fact is that my *Anatomy of a Murder* almost overnight got itself glued to the bestseller list, tapped by the Book-of-the-Month, knighted by Otto Preminger (whose subsequent movie was graced by the presence of that gentle man, Joseph N. Welch, who became a dear friend) and, as the royalties rolled in, blessed by the Internal Revenue Service.

Now the only reason I'm mentioning this is not to brag, heaven knows, but because the following story would be rather pointless if I didn't, since this background was the basis for there being any story to tell. For the painful truth is that, for all its material rewards, there is much about the trauma of best-sellerdom that is eminently forgettable. In fact if it weren't that my own immersion in it freed me to fish, for which I am eternally grateful, and allowed me to get to know some talented and lovely people I would otherwise have missed, I doubt that I would ever again mention it, even to myself.

Anyway, as my orbiting book and I joined hands and soared through the blazing hoops of national notoriety, I was naturally invited to appear and brandish my book on all manner of shows—talk shows, quiz shows, panel shows, possibly even dog shows—though here the memory bobbles a bit. Most of these bids I managed to turn down, especially after I discovered that a fisherman was more likely to raise a dead cat than a trout on the pastoral East River. But I did accept a few, and one of the most pleasantly memorable of these was when *Life* photographer Bob Kelley phoned me one day and asked if he might come up and follow me around fishing a few days, thus furnishing me with this story and starting a lasting friendship.

"You a fisherman, Mr. Kelley?" I parried cautiously.

"Yup," he said. "And I sure liked your book."

This was by now a familiar gambit that accompanied most of these invitations, and I tried not to wince. "Tell me, Mr. Kelley," I said, ever the tease, "and how did you like the movie?"

"Oh that. I don't mean your courtroom yarn, though it wasn't too bad," Kelley said. "I mean your fishing book, *Trout Madness*, which I really liked. Main reason I called, in fact."

"Well, well," I said, beginning to purr.

"*Life* wants you to write the story to go with my pictures, for which they'll naturally pay," he ran on, naming a figure so generous it stunned me into silence. "Hello? Hello?" he shouted, clicking the phone. "You still on?"

"Barely, but rallying," I managed to say, already putty in the man's hands. "When would you plan to come up?"

"Midafternoon plane tomorrow," Kelley said. "How about it?"

"Fine, fine," I said before he changed his mind. "I'll meet your plane tomorrow."

So the next afternoon I met Bob Kelley's plane, then smiling, crew-cut, trench-coated Bob himself, who in turn presented me to a curly-headed towering young New Englander called Robert Brigham. "Moose is the reporter assigned to this one," Kelly explained as I pumped Moose's big paw.

"But I thought your magazine wanted me to write the story," I said, a little shaken.

"It still does," Bob Kelley said, shrugging and widening his hands. "But when your boss assigns a reporter to a case"—Bob rolled up his eyes and snapped his fingers—"*that* reporter tags along."

"Maybe Moose was sent to translate my stuff into English," I said, a little thoughtfully.

"Barely possible," Moose admitted in his down-East drawl. "That remains to be seen."

"Well, well," I said, rubbing my chin. "I'll try not to overwork you, Mr. Moose."

Clanking with cameras, luggage, and assorted equipment, the two Bobs and I repaired to the Mather Inn in my town and then for refreshments down in the bar, where Bob Kelley proceeded to outline his general plan. This, he explained, was for us somehow to try to show in words and pictures just what magical lure there was about trout fishing that make a presumably intelligent man, one endowed with a four-karat legal education, quit a more or less permanent job on his state's highest court and write yarns about it. "What did make you do it?" Bob concluded.

"Just lucky I guess," I said, "as the whore lady told the social worker when asked how *she* got that way."

"But seriously," Bob pleaded.

"That, Robert," I said, "is something I've been trying to explain to myself ever since—not to mention to my wife." I sighed. "But I'm willing to give it another try."

For the next three days Bob Kelley and I gave it the old college try, accompanied by our reporter, Bob Brigham, who had nothing to report, and whom we accordingly pressed into service as a combined rod-bearer, camera-toter and ambulant bar. How did we make out? As my old fishing pal Luigi might have put it, "Lat me try an' tole you, my fran."

Part of the charm of trout fishing is that trout, unlike people, will respond only to quietude, humility, and endless patience, and as far as I was concerned Bob Kelley's trip richly confirmed that fact. It also proved some things trout will *not* respond to, one of them certainly being any fisherman who tries to show off and glorify himself at their expense. This sort of thing they seem to sense almost instantly by some mysterious telepathy running up through the rod and down the line and leader to the fly. Once this message is flashed the trout seem to conspire to bring the poor wayward fisherman back to humility; either that or to the brink of a nervous breakdown.

There was one other lesson all of us learned: that my Upper Peninsula of Michigan trout, at least, wanted no part of appearing in any photographic command performances ordered by anyone called Henry R. Luce. *That* message came through loud and clear.

Those first three days of fishing were a disaster as far as fishing pictures were concerned, and though I took the boys to some of the hottest spots I knew, I did not catch a single really decent trout. It seemed that I was so eager to provide Bob with a thrilling picture that I spent most of my time posing and posturing, either overstriking the few decent trout that did rise or, in my preoccupation with being photogenic, striking too late.

On the evening of the second day I did get on to one decent fighting brown when fate had poor Bob reloading his camera. By the time he'd shed that one and grabbed and focused another (he bristled with them) the bored brown had wound itself around an underwater snag and—as we heard my leader go *ping*—was merrily off and away.

In retrospect, as I write this, it sweeps over me that this sort of thing has happened so often, not only then but since, that I'm prepared to swear that a fisherman is only at his relaxed best when he knows that nothing is watching him except the scampering chipmunks and God.

Bob was most understanding and nice about the whole thing, being a fisherman himself, but by the end of the third day the strain began to tell and even I could sense—in fact *that* was a good part of my trouble—that *Life* fully expected Bob to come up with at least one thrilling picture of a trophy trout being caught by that best-selling fly-casting author of *Trout Madness* because, after all, *Life* dealt in *success*.

When on the evening of the third day we finally gave up we found Moose awaiting us back at the jeep deep in a novel, to which he'd sensibly turned on the morning of the second day when he saw how sad the fishing was.

"Any luck?" he dutifully inquired, pointing at the clinking drinks awaiting us on the hood of the car.

I widened my eyes and shrugged and raised my outstretched arms in the international sign language of defeat, and reached for my drink. "Ah . . ."

"Where to tomorrow?" Bob inquired glumly, still shedding cameras. "It better be good for tomorrow's our last day."

"Really don't know yet," I said, "but I'll brood over it during the night. Meanwhile, if you will, Moosie boy, please pass the bourbon."

During the night inspiration struck—why hadn't I thought of it before?—and early the next morning we parked the jeep on the south side of the top of a deep valley through which ran one of the most sporting and wadable stretches of the entire Big Dead River. Though I rarely fished the place any longer because of my growing infatuation with wild brook trout, I had long known it harbored some of the biggest browns around.

"We rig up here, Bob," I said, leaping out and grabbing my waders and fighting my way into them as Bob did likewise while Moose yawned and settled down with his book.

"Moose," I said, when Bob and I were just about armed and ready for the last day's fray, "it's going to be a long day. Bob and I have a lot of river to cover. Wouldn't you like to tag along?"

"I'd sure like to," Moose eagerly said, "but I don't have any waders."

"No problem," I said. "I've got an old emergency pair way too big. Wear them."

My inspirations were coming in clusters and as Moose writhed his way into my old patched waders I had another. "Hell, Moose," I said, "there's a nice big pool where our trail hits the river. Why don't you take one of my extra rods and try for a trout while we do our stuff?"

"But I never fly fished in my life," Moose confessed.

"Incredible. I thought all New Englanders were born holding a fly rod."

"Not this one. Only a little surf-casting as a kid. Never held a fly rod in my hand."

"Then why did you and Kelley bother to buy fishing licenses?"

"Routine magazine policy to appease the local gendarmes. But I still can't cast a fly."

"Tell me, can you lace your shoes?" I asked.

"Of course."

"Then you can cast a fly," I said airily. "I'll rig you up a fiberglass nymphing rod you could heave a polecat with along with a stout leader and some big flies. All you got to do is keep pelting away. What do you say?"

"I'm game," Moose said, shrugging. "Beats reading bad novels."

So I rigged up Moose and handed him a tin box of faded and tattered old bucktail streamers and the three of us slid and slipped our way down the steep river trail to the first river pool.

The omens were good. While no trout were rising in Moose's shaded pool, we soon spotted several spunky risers working between us and the first bend below.

"Let's go, master angler," Kelley said, champing at the bit.

"Bitterness will get you nowhere, Kelley," I said. "But first I got to give Moose a quick lesson." So saying, I towed Moose out into the current to give him casting room and, taking his rod, gave him a short cram course in casting a fly without impaling one's ear. "Now you try it," I said, handing him the rod, and Moose grabbed it and lashed out—and narrowly missed impaling *my* ear.

"Wait till we get out of here," I shrilled, scrambling, and Bob and I quickly splashed across to safety above his pool. "If time palls, there's beer in the car ice box and you know where we hid the key," I called out to him above the sound of the current.

Moose nodded grimly and lashed out again, caught a dead branch behind him, jerked on it mightily and broke the branch, lost his balance and, amidst the crashing of falling timber, slipped and fell on his face in the river. "C-c-cold!" he sputtered, floundering to his feet and again falling, threshing, and blowing like a beached whale. Bob and I averted our eyes and—it seemed the only decent thing to do—silently slipped away downstream on a worn fisherman's trail.

I shall mercifully spare giving any detailed account of the next four hours. It is enough to say that I fished over dozens and scores of rising browns, by far the best fish we'd seen on the trip, in fact, some of them real lunkers. But it was the same old story: in my zeal to plead and play the role of master angler I kept striking too soon, too late, too hard, too soft, too something . . . Box score: no trout. After about two frustrating miles of this I looked sheepishly at Kelley and Kelley looked at his watch and shook his head.

"Too early for cocktails, Robert?" I inquired softly.

"I'd say just about four hours too late," Kelley said. "What do you say we get the hell out of here?"

We took the shore trail upstream, resolutely ignoring all the lovely rises we saw along the way, and presently emerged on a high shaded bank overlooking Moose's pool.

"*Look!*" Kelley tensely whispered, pointing, and there in the middle of the pool, far over his flooded waders, stood an intent Moose fast to a simply massive rod-bending trout. Oblivious to our presence Moose worked the threshing creature in, lunged at him with the net, missed, and as we watched, the big brown made a mighty flop and threw the fly and dashed away.

"Oh my Gawd," Kelley moaned in anguish, bowing his head.

Moose heard Kelley's lament and looked up and waved. "Hi, fellas," he called out cheerily. "How's the ol' luck?"

"Lousy," I said. "How about you?"

Moose turned his head and pointed inshore. "Got five dandy browns dressed out there in the ferns on account of no creel. Caught 'em the first coupla hours."

"*What!*" Kelley gasped.

"Lost three or four before I got the hang of the thing, one far bigger'n the slob just got off."

"*What!*" I gasped.

"Lost track of how many I've caught and put back. Great fun, this fly fishing." With that he slapped his big fly down on the water with a tidal splash, there was a savage roll and take, and Moose reared back like a bee-stung shot putter—and naturally snapped his leader and lost his fly on another lunking trout. "That's it," Moose said, splashing his way ashore, dripping like a tired water spaniel. "There goes my last fly."

"*My* last fly you mean," I pensively corrected him.

"Let's go get a drink," Kelley said in an awed voice. "I *need* the therapy."

Hours later, back around my kitchen table, I had my final inspiration. "I've *got* it!" I said, slapping my leg.

"What's that?" Kelley said. "That we go make a midnight raid on the local fish hatchery?"

"The idea for your real fishing story," I ran on, all aglow with my vision.

"Look, fellas, it's simply perfect. Here's the master fisherman you came a million miles to photograph, the wily angler, the old fox, the guy who writes books about his art—who after four days of flailing falls flat on his—"

"Yes?" Kelley inquired silkily.

"Keister," I said, glancing over at my ironing wife.

"Go on."

"And there's good ol' Moose, who never held a rod in his life, who threshes around like a mired mastodon in one solitary pool, heaving out harpoons and flailing away for hours like a man beating a rug—and who makes the old master look like a bum." I spread my hands. "That's your *real* story, boys. It's beautiful. I love it. And God knows it's fishing."

Moose wagged his head. "We'd be fired," he said.

"What do you mean fired?" I said, looking at Kelley for support.

"Moose is right," Kelley said. "We came here to do a success story about a best-selling author and expert angler. That is our mission."

"So-called expert," I amended.

"No matter. Anything that tarnishes that halo of success—or maybe haloes don't tarnish—or dims the glittering image of our star is bad and verboten. The magazine'd never stand for it and we could indeed lose our jobs."

"Yes, I guess I see," I said after a spell, shaking my head. "In fact I'm awfully afraid I do see what you mean. But some day, I warn you, I'm going to tell it the way it was. And I do hope it won't get you boys fired."

"I'll drink to that," Bob said, and all of us clinked glasses and were shortly off to bed.

So the next day the boys caught their plane and I began working on my dubious success story, the main thing I recall about it being, as I brooded and pondered, that I came up with a thing I suspect more nearly expresses why *I* fish, at least, than anything I've written before or since. It was called "Testament of a Fisherman" which, I'd almost forgotten till now, first appeared in *Life* before it came out in Kelley's and my subsequent book, *Anatomy of a Fisherman*, now out of print.

That was at least a dozen years ago. Since then *Life* has folded its tent, of course, and Bob and Moose have moved on to greener pastures. But as I look back on it and consider my small part in it I can't help wondering whether *Life* wasn't sealing its own death warrant even then by so endlessly spinning its gilded fairy tales of "success" instead of telling it as it was. At least in its heedless death flight after this elusive will-o'-the-wisp I know of one grand fishing story it surely missed.

The Offer Trout Can't Refuse

NORMAN STRUNG

For a few seconds during each retrieve, your spinning lure can behave irresistibly. Here's how to create that momentary magic.
(November 1978)

When I first began spinfishing for trout, my technique was the scattershot signature of a beginner. I'd stand in one spot on the streambank and cast to the clock, 9 to 3. After the seventh cast, I'd move to a new spot. Initially, the fish seemed to strike at random, but as the weight of time gradually built into the wisdom of experience, I began to perceive that there was one cast that took the most fish. Stranger still, there was one moment during the retrieve that seemed magic in its attraction for trout. Although it represented only 5 percent of the time my lure was in the water, it accounted for 40 percent of my strikes.

The numbers were different but the cast was always the same; when the river ran left to right, a 10 o'clock cast was charmed. When it ran right to left, the 2 o'clock cast took fish. It was a strange puzzle, but one that I had to pursue. When the pieces finally fell together, they came up with an offer that trout can't refuse.

Trout are commonly portrayed as shy, reclusive creatures. The mention of

276

their name suggests limpid pools, lacy flies, and a quarry that is almost maidenlike in behavior. Nothing could be further from the truth.

Trout are shy, but shy like a stalking lioness, skulking in the shadows until her prey comes within range. Reclusive? Only when they suspect that they're in danger of becoming a meal for something else. Dainty? Not in terms of their eating habits. They will fill themselves to a point where forage foods from tiny midges to minnows half their size gorge their gullets, and still strike a lure. For all the romantic prose written about them, trout are no less predators than wolves, eagles, or barracudas. If they grew as large as sharks, you can bet that wading wouldn't be nearly so popular with anglers as it is today.

Just as foxes, coyotes, and bobcats are drawn to the chilling cries of a rabbit in distress, predatory fish will zero in on any extraordinary behavior exhibited by their prey. With SCUBA gear on, I've watched trout while a whole school of baitfish swam by. One brown made no move until one of the school began swimming in odd, jerky circles. The fish rocketed in and had him in a blink. Another time, a lone minnow twice swam within 2 feet of a finning rainbow who paid him no heed. The minnow came back a third time, and was either frightened by me, or he finally saw the fish. He turned and scooted, and the trout pounced on him like a cat. Make no mistake; trout, especially large trout, are hardly good guys by human standards. Their first choice in prey is always the crippled, the slow, the weak, and the fearful, and therein lies the appeal of this "offer".

It is more correctly called a presentation in that you are consciously creating the illusion of a frantic, frightened baitfish trying desperately to get away because he has come face-to-face with his maker. To make this offer, you have to be able to maneuver your lure through a three-stage change in behavior, right in front of a likely station in a stream.

Let's look at those three behavior changes first. The first stage is action. In an instant, a lure that's been lazing along at a leisurely wobble starts fluttering wildly. The suggestion is that an injured baitfish has recognized imminent danger, and now is in wild flight. The second stage is a 180-degree turnaround in horizontal direction; coincidal with the switch in appearance, the lure reverses its path and heads the other way. The third stage is vertical direction. As the lure swings around, it also rises sharply off the bottom, providing the trout with easy prey that's silhouetted against the surface. This illusion of fear, the shift into evasive tactics, and the appearance of a clear target combine to trigger the predatory urge in trout so surely that even wary browns with full stomachs can't resist the itch to strike out and snare another morsel, just because it's trying to get away.

When luck is with you, you can achieve this effect with nothing more than a 10 or 2 o'clock upcurrent cast. That's exactly how I blundered onto this technique. If you don't like to trust luck, here's how it's done by the numbers.

Begin with an upstream cast. Snap your bail shut as soon as the lure hits the water, and take in line just fast enough to keep slack out as the current helps push the lure along. Keep your eye on the slack; the current speed will probably vary, and you want to reel just slightly faster than it's moving. This translates into a lure that's slowly rotating or wobbling, and sinking as it heads downriver.

This part of the retrieve is the trickiest in some respects, because you want the lure to skim bottom, but not hang up. If you feel the tick of streambed rock, reel a little faster. If the lure blasts up to the surface as it turns around, you're reeling too fast.

If you're retrieving at the correct speed, your line should have developed a deep belly as the lure reaches a point opposite your position on the shore. Depending upon the swiftness of the current, stop taking in line a few seconds either side of this moment. The water will catch the belly, and pressure on the line will keep the lure moving on its own.

A few seconds later, the lure will begin to accelerate due to whiplash. The bellied line, your stationary rod and reel, and current drag combine to move the line faster and faster as it approaches the lure. You can identify this acceleration because you'll feel a pronounced increase in the pressure the line is exerting on your rod tip as your lure begins to work faster and faster, setting up progressively greater resistance. At this point, lift your rod tip high enough so the line clears the water. The current still has a firm grab on the lure at this point, and it takes all the slack out of the line. When the line draws up tight, the lure reverses direction and starts to angle toward the surface.

The period of maximum appeal lasts between 7 and 12 seconds. In a strong current you need not touch your reel during this time; just be ready for a strike, which brings up another dictum; don't snap your rod so high that you will be handicapped when you strike to set the hook. In a sluggish current, you might have to slowly take in line as the lure goes around and up. Again, the key is in the pressure you feel on your rod tip. It should remain constant from the point of whiplash until the retrieve is complete.

After the turnabout is made and the lure has risen, you will feel a decrease in rod-tip pressure. Water and whiplash effect have done their job and the only thing working against the lure is now current. Pace your retrieve so the lure continues to flash and flutter as it comes into shore. Although trout are most likely to strike at the point of turnaround, occasionally it just piques their interest. When this happens, they'll follow for a while, and strike later. I make it a practice to jig my lure two or three times as it's coming to me so it looks like it's trying to "escape" again. That extra little enticement has caught me a lot of fish that ordinarily would have lost interest, and it can do the same for you.

The predictable attraction of this presentation astonishes anglers who are unfamiliar with the technique, and occasionally it even astonishes me. I was once fishing with three friends from New York on the upper reaches of the Missouri River, and noticed that Eric Feldman was having unusually bad luck. We had nine on the stringer, and he hadn't felt a single strike.

"Give me your rod a second, I want to show you something," I said, and using the same combination of rod, reel, and lure that he'd found so unappealing, I lobbed a long cast upcurrent.

"You've got to pace your lure like this," I explained, cranking the lure in at a rate just a little faster than the current. "Let it go deep, then just as it swings around and starts to come back, the fish will hit. Watch the line . . . the fish should hit right about . . . now."

The word was less than a second out of my mouth when I felt a tremendous strike and set the hook. I heard Eric mumble, "You've got to be putting me on."

I was a little smug that I'd gotten the strike, but then became downright serious about the feel of the fish. It was what I call a head-shaker, a trout so large that their first reaction is not to run, but to remain in their station shaking their head from side to side to the rhythm of a heartbeat in an attempt to disgorge the puny lure. The fish doesn't budge. Sometimes you think you've got a snag, but you can always tell by that heartbeat.

"This is big," I said, sobering.

The fish moved out from his hiding spot and headed downcurrent. It was like being hooked to a huge log. His strength and bulk, compounded by the swift current, made for no contest with 6-pound-test line. I kept as much pressure on as I dared, and followed him downstream.

Twenty yards below, the fish roiled, and I could tell by the flash of a great, golden slab that it was a big brown. He bore out into the current peeling off line. I held my breath and hoped that Eric knew how to adjust a drag properly.

The line and the fish held fast, then he turned upcurrent, an encouraging sign. Now he had two forces to buck. Suddenly he turned tail and raced downstream again, but the real punch of his brutish power was gone. He swung shoreward in a sweeping arc, and entered the slow current of a bank eddy as Frank Johnson arrived with the landing net. He scooped the fish headfirst. It would not fit any other way.

The tension and excitement had me wrung out and the size of the fish made me want to grin, but I feigned a scowl as Eric marveled at the arm-length hook-jawed male.

"Now that's how you do it," I said, handing over the rod, "and I'm not going to show you twice."

Although I've never been able to prove the pudding quite so memorably as I did in that one lesson, it doesn't take the average angler too long to catch on to the technique. Learning the mechanics of the retrieve is a lot simpler than it sounds;

the difficult part lies in being able to read water, and cast accurately enough so you can guide your lure through a turnaround right on a trout's doorstep.

The first grade in this education is learning to interpret a stream in terms of places that are likely to harbor trout. You'll usually find them at home in any water that provides protection from swift currents.

Typical stations include the slack water behind submerged boulders, the deep holes at the foot of bars and riffles, the eddies that turn behind rocks and projections from the shore, and under cutbanks. Midstream channels are tailor-made for the turnaround technique, but they're tricky to identify. Look for choppy water in an otherwise smooth pool. The chop is brought about by swift water from shallower parts of the stream bed overriding the slower, deeper water down in the channel. On a small scale, this troubled water looks very much like the waves churned up by a rip tide.

Shaded water is another place that's worth a turnaround or two. If it's not over holding stations, hungry trout will still locate there while they're on feed because of the camouflage afforded by shadows. Rising fish are another good bet. Even if they're plainly after flies, the thought that an easy meal might get away is often too much for them to bear.

Once you feel you've found a spot with promise, move upstream. How far to go is a function of two things: the swiftness of the current and the distance the station is from you. The swifter the stream or the more distant the station, the further ahead of the target you must be.

Although the following rules of thumb leave something to be desired in real application because of variations in current speed and crosscurrents, here's a sampling of stations, and how to construct a turnabout cast for them. (This hypothetical stream would be running at a speed of 3 knots.)

Hole under cutbank on your side of the stream. Position yourself 5 feet upstream of the hole, taking care not to spook fish through your shadow, profile, or bank vibrations. Make a short, 30-foot upstream cast, 2 to 5 feet out from the bank. Note that the turnaround will occur within 5 to 7 feet of your rod tip, so make sure your drag is set accurately. When working this kind of station, I usually switch my reel to free reverse so I can quickly put some cushioning line between me and a large fish by reeling backward.

Small bank eddy, your side of the stream. Position yourself 5 feet above the start of the eddy. Cast 20 feet upstream, 5 feet beyond shore. As the lure enters the eddy, reel slowly to make the turnaround. Otherwise the lure will sink in the slow water.

Large bank eddy, your side of the stream. Position yourself on the point of rocks, river bar, or log jam that's creating the eddy. Start with a cast that's identical to the one used for a small bank eddy. Make progressively longer casts that reach out into the main current in 3-foot increments. The idea is to present a series of turnarounds, each occurring 3 to 5 feet below the one preceding it, along with the eddy fence (the ill-defined line where fast water sweeps by slow water). Keep casting until you reach the spot where the fence fades out. Fish could be stationed anywhere along the fence.

Midstream boulder, showing above water. Emergent boulders, stationary logs, and other above-water obstructions to the current create two eddy fences that border the slack water behind the object. Here again, you should probe the entire eddy fence closest to you, but the technique is a lot different than the one for bank eddies. Stand opposite the place where you want the turnaround to occur, and cast your lure in the middle of the calm pocket, so it lands approximately 45 degrees upriver of the planned turnaround point. Close your bail and jam your rod tip into the water. The current will seize your line, and pull the lure through the calm water in a downstream direction. When you want the lure to turn around, snatch the rod tip up. It will yank the lure across the eddy fence. Once the crossover's made, the current will turn the lure upriver, and it will begin to rise.

Submerged midstream stations. This term refers to things like submerged boulders, channels, holes, and the pocket of water before an emerged boulder. Since they could be any number of feet from shore, let's discuss them in terms of degrees of angle between you and your target.

Stand approximately 30 degrees above the place you think holds a fish, and cast upstream at a 30-degree angle. Drop your lure half again as far as the station is from you. If it is 20 feet away, make a 30-foot cast, if it is 30 feet away, make a 45-foot cast, and so on. Keep your rod tip pointed at the moving lure, not where the line enters the water. This helps develop the belly.

When your rod tip approaches the spot where you suspect a fish is hanging out, lift the line clear of the water and turn the lure around.

There are two guidelines that will prove useful when sizing up these potentially long casts. First, 30 degrees is about the maximum angle that will allow the turnaround to occur. If you go beyond it, your lure will trace a path that scribes a long, lazy arc with very little change in the speed or direction. Remember, however, that the 30-degree rule is in relation to the current flow, not the stream bank. It's often possible to make a 90-degree cast in relation to the shore, that enters the current at a 30-degree angle. A sharp bend in the river is one common example.

When trying to figure out where to point your rod to develop a belly, and to estimate where the lure is so you can turn it around, use a five to one ratio. If you have 20 feet of line that you see, the lure will be around 4 feet beyond the point where the line enters the water. If you have 40 feet of line above water, the lure will trail the entry point by 8 feet. Note: this is only true on a slow retrieve with the current. Across-current or upcurrent retrieves have a much higher ratio.

I can say without reservation that this spinfishing technique is the most dependable trout-tempter I've yet to find, but I'd be less than honest if I said it was simple to master. Don't expect to exhibit marksmanlike accuracy and a turnaroud that's right on the money on your first try. Gauging river speed, lure depth, the feel of different terminal tackle at work, and drift vectors are all crafts that require practice and time to perfect. But that's one of the many joys of angling; unlike football or baseball practice, when you score at fishing practice, it really counts. And as your strikes and successes mount up, you'll develop a feel for the technique. Your eyes and hands will join forces and they'll tell you where your lure is, how fast it's going, and you'll begin to sense that marvelous moment of anticipation when a strike is most likely to occur. At that point, you'll be hooked as surely as the fish on the end of your line, for once you learn to make it work, the offer that trout can't refuse is impossible for a fisherman to turn down as well.

A Brookie for the Wall

PETER KAMINSKY

Some dreams are better than others—especially those that come true.
How about one where trophy-sized brook trout rise all day long?
(January 1982)

In Labrador, you will find the *real* world. It rests secure from the works of man. Even if you've never been there (few people have), I think you could describe it for me. "Tell me," I would say, "of a perfect place to fish for trout."

And you might answer: "Take a few thousand miles of evergreen forest and carpet the ground with pale green moss the color of oak leaves on their underside in early spring. Then scoop out enough forest to give you lakes beyond numbering. Arrange the lakes in chains so that they flow one into another, connected by river courses, a mile in length, riffled and pooled. Sprinkle the shoreline with some caribou to catch the attention, now and again, of the weary fisherman. And, for the same reason, place some loons on the water to break the Northern silence with their whinnying calls. Fill the waters with mayflies, golden drakes the size of Spanish doubloons. Let the sun shine long and the nights be short, and let the insects, warmed to activity, hatch by the billions all day long. And, oh yes, put in a race of giant trout with fins as meaty as a dog's hind leg."

We had flown in by chopper the night before. From Goosebay to Anne Marie Lake, we covered about 80 miles, crossing two ranges of low mountains. I had looked forward to an ample, old-timey Adirondack lodge—you know the kind: a fireplace big enough to garage a Chevy Blazer, and walls of amber pine festooned with the heads of twelve-point bucks watching over a mahogany bar.

Instead, we found a small house, a couple of bunk beds, one wood-burning stove, a shower, and two dog-eared copies of *Valley of the Dolls*. Makes sense too, when you think about it. Everything had to be flown in. Each charter cost about $800. That being the case, our hosts, Jack and Larraine Cooper, outfitted their lodge the way NASA rigged Apollo I: safe, adequate, and *spare*.

We set out early, Tony Atwill, myself, and a guide who tillered the small outboard that powered our square-stern canoe. We raced across the open water of Anne Marie Lake and cut up through a channel called Lover Boy. Skirting some whitewater, we anchored above a weedbed at the lip of the rapids. Tony cast a Royal Wulff over the slick. I short-leadered a Mickey Finn to my sinking line and was rewarded with a tug that bent my rod double. This was a new experience. Once I had caught a 17-inch rainbow on Long Island, but nothing ever punished my rod like this. Leaning over the gunwales, we peered down for a glimpse of the fish. But brookies in Labrador get so old and dark on top that they seem to suck up the shadows and disappear. Finally he came up. A bow wave, followed by an eye, then a big body. I thought of the giant squid in *20,000 Leagues Under The Sea*. The scale read 7¼ pounds. I wanted a brookie for my wall, but not that one, not yet.

Next day we swapped guides with the three fishermen with whom we shared the lodge. We were now under the stewardship of one Howard Guptille, a man of astringently dry wit. Our route lay south, to Woody Pond. To reach it we ran downstream, to the outlet of Anne Marie Lake, and then portaged our motor along an old trapper's trail to a second boat (which in the watertightness department would have run a distant second to a screen door). After that came yet another portage to a third boat at the inlet of Woody Pond.

Midlake, a trout rose. We eased up to him, cast, and discovered a trick. There isn't much current through the pond, so the trout don't wait for the mayflies to come to them. Instead, they follow the flies. When you see a rise you cast to where you *think* the trout is headed. There are four directions to the compass, so figure you have a one-in-four chance of nailing a riser.

We devised a way to even up the odds. We called it Brookie Bracketing. After the rise, Tony would cast a few feet ahead. I'd do the same, but to one side. The permutations are endless. We felt the flush of inspiration wash over us . . . true angling pioneers. We named our casts. There was a Right-Angle Bracket. A 270-Degree Bracket. An Ascending Bracket, a Descending Bracket, and an Ascending Descending Reverse Bracket. We even caught some fish. Great fun, this bracketing, but as we later found out, totally stupid.

There are times when Labrador trout won't rise. Their logic often runs contrary to our experience in more southerly waters. If there's an overcast, forget it. If it starts to drizzle, forget it. If the gentlest wind ruffles the water, ever so slightly, forget it. Insects hatch with such consistency and in such profusion that the trout simply will not feed unless wind and weather deliver their food on a sun-dappled platter.

All this is nice to know, but what do you do when you have come 1,500 miles to fish and the trout ignore you? You put on a bass bug and you pop up some pike, dismissing any thoughts you may carry that pike give inferior sport. Pound for pound, inch for inch, as the saying goes, they are unquestionably gamer than brook trout by a good long margin.

We came upon our first pike by accident. On the return voyage from Woody Pond we stopped at the head of the lake to sample the weedbeds on either side of the inlet. Howard, our guide, advised that it was too shallow for trout. But this time Howard had just delivered himself of the opinion that Brookie Bracketing was for the birds, while Tony and I *knew*, with the faith of the newly baptized, that it was surely the greatest angling advance since the reel.

So we cast some streamers toward shore and snaked them through the weeds. And there he was, a nice little pike following the fly. He wasn't without caution, darting into the weeds or behind a rock, ever the stealthy hunter. Somewhere along the line he made up his mind to attack, fired up his after-burners, and slashed at the fly like jet-propelled lightning. What a strike! No sooner had we brought him to the boat than he took off again, a splendid little fish, finally cutting the leader with his teeth.

We were fresh out of streamers, so Tony tied on a bass bug. The pike went bananas. It was surface strike, sight fishing, all the way; North Country bone-fishing, so to speak. We landed some, but lost more to the pikes' sharp teeth.

Back at the lodge, we struck a deal with one of the guides. We needed wire to fashion leaders. He needed tobacco. He played guitar. For two pouches of tobacco, plus one Havana cigar, we acquired one 0.10-gauge high E string from his guitar.

The following day was right out of the Duck Hunter's Prayer Book—cold, windy, wet, and generally awful. The lake heaved whitecaps like bales of hay. The trout stayed down and sulked. Rigging up our 9-weight rods, we tied on 6 inches of 24-pound mono followed by the same length of guitar wire, terminating in a big green popper, ugly as Quasimodo. By noon we had taken (and returned) more than a dozen pike, including one 11-pounder who fought for 30 minutes. Truly marvelous fish, those pike.

Late in the season, spawning brook trout enter the flowages between the lakes; and though it was still a bit early in the year (the first week of August), on the same day that Tony and I had gone pike popping, another member of our party had taken a supremely beautiful spawner at the outlet of Woody Pond.

Next morning, guides and fishermen took up their stations in the flow below Anne Marie Lake. This was trout fishing as I had dreamed of it. Waist deep in rushing water, I slid, stumbled, and butt-walked to midstream, quarter casting my Muddler down and across. On the downstream swing of just such a cast, the trout took—with authority. It was impossible, in that heavy water, to circle below him. The trout turned broadside to the current, using it to his advantage. Brookies, even giant ones, aren't the world's spunkiest fighters, but when you add all that mass to moving water I imagine the feeling could be compared to trying to drag a throw rug through the tail race of Grand Coulee Dam—on 6-pound-test.

I don't know how long it took to bring the trout to net. Maybe 10 minutes. Maybe a year and a half. I was flying on a cloud, totally outside of time, lost to the world.

When I did net him, I snatched him from the water and expelled the breath I had been holding all through the fight. A magnificent 6¾-pound fish, not the biggest of the week, but to my mind, the best. From his fat belly, the crimson flush of spawning billowed up his flanks, capped to a scarlet swatch that ran clear across his shoulders, like the gaudy epaulettes of a Russian field marshall. And layered below the red, as if seen through a stained-glass window, green and yellow and blue mottling, criss crossed with the blackened scars and tracks of age.

Best of all, sometime in this trout's careless infancy, a predator had taken a bite from his tail, 2 inches deep and the same across.

From far away one of the other anglers called to me. "Don't fret about the tail, the taxidermist will fix it good as new."

"Fix him?" I screamed across the torrent. "Fix him? No way, pal. This fish has character."

And then a laugh started in me, way down below my knees: I was bursting with happiness. It worked its way up through my guts and wrenched my mouth wide 'til the sound filled all of western Labrador, I'm sure.

If a stranger had happened upon me just then, he would have thought me mad.

There was no urgency in our last day. We had caught fish and we had caught them in numbers. They were locked in our memories, and nothing could dislodge them. So, Tony and I just took things nice and easy.

The weather grabbed its cue from our emotions. Flat, calm water, warm summer sun, the air full of pine fragrance, hatching flies luring trout to feed. We discovered then that you don't have to outguess brookies. You don't have to bracket them, either.

Really, all you have to do is strip out 30 feet of line and send that fly sailing just as soon as you see a rise form. If you're fast, if you don't false cast a lot, you'll catch many trout. The trick, if there is one, is to catch a trout with every cast.

We did. We caught and caught and caught, one after the other. And we grew blasé, just like those stories you read of bored anglers in Fisherman's Paradise.

Just before the plane touched down to take us home, we sallied forth for one last fling. Tony impaled a Marlboro filter on his hook and cast it out. He caught a fish.

It was time to leave!

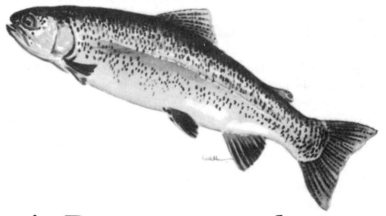

A Day in Paradise

RUSSELL CHATHAM

An author/artist's vivid portrait of fishing in a far-off, promised land.
(February 1983)

I would call the river delicate. It flows generally to the southwest, coming out of a long, broad, seemingly arid valley to finally join a much larger river, which subsequently empties into a lake. The system, in common with so many others on New Zealand's South Island, is full of rainbow and brown trout.

The fish are generally large: 3 pounds is probably about average, and every day you will cast to fish of 7 or 8 pounds. In a week's fishing the lucky angler will see at least one trout in the double figures.

The gradient of this particular river is not at all steep. In places it riffles along, wide and shallow, then suddenly at the corner of a hayfield it will cut a high bank, turn, then move slowly and darkly through a long, deep pool. The big fish are in the pools.

In the vicinity of the little town of Te Anau at the southern end of the South Island where this river runs, you might easily convince yourself you are in Northern California, Marin and Sonoma Counties in particular. Part of it is the rolling hills, gentle valleys, and ample vegetation. Annual rainfall is around 30 inches, similar to that of California's wine country.

A larger part of it is the distinctive eucalyptus tree, so widely transplanted in California from New Zealand and Australia. Californians think of the trees as native because we grew up with them. Thus, oddly, seeing eucalyptus in their true native land makes you think of home. One can imagine New Zealanders also thinking of their trout as being native, so important have the fish become to their lifestyle as well as their economy, even though the browns originally came from Europe and the rainbows from California.

It is hard to imagine this lovely island paradise without the overwhelming numbers of fish and game it now supports. But, in fact, before the islands were settled by Europeans there were no game animals and no trout.

Certain birds were native or self-introduced from Australia: the mountain parrot or Kea, herons, bitterns, paradise and gray ducks, rails, harriers, and a few others. The more familiar birds, at least to North Americans, such as mallards, Canada geese, pheasants, pigeons, owls, sparrows, quail, blackbirds, thrushes, finches, and sparrows, to cite a rather incomplete list, are all introduced.

Among the native fish are the eels, smelt, whitebait, assorted mudfishes and bullheads, and the grayling, considered to be extinct since about 1920. Brown and rainbow trout are very widely distributed throughout both north and south islands, and other introduced species include Atlantic salmon, sockeye salmon, king salmon, char, Mackinaw, perch, catfish, and carp.

Among the mammals, none of the major species now on the island are native. As there are no predators, the deer and elk populations ballooned out of control until finally commercial hunting became necessary as a means of control. Deer are now ranched much like cattle or sheep. In spite of extensive and sophisticated market hunting, deer are still more plentiful on the South Island than in even the most remote forests of North America.

To give some perspective as to the truly rural ambience of the South Island, it is nearly the size of California and its entire population is less than half that of the San Francisco Bay Area.

One day a year or so ago, just before Christmas, Frank Bertaina and I decided to walk 5 or 6 miles of that little, delicate river mentioned earlier. We had our friend and guide Bob Speden drop us off with an understanding he would pick us up about 8 hours later at a designated place upstream.

From the road we crossed a broad meadow that stretched a thousand yards to the river. It was knee-deep in sheep, New Zealand's principle export.

"This is the land," Frank smiled at me, "where men are men and the sheep are nervous."

Soon we struck the river and started upstream. The first mile was somewhat discouraging. Floods earlier in the year had altered the river's course, moving it out of its former bed so that it was now thinly spread over barren gravel. The old, scoured pools, willow lined and deep, were stagnant and isolated from the flow. There seemed to be no place for the kind of fish we were looking for to find cover.

We had been having weather problems and today was no exception. Heavy rains earlier in the week had put many of the streams out of condition even though it was mid-December, the beginning of summer.

Te Anau lies immediately to the southeast of Fjiordland, a steep, mountainous band of country along the west coast of the island. These rugged mountains receive vast amounts of rainfall, as much as 300 or 400 inches a year, brought by storms sweeping in from the Tasman Sea. Once over the mountains in Te Anau itself, precipitation decreases dramatically to 30 inches, give or take 10. As Frank and I began our walk, a fair portion of the year's total seemed to be falling on us, driven into our faces by a relentless wind.

Visibility was poor to impossible, no small disadvantage since the fishing here is entirely dependent upon locating and casting to individual trout. In some ways it's very much like bonefishing: seeing and stalking are as important as casting, and you can't have one without the other.

"I try to tell people exactly what to expect down here," Frank tells me. "If they just want lots of big fish and don't particularly care how they catch them, I suggest they go to Alaska. But what you have in Southland New Zealand is not to be found anywhere else: sight fishing, one on one, with light tackle and a dry fly, for fish which will average 3 or 4 pounds, and realistically speaking, go to 8 or 10."

Frank arranges trips for fishermen to New Zealand and is himself a consummate angler. He worries about giving his clients information that will not leave them, in the end, dissatisfied. Strictly speaking, it is probably an expensive mistake for someone who is not at least somewhat seasoned to plan a trout fishing trip to New Zealand. Of course, you can rent a boat and go out on the lakes and troll and catch plenty of trout. But you can do that just as well in Minnesota or a hundred other places close to home.

After 2 hours of fighting wind and rain without seeing as much as a fin, we came upon an enormous pool which Frank knew held about two dozen fish from 3 to 12 pounds. We stood a long time studying the broad tail, but because of the wind and glare, could not locate a trout. Then, inevitably, we spooked two big fish out of the shallows by walking past them.

At the center of the pool, close in against the far bank where the water was barely gliding, there was a dark slick and in it a fish was rising at intervals of 30 or 40 seconds.

At Frank's insistence I eased out on the spacious sandbar, crouching very low until I was kneeling at the water's edge. It was here that I first began to regret my choice of tackle for the day. Because of the river's small, seemingly manageable size as well as its extreme clarity, I had brought along my favorite rod, an 8-foot graphite model designed to cast a No. 4 line, and on which I use a No. 3.

I was looking at a 40-foot cast with a long leader in a gusty side wind. You could do it but it wasn't pretty, and I think I tore my favorite shirt while performing the essential double haul.

The No. 16 Elk Hair Caddis landed right though, and as it floated over the fish, he took and I tightened. A few seconds later I gently freed the 6-incher. It was the only immature trout I saw in two weeks. We never did see any of those big ones at this pool; they just weren't out feeding.

The rain let up a bit, so we did some harder walking to reach a series of pools that lay tight beneath the gorgeous, terribly high, mossy cliffs. In one of the pools—a dark slot, really, where flecks of white foam passed slowly over the black water—a 4-pound rainbow drifted up out of the darkness to gently sip in an insect. Frank fished to it but nothing happened. We waited.

Ten minutes later a fish rose again, this time charging 2 or 3 yards upstream in a violent rush. This fish, though, was a 6- or 7-pound rainbow, an entirely different trout. I tried casting to it, but with the short rod, light line, wind, and brush behind me, the fly never got wet.

The only way I could see a clear backcast for the relatively long shot needed to cover the fish was to get into the water and cast upstream. Frank advised against it but I plunged in.

Just as I reached a good position and began false casting, Frank cautioned me to wait because the trout had come out into the shallows to actively feed, and it was swimming all over the place. From my low position I couldn't see under the water at all.

Up on the bank, Frank could see clearly and he told me to stay very still because the fish was slowly cruising right toward me. Soon enough I saw it, a beautiful rainbow about 5 pounds and I could only stand and watch helplessly as it swam right past my nose and disappeared downstream, spooked.

"That's one of the reasons you don't want to get in the water if you can help it," Frank said with a little laugh.

The rain started up again and the sky became more ominous than ever. Frank wanted to reach three or four big pools which were stil several miles upstream so we began walking at a pretty good pace.

As we passed pool after delightful pool I couldn't help but be impressed with the vicissitudes of this deceptively simple stream. It is not inaccessible or remote in the least. In fact, for its whole length it runs through ranches and farms. It's just that you forget how very sparse the population is because the countryside really does look like someplace you've been before: California, as

I mentioned. And in California, streams like this one were abolished years and years ago.

What you forget is how little time and pressure it takes to change the fragile essence of nature. For instance, as recently as fifteen years ago, the much talked about Armstrong Spring Creek, which is only 10 minutes away from my front door in Montana, was a wild, seldom-fished jewel of a stream. Five or six years ago, the late Dan Bailey told me he couldn't bear to go there anymore because of what had been done by thoughtless landowners and a healthy cross-section of the angling public.

Today, the stream is badly overfished, its banks so heavily trod that in places the vegetation can't even grow back. This once free-flowing stream full of large, wild fish, is now changed, channeled, and dammed; its banks have been ruthlessly stripped of vegetation, and hatchery rainbows have been carelessly released into it. And while some large fish do remain, the trout are generally smallish and nearly all have been caught and released at least once. And it now costs $25 a day to fish it.

Trout Unlimited tried to protect it, but when a stream reaches the point where it requires protection, it is already too late because its wildness is gone. I don't want to be misunderstood: trying to preserve and protect Armstrong Creek was certainly admirable and, obviously, necessary. But even at the time, which was several years ago, what had made the stream famous and legendary among fly fishermen remained only as a myth. Its wildness is gone forever and the fisherman is no longer free on its banks.

I thought about this as Frank and I were walking along what was so obviously a wild yet accessible river. What is it essentially that destroys wildness? The answer is obvious: pressure. We walked through many farms yet saw no farmers. We walked on, and crossed a number of roads but saw few cars. Nor did we ever encounter a single other fisherman, not only on this day, on this river, but in three weeks on three dozen rivers. One excellent pool flowed right by what appeared to be a gravel company, but the equipment looked unused and no one was around. There you have it: no one was around.

Of course, to be perfectly fair, the fishing in this little stream, especially with the water as low and clear as it was, is simply not for the occasional fisherman. A guy with a Saturday off, throwing a 2-ounce devon spoon on 15-pound line, is merely going to put the trout under the banks for a while. And a clumsy fly caster will do likewise.

Presently, we came to a substantial pool with a high clay bank rising steeply on the outside of the curve. The tailout was perhaps a hundred feet wide, coming very slowly up so that its mean depth was about a foot. Farther up, beneath the high bank at the center of the pool, the water was 7 or 8 feet deep—slow, dark, and promising.

We looked cautiously over the rim. It had stopped raining and the wind had let up, but the skies were still dark in what was now late afternoon. But the tailout was so shallow you could see most of it pretty well. Right away, Frank spotted a brown of at least 7 pounds nymphing in about 10 inches of water clear over on the far side.

"Look at this." He nudged me.

Another brown, clearly several pounds larger than the first, was slowly cruising down out of the deeper water. It passed the first fish, and moved into the shallowest part of the tail where we lost it in the glare.

"Go ahead," I said.

"No way. Go around and try them. I'll spot."

Walking downstream, I crossed in the fast water well below where we'd last seen the biggest brown. Upon reaching the beach, I stayed back away from the pool until I was opposite Frank, then crawled right to the shallow edge.

"Look," I heard Frank say softly. Upstream I could see the heavy rings. With the wind down, a big fish had taken something off the top.

"Okay now," Frank directed. "The bigger brown we saw come out of the pool is slowly working up toward you. He's taking nymphs every 10 or 15 seconds."

I checked my fly and leader: a No. 16 dark, impressionistic, weighted nymph on 5X. If only a nagging wife had been there to tell me how stupid I was, I might have gone to something more stout and sensible. As it was, I kept thinking about the still, shallow, crystal-clear water and stuck with the fool's choice.

I made the cast as Frank directed, across stream and slightly down. Slowly the current pulled the line around and I stripped in a bit so the fly would swing in front of the trout.

"Retrieve," Frank said. "He just took something."

He had just taken something all right, namely my fly. I came up gently and felt him for about 1 second, but the 5X leader had been reduced to no X by false casting or whatever, and the biggest brown trout I'd ever hooked sprinted for deep water with a tiny fly in his lip.

Upstream another fish rose. "I'll go to a dry fly and try that one," I said, hoping to overcome the mortification and disappointment I so totally felt.

Frank moved up and cautiously looked over the edge just as the fish rose again. "It's a beautiful male rainbow. A good one, too. Six or seven pounds."

The water was now extremely calm. Looking across, I could see Frank silhouetted against the sky. Below him the cliff was almost orange in the fading light. Against it, the water drifted slowly, a black green, with just a few flecks of white foam to indicate its speed. The trout rose again.

There was a decision to make. I pulled out the 4X spool. There was only about a foot left on it, so I took some new 5X. One thing about these fish—while they are not particularly selective, they are touchy, and you really have to make your first shot a good one. I put the Elk Hair Caddis back on, greased it a little, and started working out line.

This would be about a 50-foot cast. I was kneeling, and it was all I could do to control so much line. But the loops stayed open and suddenly the fly appeared on the water. It seemed to shine like a light. The drift seemed endless, moving slowly by me.

Frank saw the big rainbow elevate. Then I saw its substantial jaws come right out of the water, and I let them disappear before easing back. There was no resistance and the trout was gone.

"What the hell happened this time?" Frank called. "He took it perfectly."

"I know he did. I thought I gave him time."

I flipped a backcast and caught the leader, bringing the fly up close. The tippet had fouled under the hair wing so that the leader was pulling the fly backward, making it impossible to hook a fish.

I felt like a frustrated child, very much wanting to snap the rod into numerous small sections. Instead, I screamed an inner scream and slumped onto the muddy beach.

"Wait a minute," Frank said. "Another fish just rose up above." He walked up the bluff and looked over. "It's another rainbow, a female, not as big as the other one but still a good 5 pounds."

Pulling myself together, I crawled into position, checked the tippet for knots, and tied on a fresh fly. I did what I could to keep the loops tangle-free, putting a clean point on the delivery, and once again the fly landed just right. It drifted slowly, the trout rose and took it. Resistance—what a feeling!

At first there was a bit of furious head shaking, and then the rainbow made a smoking run upstream, taking the entire fly line and 10 yards of backing in a matter of 5 or 6 seconds. It was a big pool, and all I had to do was keep a light but steady hand.

Frank called from across the way, "There are some big rocks up there where the fish is."

A fair warning, but the leader was already broken.

In order to reach the road and our ride, which was a couple of miles away, we would need to start moving. I wish I could describe just how I felt. The last hour had been a kind of emotional roller coaster; I'd hooked, or at least had takes from, the three largest trout of my life right in succession.

I was disappointed and embarrassed at my own clumsiness, yet at the same time there was also a sense of exhilaration and even, in a perverse and perhaps incomplete way, accomplishment. After all, these weren't exactly minnows, and it had taken all day just to locate them. Had things gone even a hair differently

I might now be able to give you the weights and lengths of three huge trout even though I certainly had no intention of killing any of them. As it is, I have a very thrilling and precise memory to carry with me forever.

The last thing I remember about that day in paradise is that it rained very hard on us all the way back.

Cast to a Rhythm

JIM BASHLINE

Why are trout usually so difficult to take during a glut hatch? An expert tells how to make your artificial be the chosen mouthful. (July 1985)

Each August, like lemmings, dry fly anglers from across the nation descend on Yellow Breeches Creek to witness the hatching of the white fly. The scholarly call it *Ephoron leukon*; the just plain fishermen call it that *blankety-blank* white fly. Though a handful of other streams hold the same mayfly, this famous Pennsylvania limestone creek has them in battalions, and for ten days to two weeks, beginning about August 20, the number of size 15 insects boggles the mind. Many trout are caught during this annual phenomenon, but these fish are caught only by a handful of anglers—the ones who consciously or subconsciously have learned to cast to a rhythm.

Many anglers are under the impression that rhythmic casting is confined to the Yellow Breeches; trout elsewhere simply rise when food presents itself or when they jolly well feel like it. This is true enough in a number of dry-fly fishing situations, but when large numbers of insects are available, as they are during the white fly hatch, the trout fall into a special feeding pace. The angler must understand this pace and fish accordingly.

It's not easy to hold back from making cast after cast when so many fish are

296

rising, but it must be done if you desire consistent success. Fortunately, back in the 1950's I enjoyed many sessions with a group of fish that I chose to call the "concrete trout," and these fish taught me the value of timing the cast to meet their next trip to the surface.

The concrete trout were the result of a terrible event that occurred while I was serving my draft hitch during the Korean conflict. The famed Goodsell Hole, located in the center of my home town of Coudersport, Pennsylvania, was wiped from the face of the earth during the summer of 1953, when the Goodsell and 2 miles of the upper Allegheny River were relocated and converted into a concrete trough for flood-control purposes. The trough has since proved to be of some value during spring flood season, but the loss of migrating trout from the big water downstream still pains me.

Yet, for a half-dozen years following the construction, the old instincts were strong, and each summer some sizable brown trout entered the trough and attempted to breach the retaining dams that blocked their passage. The big fish would congregate in the lower reaches of the trough and lay there like so much cordwood.

When spinners returned for their egg-laying chores on the river above the concrete, millions of the insects would funnel down the chute. As this abundance of food drifted over the browns, the big fish would rise and sip—not in a frenzy, but with a measured cadence. Any attempt to catch one of these big fish was made more difficult because I had to cast from the edge of the trough, which was 15 feet higher than the surface of the water. Talk about drag! With 15 feet of line hanging from the rod tip, another 20 feet on the water, plus a 10-foot leader, a good float was difficult to manage. If the fly drifted for more than 30 inches without being jerked by the current, the wind, or a nervous hand, I felt more than lucky.

Clearly, casting from the top of the trough wasn't going to work. I had to get down to the fish. This part of the trough ran through a residential neighborhood, so I simply appropriated a suitable tree in someone's lawn, tied a rope to it, and lowered myself hand-over-hand down the inclined slope of the concrete. The water was about 30 inches deep—just right for hip-high boots. But once there, I didn't do well on these fish until I discovered that simply putting a good cast over one of the browns was fruitless. The water was mirror smooth, and the fish wanted that fly delivered at precisely the right moment.

Good spinner falls of pale evening duns were common in June and July, and the number of dying insects, wings flat on the surface, was amazing—there would be a veritable scum of flies. By tipping and sipping, the trout could rise and actually suck in two or more spinners in one gulp. This tipping and sipping could be timed, I eventually discovered, and some very large brown trout came to the net. The trick was to pick a fish and watch it as you waited for the ripples from your boots to subside. Each fish had its own feeding channel and its own self-contained metronome. Some went waltzlike—one, two, three . . . rise—while others went for a count of eight or more. Little fish of a foot or less came somewhat more sporadically, but even they would eventually fall into a specific rhythm. I learned to false cast in a slightly oblique direction to avoid waving the fly directly over the target fish. Then, when I felt the fish was about to do its thing, I tried to kiss the surface as softly as possible with the delivered fly. As I recall, about one cast in twenty-five brought a rise. Not bad for trout that knew what tapered leaders were all about.

An aside worth noting is that the flies I used to suggest the spent spinners were actually no-hackle creations. Since there was no severe ripply water to sink a sparse dry, I experimented until I settled on hackle tip wings that had most of the underneath and top hackle trimmed off. About all it had was a pair of wings and a body. To make them float better my friends and I tied size 16 flies on size 18 and 20 hooks. The little flies hooked well if pulled, rather than jerked, at the moment the fly vanished in a closed mouth. We did break some leaders, however. Brown trout of more than 20 inches require a soft hand with 7X leaders.

It was my nephew, Doug Frederick, who demonstrated another amazing fact about trout that are in this count-cadence feeding pattern. The fish seemed to get so enthralled with the large amount of food that they could be approached within a rod's length without spooking. While rigging a new leader before climbing down the rope one evening, I watched Doug hook and net two browns (18 and 25 inches, respectively) while he was nearly standing on their tails. He was dapping no more than 5 feet of leader in the same manner one would lower a worm into a pot hole. The fish saw no floating leader and apparently made no connection between the floating fly and a pair of rubber-clad legs less than 8 feet away.

About two years ago, my wife and I relocated to central Pennsylvania. On the property is a trout stream. It is a mix of limestone and freestone water and holds an amazing variety of insect life. To my delight, the trout surface-feed here during all but the coldest months, and the number of flies on a given evening can be prodigious. When the early blue-winged olives or the later pale evening duns and little "tricos" appear, they usually do so in abundance. I quickly discovered that random casting was not productive. These little native browns would have no part of a haphazard presentation. I had to watch an individual fish and put the fly in the right feeding channel at the proper moment.

This rhythmic approach to angling is, in my experience, limited to trout. No other fish in streams, ponds, or lakes operate in such a "by-the-numbers" manner. Largemouth bass certainly don't, and even the stream-bred smallmouth, which eats many of the same creatures that trout eat, is not a sequential feeder.

Timed feeding in lakes and ponds features another variation that can cause a thoughtful fly fisherman to consider another sport. Instead of staying at the same feeding location, pond fish are on the move during a good hatch. The current does not bring food to them in an orderly fashion, so the fish must stay in motion to take advantage of the windfall. These cruising trout rise and then swim on to the next insect. If you cast to the ring you'll miss the fish. But there is a pattern here too, and the trick is to determine which way the fish is moving. While some fish tend to move in a more or less straight line (usually away from your canoe, boat, or shore location), many fish move in lazy yet well-defined circles. Watch the rise patterns and try to guess the direction and the timing. Drop that fly at about the spot you guess the trout will surface next and the battle is half won. Being on a glassy lake when fish are popping all around is one of the most beautiful experiences I can imagine.

The rhythm method of fly fishing is not limited to dry flies. Subsurface nymphs or drowned surface flies can trigger such behavior, causing the hard-to-define "hump" rise. This occurs when a trout rises almost to the surface, grabs a morsel, and then quickly turns, leaving a bulge, or hump, on the water. Dressing the leader a couple of feet behind the nymph or wet fly with flotant is a common approach for those who have good eyes and reflexes. When the leader twitches or ducks under, the strike is made. If this sounds difficult (and it can be in fading light), glue a tiny piece of plastic foam the size of a pea about 18 inches behind the fly. Stick it fast with contact cement. The speck of foam acts as a combination bobber and strike indicator and won't cause any trouble on short- to medium-length casts.

So remember, when trout are rising by the numbers, they eventually get into their own rhythm. Curiously, it seems to end up being a "waltz time" or a slight modification of it.

Even if you have no music in your heart and can't carry a tune in a burlap sack, think about doing more watching than casting for the first few minutes when you next encounter a lot of rising trout. If casting here and there without results finds you wondering, pick a trout and discover its rhythm. But by all means try to count without moving your lips; non-anglers would never be able to fathom what you're attempting to do!